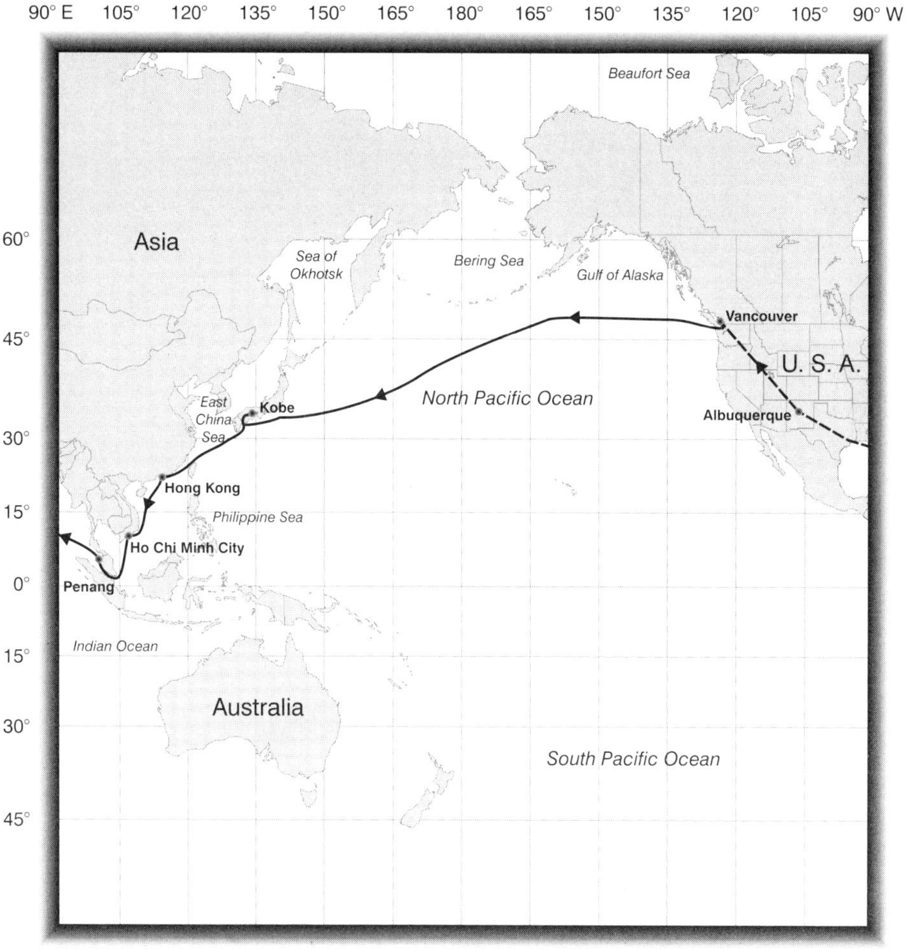
90° E
105°
120°
135°
150°
165°
180°
165°
150°
135°
120°
105°
90° W
60°
45°
30°
15°
0°
15°
30°
45°
Beaufort Sea
Asia
Sea of Okhotsk
Bering Sea
Gulf of Alaska
Vancouver
U. S. A.
North Pacific Ocean
Albuquerque
East China Sea
Kobe
Hong Kong
Philippine Sea
Ho Chi Minh City
Penang
Indian Ocean
Australia
South Pacific Ocean

At Sea at Sixty
Reflections from a Round the World Voyage

Catharine Stewart-Roache
&
Patrick J. Roache

P. O. Box 9110
Albuquerque, New Mexico 87119-9110
USA
http://www.hermosa-pub.com/hermosa

Copyright © 1999 Hermosa Publishers
International Standard Book Number 0-913478-10-5
Library of Congress Card Catalog Number 99-64269

"Sea" by Catharine Stewart-Roache
Copyright © 1999

All rights reserved. No part of this book may be reproduced or transmitted in any form or by any means, electronic or mechanical, including photocopying, recording or by any information storage and retrieval system without written permission from the copyright holder, except for brief quotations in a review.

Acknowledgments

We are grateful to Sandy Schauer of Montanita Publishing, Dr. Muriel Latham-Pfeiffer, and Dr. Manfred Kurt Wenner for copy editing and many substantial suggestions that improved this book. Milton Lau of Lau3 Designs handled the layout and book production. Our fellow senior passenger John Norell graciously provided one of his many drawings done at sea. (The rest are Catharine's.) Thanks also to our friends Marvel Harrison and Terry Kellogg for their encouragement regarding the Semester At Sea program. Finally, we sincerely thank each of our shipmates, young and old, for sharing this part of their life's voyage with us.

Dedicated to our children - who understand when we run away from home - so they might share some enjoyment from our trips.

    Whenever I find myself growing grim about the mouth, whenever it is a damp, drizzly November in my soul, whenever I find myself involuntarily pausing before coffin warehouses and bringing up the rear of every funeral I meet; and especially whenever my hypos get such an upper hand of me that it requires a strong moral principle to prevent me from deliberately stepping into the street and methodically knocking people's hats off - then I account it high time to get to sea as soon as I can.

    Herman Melville, *Moby Dick*, 1851

Table of Contents

Chapter 1. Introductions 1
Sailing into Old Age 3
Dreaming from a Desert 6

Chapter 2. Port of Embarkation:
Vancouver, British Columbia, Canada 11
Our Neighbouring Country 13

Chapter 3. The North Pacific Ocean 17
My First Ocean 19
Crossing the Deep in Storms 20
Getting My Bearings 23

Chapter 4. Kobe and Japan 25
A Coast of People 27
Reconstructing in Japan 30
Polite Japan 32
Communicating in Japan and the World 33
My Urban Problems 35
Modeling the Experience of Aging 36
Passing Thoughts 40
Sayonara 41

Chapter 5. The China Seas 43
Reflecting After Kobe 45
Apologizing for Hiroshima 46
Guilt and Personal Battles 52
Religion as Poetry, Religion as Politics 54
Core Matters 60

Chapter 6. Hong Kong and China 63
Land of Many Dragons 65
Ferrying in Hong Kong 67
A Work of Art 73
Cruising The Li River 75
Capitalist Hustle in Communist China 79
Hong Kong Farewell - Auf Wiedersehen 87

Chapter 7. South China Sea 91
Conversations, Reflections, and Diversity 93

Chapter 8. Ho Chi Minh City (Saigon) and Vietnam 97
"Madame, Madame, Postcards" 99
The World Heritage Site of Halong Bay 101
The Bottom 107
Puzzling Out Vietnam 108

Chapter 9. More South China Sea and The Straits of Malacca 111
Calm Waters, Unsettled Thoughts 113
Preparing for an Islamic Country 114

Chapter 10. Penang and Malaysia 117
Equatorial Diversity 119
"Take Care" 122
Searching for Beauty in Malaysia 125

Chapter 11. The Adaman Sea and Indian Ocean 129
Preparations for the Indian SubContinent 131

Chapter 12. Chennai (Madras) and India 133
India, Ready or Not 135
Flunking India 141

Table of Contents

Chapter 13. The Indian Ocean and Arabian Sea............157
Time for Some Heavy Thinking...............159
Dying in India...............166
Healing Waters...............167

Chapter 14. The Sea of Aden, Red Sea, Suez Canal, and Mediterranean Sea...............169
Imagining the Past...............171

Chapter 15. Haifa and Israel...............177
Not So Safe Harbor...............179
Misinformation Galore...............179
Baha'i...............183
Exploring...............187
Curfews...............188
Beautiful Galilee...............189
On Our Own...............191
Praying in the Evil Land...............193
My Last Time...............197

Chapter 16. The Mediterranean Sea and Aegean Sea...............199
My God, Your God...............201
Shalom...............208

Chapter 17. Istanbul and Turkey...............209
Crossroads of the World...............211
The Bosporus River - Awaiting Armageddon...............215
Sufi Chanting...............218
Buying in Turkey...............222
Big City Danger...............224
Last Day in Istanbul...............225

Chapter 18. The Aegean Sea and Dardenelles 229
Sore Throats and Hailstones 231
Gawking at Rainbows 232
Grandmother Sea 233

Chapter 19. Civitavecchia and Italy 237
Bon Giorno, Italia! 239
Motoring in Italy 242

Chapter 20. The Mediterranean Sea, Again 247
Enduring Sea, Enduring Art 249
Landmarks 252

Chapter 21. Casablanca and Morocco 255
Last Port and New Continent 257
Disappointing Casablanca and Moroccan Manners 257
Roman Volubilis, on the Way to Fes 259
You Must Remember This 260
Leaving for Home 262

Chapter 22. The Atlantic Ocean 263
Crossing the Deep in Tranquillity 265
The Last Ocean 265
Searching for a Mobile Sea 266
Degenerating Diets: Food and Other Fads 267
Exercising and Eating 271
Panning the Crowd 275

**Chapter 23. Port of Disembarkation:
Miami, Florida, U. S. A.** 279
Docking in Miami 281

Table of Contents

Chapter 24. Afterthoughts 283
Missing Our Floating Village 285
"Extreme" Lists and Currencies 288
Action Items 290
Confessions of an Optimist 291
So! What About Aging? 292
Sea Moods 294

Chapter 1
Introductions

Chapter 1 – Introductions

Sailing into Old Age

pjr

Sixty is *old*. Fifty was pretty darn old, but you can't fake it at Sixty. If the categories are just young and old, and you live to the ripe old age of ninety, you would say forty-five is the dividing line. If your categories are youth, middle age, and old age, you would say that middle age begins at thirty, and old age begins at sixty. That's our perspective, anyhow.

In September 1998, we (Catharine and Patrick) both turned sixty. Ten years earlier, we had celebrated turning fifty with a six-week bicycle trip down the west coast, Canada to Mexico, unsupported, just the two of us. Although we both had serious doubts (not shared until after the trip) about spending that much time together with little other social contact, it turned out to be wonderful. We did several other bike trips in the intervening decade, some by ourselves, some in groups. For our rite of passage into old age at sixty, we first thought of another bicycle trip, this one down the Mississippi River from the headwaters in Minnesota all the way to New Orleans. We still may do it (at seventy?), but something better came up. Our good friend, Dr. Marvel Harrison, had spent the spring of 1995 as the mental health counselor on board the Semester At Sea program. She told us about it, showed slides, and we sought more information.

Semester At Sea is an undergraduate exchange program, something like spending a semester studying in Europe. The class work is set up by the University of Pittsburgh, so most of the class credits are transferable to the students' home institutions. The program has been in existence with various university connections for over thirty years. Students from all over North America and a few other countries go around the world while they take regular undergraduate courses onboard a ship. They sail around the world, East to West in the spring semester, West to East in the fall semester. The university obviously cannot offer the full range of courses, but does offer a surprisingly broad menu of seventy courses, especially in the politics, economics, international business and marketing, sociology, geography and cultural study of the ports visited. The 16,000 volume library on board their ship is the most extensive library afloat - this is no tourism and gambling cruise!

About half of the one hundred days of Semester At Sea are spent in ports. Some activities are simple tourism, which is educational in itself, but some are more focused as educational field trips. The course offerings are quite impressive. The most unique and, for us, attractive educational offering is the one everyone takes, the Core Course that meets every day at sea, covering the geography and politics of the countries visited. The cost is about that of a semester at a fairly expensive university plus side trips in the port countries. Intrigued by the information on the Web site (*www.semesteratsea.com*) and by Marvel's endorsement (she is one of the most traveled people we know, and we trust her evaluation) we signed up.

On September 8, 1998, we flew from our home in New Mexico to Vancouver, and two days later we sailed on the *S. S. Universe Explorer* with some 640 undergraduates, 42 other "adult passengers" many of whom like ourselves were in the "senior citizen" category, that is to say *old*, about 50 faculty/staff, 16 younger children of the faculty and staff, and a crew of a couple hundred. In all, just under 1,000 people. Our experiences were shaped as much by the life in this floating village of unusual people as it was by the port countries visited. This book developed from our reflections on the voyage. The eleven ports were as follows.

Vancouver, British Columbia, Canada
Kobe, Japan
Hong Kong, China
Ho Chi Mihn City (Saigon), Vietnam
Penang, Malaysia

Chapter 1 – Introductions

**Chennai (Madras), India
(Suez Canal)
Haifa, Israel
Istanbul, Turkey
Civitavecchia, Italy
Casablanca, Morocco
Miami, Florida, U. S. A.**

We have been married 35 years, living together, raising five children together, and spending a great deal of time together, but we do not believe in "togetherness" in all things. We have taken separate vacations. Although we have much in common, especially values, we are different. Catharine says we don't argue well together, but we play well together, and if we could only have one or the other, we'll take playing together. We saw no advantage, and a likelihood of considerable problems, if we tried to co-author every paragraph. The simplest approach has been to write more or less alternating sections of chapters, which we then edited afterwards to remove some (not all) the redundancy. Any themes the reader detects arose naturally during reflections on the voyage, rather than being pre-conceived and pre-planned.

"None of your business" is a phrase not heard often these days. Politicians should use it every day. In a way, we would enjoy writing gossipy stuff about our shipmates, with character analysis and personality sketches - after all, there is nothing as interesting as people - but it would be a violation of their implicit trust. So the only "exposures" contained herein are of ourselves.

It was a big, wonderful trip, more dangerous than we thought it would be, more stressful, and much more interesting. Kind of like marriage, and life itself, actually.

Dreaming from a Desert

csr

I wake up. I sense, before I actually hear, the rain. With a smile I get up and go into our living room, which has skylights. Yes. It is rain, the first I've heard since the ship. There, water came from the sky and also surrounded us. It moistened my very soul. I suppose people who don't live in the desert don't have this need to water the soul. But I do.

To a great extent the trip around the world on a ship was a voyage for my spirit. The sea has something very special to offer and it has been offering this to humans for millennia. Some fear it, hate it; others are drawn into it and its power never leaves them, even when they are on land . . . or in my case, a desert.

I remember with such clarity the first time I saw an ocean. It was the Pacific. I marveled. Then I *had* to get in it. I loved the taste and feel immediately. I was about thirteen and knew I would be going back to Texas after our family vacation, but I knew that a relationship had begun.

It was years before I could develop that relationship. A few university degrees and five children came before I became more involved. This second encounter was also in the Pacific. I went snorkeling for the first time in Hawaii. I was hooked. Dangerously hooked. I was so mesmerized that I got a horrible sunburn on the backs of my legs . . . and learned a valuable lesson: don't take the sea and sun lightly. They are powerful and demand respect.

Eventually, I learned to scuba dive, and lived part of each year on the Caribbean . . . but I knew there was a whole blue planet out there. I wanted to "sail the ocean blue" as in the childhood song. I had learned to sail a very small boat and knew that for me it was too late to learn to sail a boat big enough to go around the world on my own or even with the two of us.

They say to get anything done you need the desire, the opportunity, and the means to make it happen.

Chapter 1 – Introductions

Pat and I surely had the desire to sail around the world, which had grown stronger as we got older. Without the responsibilities of jobs and children we had the time. The opportunity came when one of my best friends, who had worked on the Semester At Sea program, told us about it; we made inquiries, and space was available for the Fall of 1998. And now as we turned into retirement we had the means. This is fortunate and we know we are very lucky to have the means and the motivation to use them.

Desire, opportunity, and means. So we made our reservations and set sail from Vancouver, British Columbia on September 10, 1998.

In the North Pacific we would both celebrate our sixtieth birthdays. I recently saw a TV program based on the writings of the beloved Pope John XXIII who had said when he turned sixty, "Sixty is the beginning of old age." It is something to think about upon turning sixty. My old age. Time to review, reflect, plan for the future.

So we call our book *At Sea at Sixty*. Not *Adrift at Sixty*; there is a difference. For me the phrase being "at sea" implies that one is a small part of something much bigger. It implies that you're on your own in an important way. Have you brought what your need? Water, fuel, food, skills, strength, attitude, confidence? Do you know your seafaring limits? When to be afraid? When to "batten down the hatches," or wait out a storm, or head for a safe harbor. All of these images conjure up in my mind life situations as well as sailing situations. Situations having a lot to do with old age.

Actually, at about age forty I began to encounter my limits both physically and mentally. I did have to get those reading glasses that "old folks" used. I did have to write more things down. But I also learned I could aim for new limits. My bicycling took me way beyond what I imagined my limits were. Pat and I rode our bikes from Canada to Mexico to celebrate our fiftieth birthdays; we both rode two hundred miles-in-a-day events. We stretched. We both wrote books, and made moves, and ventured out into the world as pilgrims, travelers, tourists.

In these adventures we learned the importance of fear . . . it really can be the beginning of wisdom, or it can paralyze you. But it is not helpful to ignore it or try to deny it. Fear can get you to stop when it is dark, when you are tired or hurt. Pretty important if you want to stay alive. Fear can prompt you to stop and think and set a new goal.

We learned the importance of confidence and the "I think I can" philosophy of that children's classic we read so many times to our little ones. While on a major trek in Nepal in 1987, I thought I could finish the trek even though I was injured, and with help, I did. Not with much style, not as I had first imagined, but I did make it.

And that bit about batten down the hatches . . . wait out a storm. We learned that through the death of one of our children. It was time to find a safe harbor for ourselves so that we could figure out how to live our lives in the face of such chaos. We found the safe harbor with each other and our friends . . . and work. And God's tender mercy. A hard lesson. A lesson that life is hard, not just for us, but everyone.

Some of the questions we set before us as we sail into old age are: What are we taking on this voyage that is useful? (Maybe as useful and necessary as water.) What attitudes, insights, will nourish us? What skills do we need?

In this book of our voyage around the world, we will of course describe where we went and what happened. But we will also look into ourselves and see what we have learned about being "at sea." Each of us will age uniquely, will be at sea in the aging aspect of the human condition shared by people in every latitude and longitude. But did we find anything on the sea or in port that might be perceived as of particular use to me as I sail into old age? Did we

Chapter 1 – Introductions

find anything within ourselves on this voyage that might help us as we age . . . not necessarily gracefully but surely with grace?

Some of the insights of the trip occurred as we went along; others as we have reflected. Others are yet to come. A journey of this nature is not grasped so quickly. I am curious about what is yet to come. I invite you to also be curious about what went on during that one hundred days.

Chapter 2
Port of Embarkation: Vancouver, B. C., Canada

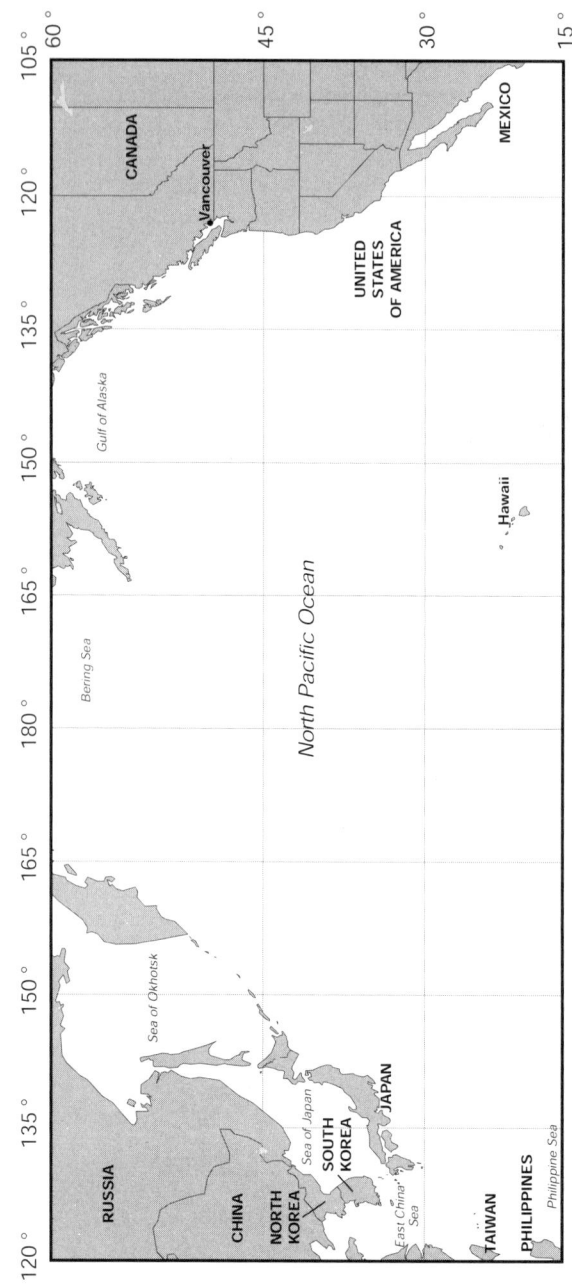

Vancouver, British Columbia, Canada
Latitude 49.1°N Longitude 123.1°W

Chapter 2 – Port of Embarkation: Vancouver, Canada

Our Neighbouring Country

csr

We had planned and looked forward to our great adventure at sea for well over a year. It would be exciting, profound, we would question ourselves, our world.

Instead of all this intellectual stimulation, I was standing in the shower stomping on clothes in a cloud of soap suds. I had violated the very first rule of air travel and I was paying the price. *Never pack liquid soap without putting it in a sealed container.* Somewhere in my brain I knew this, but I had not abided by it.

Packing for this trip had been careful and deliberate. What do you take in three bags which will be the right choices for three and a half months and many different climates? What cassettes, medicines, books, clothing, supplies are really necessary? I had decided that a giant-size bottle of Woolite would be the answer to hand laundry and we both thought that we might be doing a great deal of this because of the probable shortage of laundry facilities on board. I had packed the fatal bottle in with my Polartec clothes and next to sweatshirts and pants. Can you imagine how much liquid soap these items absorb? I couldn't. But I can now.

Hours after rinsing and wringing, and wringing, and wringing out my clothes I was ready to take them to a laundromat to see if they could finish the job. More than half a day was used up in this whole process. By noon of the day before sailing we were both ready to see something of Vancouver besides our bed and breakfast room and the neighborhood laundry.

Vancouver really captured our interests: good food, water, museums, and friendly, helpful people. On a bicycle trip the year before in the Pacific Northwest we had been excited by the art of totems and First Nations carving which we had seen in the provincial museum in Victoria. ("First Nations" is the Canadian term for what we more temperate North Americans refer to as Indians or Native Americans; the Canadian term seems to us to be more respectful in explicitly recognizing that they are independent nations.) Pat had more exposure to this art than I since he had gone up the west coast ferry to Alaska in the early 90's. The anthropology museum in Vancouver offered terrific examples of First Nations artifacts and recent art works. I am a sculptor and, though I work in stone, I appreciate the wonderful work in wood. Some of it was very small and detailed, others were huge and imposing.

After our taste of the port city we dressed up and went to the harbor to tour the *SS Universe Explorer* and to a welcoming party for us senior passengers and parents of the students who would be our shipmates.

When I first saw the ship it looked huge to me. All I could think of was that I would be lost at sea in three dimensions. As a child growing up in north Texas, living space was one-story ranch style. Pat and I had lived in two-story houses but now we had six stories! *Decks*. And bulkheads and fore and aft and port and starboard. A whole lot of newness faced us.

We met a crowd of people and nibbled on hors d'oeuvres as we listened to talks from the dean of students, the academic dean and the captain. We had time to walk around - and up and down - and get some sense of our new home and the layout of the ship. Our first impressions were very positive.

The next day was pretty much a blur of activity. Lines, boarding protocol, finding our cabin, figuring out where to stow our gear and how to get in and out of which door. Loading all of us took most of the day. As we waited for the moment of casting off we were entertained by the port activity. Tons of logs were being loaded onto a ship docked next to us. It was easy to imagine that the cargo was also destined for Japan, our next port.

Most of us were outside to watch the moment we had waited for. Parents waved good-bye from the dock to their children going so far away for so long. Some students had never left home. What an initiation for them. And then there were us oldsters. By and

Chapter 2 – Port of Embarkation: Vancouver, Canada

large, we were retired, and seasoned travelers, but few had gone around the world. Some of us were married couples, others single, widowed, or leaving behind spouses who understood their wanderlust and wished them well.

We were as excited as the young people when the very loud horn blasted our readiness to depart. The crew scurried around on the fore deck and quickly we were on our way West. *All the way West.*

Chapter 3
The North Pacific Ocean

Chapter 3 – The North Pacific Ocean

My First Ocean

csr

This North Pacific was the first ocean I had ever seen as a child; now I would see it for twelve days and get to know it better than any of the other seas and oceans of our 100 day voyage.

It is by far the largest, the deepest, and the most diverse of all oceans. Crossing it is an experience of a vastness second only to the sky. It seems to me much more than the expanse of land I see when I'm on the top of the Sandia Mountains in New Mexico and look either east or west. Granted, there is only so much I can actually see before me and around me, but when I'm on Sandia Crest, my mind does influence my experience. I know that all of this land ends on the east or west coast but the Pacific stretches out much farther than either coast. And, as I looked at the globe, I realized that we would be crossing at a very narrow part of this vast ocean . . . not the wide waist of the equator; not the long diagonal route of Cook or many of the great explorers.

The clue to all this vastness is the crossing of time zones. For us in New Mexico we just cross through Mountain and into Pacific time to reach the coast. On the ship we turned back our watches every 15 degrees of longitude. We "retarded" our clocks almost every other night while sailing. The twenty-five hour days were a gift of time to be enjoyed. Something to think about for all those times I've said, "I don't have enough time in my day." When I was younger it was more difficult to realize that human beings *made up* time. We are in charge of it. We made up the significance of 24 hours, of a week, of a millennium. Time is our arbitrary invention. For so long it determined so much of our lives: work schedules, school, weekends. As we have aged we have become more in touch with other aspects of set times. We remember for example, that the Sabbath was made for people, not people for the Sabbath. An old wisdom needed to be remembered, even by the young.

At Sea At Sixty

the sea rocks her child
planet earth wrapped in wet blue
we clutch her mantle

The captain had set a northerly course which would take us just south of the Aleutian Islands. This plan was changed because of the intervention of Typhoon Stella. It was an important occasion for becoming flexible, adhering to the admonition of the Dean of Students to "be flexible on this voyage."

As a group we of the *SS Universe Explorer* had proved to be minimal sailors. Our first lifeboat drill was a fair warning that we better shape up if we were to be able to perform the basics that marine life demands. Added to this was a pretty seasick bunch. Before we got to Stella, we had no sea legs. As we snuggled up to her, we discovered her rocking and rolling power.

Crossing the Deep in Storms

pjr

Second day out, sea-sickness for many. Long, long swells,
Even experienced ocean travelers say these are bad. Not rough or

Chapter 3 – The North Pacific Ocean

dangerous, but a long wave-length pitching and rolling that demands attention. Fairly chilly, too. We are glad to be out and on our way, leaving some family stress behind for a while. No mail or e-mail until the ports, no telephone calls unless it is really bad news.

Then, a warm flat day, and the students start looking like students, lounging in the sun. There has been some heavy drinking, but not as much as I might think. Bear in mind that I attended Notre Dame in the late 1950's, so my standards are pretty low. Noisy, but not terrible. Fortunately, we live on the top (Observation) deck, far away from the bar and the rap music, which I despise.

The seventh day out, we get some real action. The tail of Typhoon Stella, or maybe it was Hurricane Stella. Same phenomenon, same physics, but in the Atlantic and Eastern Pacific, they are called hurricanes, and in the Western Pacific, typhoons. Big stuff, heavy pitching. I am not bothered much in the daylight, but at night, my imagination is a little more active. My idea had been to try to sleep in the middle of my small single bed, but after some experimentation, it turns out to be better to move right up to the bulkhead. I move with the ship, but my motion is not amplified like a buggy whip. Neither of us has been ill, but I have some mild nausea.

The storm passes, a few more nice days, then some more heavy action with Typhoon Vicki. We can hear the waves crash and churn under the ship. I think the screws (propellers) are cavitating, but others doubt it. We are looking at 33 foot (10 meter) high waves. St. George's Watch, the lounge at the bow of the ship, is on our Observation deck, six decks above the water line, and spray hits the windows. In my geohazards course in the theater on Bali deck, just one deck above the water line, a set of drums crashes to the floor. Later, at an informal lecture on the Law of the Sea given for our senior group in another lounge on the aft end, I watch the horizon pitch wildly up and down in the wall mirror. Furniture is moving. People are laughing it off, but I am frankly worried. In Vancouver, people joked about the Titanic, but of course that happened in still water. A better model would be the Edmund Fitzgerald, the 729 foot long Great Lakes ore freighter that simply broke in half during a November gale on Lake Superior in 1975. Here, lowering the lifeboats four stories on cables on a pitching, damaged ship would be a joke. "Women and children first!" I couldn't agree more - I'm not trying to climb into that thing. Then, a big one hits. The captain later estimates it as 45+ feet. The screws definitely come out of the water. I swear we are surfing on a 23,000 ton, 618 foot long surfboard. I am not happy to see the sun go down. I finally decide that there is no virtue in toughing out my incipient nausea naturally, and I would rather have my equilibrium in a disaster, so I take a sea sickness pill. It helps almost immediately. A wild night of sleeping - a friend's bed broke loose and he went sliding across the cabin, and their chest of drawers dumped. In the dining room, a steward gathered armfuls of spaghetti off the floor. Some people got a bit banged up. Things are better in the morning, but the rough seas continue for several days.

John Norell

After Kobe, we play tag with our third typhoon, at one point heading north instead of south to avoid the worst waves. All in all, I feel I have maxed out on my experience of typhoons at sea, and would just as soon pass on the next ones. It was exciting, but I've done it, thank you very much.

Chapter 3 – The North Pacific Ocean

Getting My Bearings

csr

    I was a lucky one. Instead of being sick, I was mesmerized by the storm. I could hardly believe my eyes. I was experiencing a major storm at sea, something I had read about and tried to imagine all my life. It was more amazing than any writing could present. It was beautiful, scary, mysterious, beautiful, horrifying. And noisy.

    I was excited about my classes, especially marine biology and oceanography. What an opportunity to study the oceans and seas while *on* them. First of all, I was curious about the difference between an ocean and a sea. It turns out, the only difference is size. The "true" oceans of the world are few, namely, the Pacific, Atlantic, Indian, Arctic, Antarctic. The seas are many: East China, South China, Adaman, Red, Mediterranean . . . you get the picture. The western edge of the Pacific is very influenced by two currents which we now approached. The one to the north of us is the Kamchutka current. It is cold and not very diverse in marine life, therefore it has good fishing. The current off of the eastern coast of Japan is the powerful Kuroshio current. In this northward flowing three knot current there are few nutrients, the water is warm and a beautiful shade of blue and the fishing is not very good.

    As we moved closer to this current the sea was calm, but this did not last long. We hit the edge of our second typhoon, Vicki. She was as impressive as Stella. The captain described her force as eight on a scale of nine. The spray from her waves splashed in the windows of the St. George's Watch, six decks (stories) up on the ship - and the first deck is well above the waterline. Later some crew agreed that one wave must have been 45 ft and that the propellers came out of the water causing a terrible sound and shudder.

    The decks were closed; I listened to opera music and absorbed the power and beauty of a storm at sea.

Even in the storm we were able to catch a glimpse of our first sight of land since Vancouver: Mekurajima and Meijukajima. It seemed somehow strange to see something as stable as land after all that moving water.

But all of this excitement had a time price to pay. We were four hours late arriving into Kobe, our first port.

Chapter 4
Kobe and Japan

Golden Pavilion

At Sea At Sixty

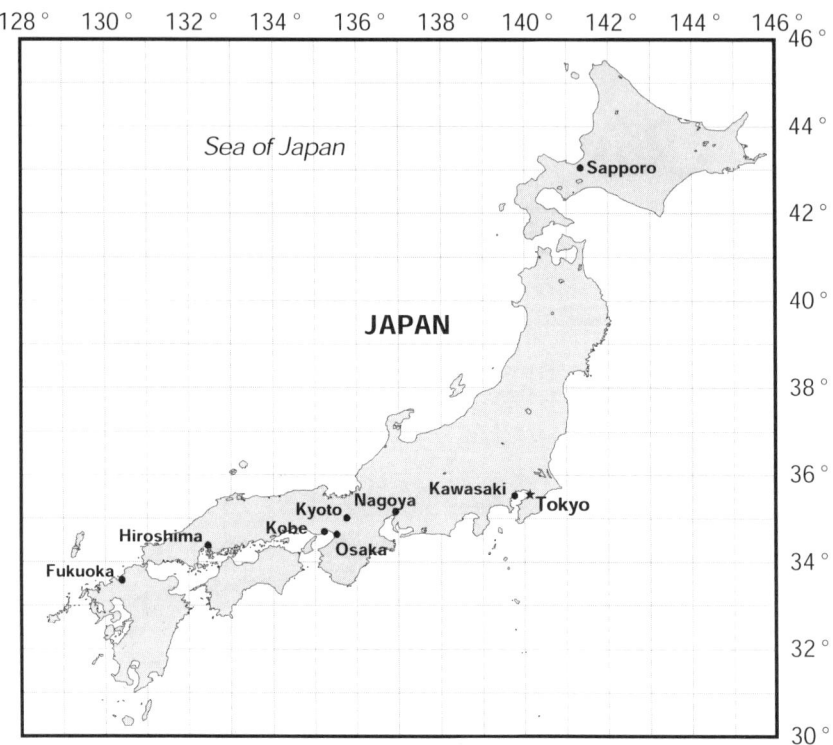

Kobe, Japan
Latitude 34.4°N Longitude 135.1°E

Chapter 4 – Kobe and Japan

A Coast of People

csr

Our first port on the Semester At Sea voyage was Kobe, Japan. Kobe is located in a very protected harbor on the Sea of Osaka - in fact, it is not far from the city of Osaka. It is a protected harbor, but Vicki, which the Japanese simply designated "Number Seven" had disturbed Japan enough to shut down all trains and many highways. At sea, we saw flotsam hours before we docked. During our stay we saw downed branches and other effects of this storm. We also found out that Japan has come to expect (and even depend, in regard to agriculture) on the seasons of typhoons which strike their coast many times a year.

As I think of how my experiences on this trip relate, or symbolize in some way my own aging, I realize that I have weathered many storms and they, with all their force and sometimes great pain and loss, are a way of life. They have blown through my years, and will continue to be a way of life. Personal storms, like typhoons, also get our attention and force us to change plans and make adjustments in day-to-day living. Because of them we discover our strengths and we begin also to appreciate the ordinary, something often missed by the young. Life has taught me that ordinary things are precious. The ordinariness of sunrises and sunsets, silence, water, mountains, deserts, bread, friends, children, and my marriage. To have a marriage is universally ordinary. To transform that into something extraordinary is a small miracle. As I grow older I want to celebrate my ordinary marriage as the extraordinary, surprising, resilient miracle which it is. I want to jump for joy over my husband; I never think of him as ordinary. As a statistic, I suppose he is; as a partner, he is not.

As we docked in Kobe, I tried to remember all the pre-port and cultural port instructions: be polite, bow, use what phrases you know in Japanese, use chopsticks, give gifts. The latter was a moot point since all the opportunities for in-home stays were taken by others on the ship. One thing that was apparent was that we should have applied for home stays months ago, before we even began our voyage. Much is available only as a pre-sale. I had thought that this applied mostly to side-trips in each port. That was also true, but the more difficult arrangements to make were the home stays. By this first port we knew we would miss out on all chances of home stays in any port. From reports of students and passengers these were usually enjoyable and informative. Since the Japanese people that Pat had met on two previous business trips to Japan had never invited him to their homes, it would have been a rather rare opportunity to learn more of the inside Japanese way of life.

After everyone had been cleared through customs and immigration, we left the ship and did a bit of exploring. First we traveled on the electric commuter train around a newly built island constructed after the terrible earthquake of 1995. Here there are many large and fancy hotels, offices and shops. Then we continued to the Sanynoma Center and its malls. Streets and streets of malls, much like anywhere in the Developed (and Consuming) World. Makes me think that instead of using terms like First, Second or Third World countries, or Developed, Undeveloped, or Developing, we could classify countries as Consuming, and Conspicuously Consuming. The USA and Japan fall into the latter. I have never seen so many cell phones or electronic gadgets in my life. I must admit, I don't hang around electronic stores at home, but they did kind of jump out at me.

For the following three days I had bought tours in Kyoto and Nara. On the first day I was to see gardens and landscapes and then, the following days, temples. Pat was going on an earthquake tour.

I had not realized how much time on a bus this would mean - after all, Kyoto was only about 70 kilometers (42 miles) from Kobe. Traffic in Japan is every bit as complicated as in large cities in North America. I have a low tolerance for freeways anywhere; I

Chapter 4 – Kobe and Japan

didn't develop an enthusiasm for them just because they were foreign.

I could hardly believe my situation. There I was following a Japanese tour guide - following her *flag*, no less. I thought of all the times I have been amazed seeing Japanese tourists coming off buses in our national parks and in various places of interest in New Mexico. Now I had become one of those tourists on a bus which had taken two and a half hours to go 42 miles! But bus touring seemed the only way to see what I wanted. If I were to go again, I would deal with my discomfort of not knowing the language and not really knowing for sure how to use the train and bus systems, and I would try it without an organized tour. However, those who did go it alone had to deal with traffic delays, too.

Kyoto is a huge busy modern city, but it had been the capital of Japan for 1100 years so there are many temples (more than 1000) and shrines (300 plus) which make it a very attractive destination. For two days I dutifully followed the guides and gazed at ancient and amazing structures, including temples, shrines, and gardens. We tend to think of gardens exclusively in terms of plants and flowers, but some of these Japanese gardens were far from lush. I reflected on dry landscapes of white gravel and carefully placed rocks - spaces created for prayer and meditation. But as we hurried along it seemed a contradiction. My impression was *not* one of a Zen consciousness. It prompted me to get in touch with the contradictions of my own culture: the love that was a foundation of Christianity, so often violated by war; principles of mercy and justice shared by my tradition and others, ignored by righteousness and over-consumption. We humans have some terrific, even divinely inspired ideals, but we have a hard time living them out. We are not alone in this inconsistency, as I discovered country by country, religion by religion.

One dry landscape at a shrine in Kyoto had a very thought provoking feature for me. There were fifteen stones placed in a well-raked area of white gravel. I sat in many different places and from no one place could I see all fifteen of the stones. I realized that an appreciation of what I can see is always going to be limited. A perspective on my life (or the world for that matter) is much like that too. I cannot see all my faults or virtues at the same time. I cannot see all of my lived experience at any one moment. I can only get one view at a time. To ask for more is a form of spiritual greediness. The lesson I learned looking at that landscape was : pay attention to and enjoy what *is* before me and what *is* me right now, don't demand perspectives of another time or another place.

At the entrance to one of the most visited temples in Kyoto, Kinkaku-Ji, there were posted five commandments of Buddha. Do not kill. Do not lie. Do not steal. Do not commit adultery. Do not drink too much. A very good life and a good society can be built on these five as well as my traditional ten. Two obstacles to enlightenment were also posted: greed and avarice. I can go along with that, especially if they include aspects of spiritual, physical and mental as well as monetary greed and avarice.

Reconstructing In Japan

pjr

Kobe is a major port city of Japan. The entrance to Kobe harbor was beautiful, with a city fireboat display (less violent and more graceful than fireworks, for my taste) accompanying our ship into the modern, spacious and spotless berth, rebuilt since the major Kobe earthquake.

Kobe had been devastated by an earthquake in January 1995, less than four years before our visit. As part of the Semester At Sea philosophy of education, every port involves "practica" field trips for various courses. As part of the Geological Hazards course taught by Professor Bill Orr, I participated in a tour of the Kobe earthquake reconstruction area, including a presentation by the city councilman who supervised the reconstruction effort.

Chapter 4 – Kobe and Japan

Television coverage of the quake in the states implied the "hubris" theme so popular in our increasingly anti-science culture. The reporters said that the Japanese thought they could predict the quakes, but could not, and that the death and destruction had been high despite the Japanese claims of earthquake-proof building codes. The truth is more interesting, as is often the case. Obviously, no one would ever claim an "earthquake-proof" building without some qualifications, but the term "earthquake-resistant" is properly used. In fact, the new buildings in Kobe, including tall office buildings, survived very well. It was the older small buildings, as well as elevated roads and docks, that were devastated. Most of the almost five thousand deaths occurred in the old parts of town, small houses with slate roofs. A sad statistic on the demographics of death indicates the situation - 60 per cent of the deaths were of people 60 years or older. Most of the people who died were old people living in old housing areas with old construction techniques, old people not strong enough nor able to move quickly enough to get out of the houses after the collapse. No one could move quickly enough to *avoid* this quake. At 5:45 am on January 17, 1995, the magnitude 7.2 (Richter scale) quake struck, and the whole thing was over in 15 seconds. The worst earthquake in half a century, in a country doomed to earthquakes, being located on the infamous Pacific "Rim of Fire." (In the 1923 Tokyo earthquake, 150,000 had died, about 30 times as many as the Kobe quake.)

The "failure" of prediction was more interesting than reported. The earthquake just was not the *type* expected. All of Japan, being located on the border of two converging tectonic plates, is subject to quakes from the subduction of the tectonic plates, as the underwater edge of one plate dives (in geologic time scales) underneath the other. This is the phenomenon the Japanese geophysicists study and closely monitor. But that is not what happened in 1995. The Kobe quake was not a subduction quake. Its epicenter was not even at Kobe, but near a small island perhaps ten miles offshore. The type of motion was not that associated with a subduction quake, either.

The relief effort was somewhat slow, and neighborhood people had to fend for themselves for several days. Fires were difficult to tackle, because roadways and communications were crippled, all the infrastructure city dwellers learn to take for granted. Even in the long term, there was little government assistance to rebuild individual homes. The rebuilding of the Port of Kobe was remarkably rapid, driven by its economic importance to the entire nation. With some cost sharing between Kobe and the national government, the Port of Kobe reopened within three months.

The films of the disaster showing fires, toppled roofs, displaced and collapsed sections of expressway, rescuers searching through rubble, bring home the human tragedy. But the force of nature involved is more forcefully brought home to me in the waterfront area, set aside by the Kobe city government as a disaster memorial. No deaths here, no rescue efforts, no toppled buildings. Just a reinforced concrete walkway along the edge of the old harbor, extending well out from the shore with little noticeable damage, hardly any vertical displacement or waviness, until one point, where the walkway simply shifts south about two meters (six feet), the concrete sheared and displaced in a discontinuity, then continues parallel to its original direction. Contemplating that displacement, I marvelled at the skills of the architects and engineers who built skyscrapers that withstood the cataclysm.

Polite Japan

pjr

What would the Japanese do if the rest of the world suddenly decided they didn't need their stuff? What will we all do? The world is into making stuff, and using up stuff, and we cannot get off the merry-go-round.

Chapter 4 – Kobe and Japan

The Japanese we encountered generally were polite, kind and generous, but aloof. This agrees with my own experiences on two previous trips to Japan, and with the experiences of several colleagues who spent an academic year or more there, and with many other observers of Japanese culture who agree that the Japanese are very polite, but not close. That is OK; "polite" goes a long way. Politeness is highly under-rated in America, I think. (Even in marriages.)

There were also many stories from our shipmates of Japanese being more than polite - perhaps not "close," but genuinely hospitable and generous. We met one decidedly non-aloof fellow at the beginning of a hike in the mountains. His fruit truck was parked at the end of a parking garage, the incongruous entranceway to a popular hiking area. Seeing that we were westerners, he enthusiastically engaged us in conversation, gave us gifts of tangelos from his truck, told us of his visit to the United States. His English was minimal, but his enthusiasm made up for our lack of knowledge of the Japanese language. The encounter was surprisingly warm, and left us with an appreciative glow. Other Semester At Sea people had good experiences, too. During a mild but cold rain, an unprepared woman student was taken aback when a Japanese woman came up to her on the street and handed her an umbrella, "a gift from us to you Americans," then walked on, herself unprotected. The Japanese are also tolerant of drunks, foreigners as well as their own, I would say to a fault. We heard of drunken Semester At Sea men students who were abusive to an old Japanese man, taking off his reed hat and trying it on themselves, in a downtown street mall. No one protested or called the police.

Communicating in Japan and the World

pjr

From later ports, we would look back fondly on Japan, for its health and wealth, for its cleanliness, its politeness and hospitality -

and, surprisingly, for its ease of communication. It was relatively easy to communicate at a tourist level in Japan, either in their partial English, or in our bits of Japanese, which is a very easy language to pronounce. At a more engaged level, Japanese becomes difficult, set with pitfalls of manners and offenses built into the structure of the language. Different verb forms are used depending on the relative stature of speaker and listener, far beyond our almost archaic words like "sir" or the Spanish distinction between *usted* and *tu* and their verbs. Westerners are often amused by the Japanese professional's formality of exchanging business cards, but in their highly structured society, they literally do not know how to talk to people (that is, what verb forms to use) until they know the listener's title and position relative to their own. For tourists, they cut us more slack.

Also for tourists, Japanese is very easy to read when written in Romanji, the phonetic transliteration using our western alphabet, commonly used on street signs, subway stations, etc. Unfortunately, the written Japanese of newspapers and books is impenetrable without years of study. The Japanese themselves waste years learning their written language. Of course, it is not a "waste" if you consider it as an art form, but for utilitarian communication, it and other non-phonetic languages (like Chinese) are terribly inefficient. The well-known absurdities of English, which frustrate people around the world, pale into insignificance compared to the problems of written Japanese and Chinese. Dependent on world commerce as they are, most Japanese professionals study English diligently. Any native English speaker living in Japan can make a nice supplementary income teaching adult English classes. The results are not very successful - the Japanese have a very hard time with English, even after years of study. Catharine and I once met a Japanese engineer who had studied English for ten years. We met him off-road in Catalonia, where we had all stopped to walk over to a Roman aqueduct. He had been working at a firm in Barcelona

Chapter 4 – Kobe and Japan

for less than one year. We conversed pretty well, at a casual tourist level, but not in the English that he had studied for ten years, but in Spanish, with its regular pronunciation, dependable phonetic spelling, fairly regular declensions, and lack of absurd words like "get." (Have you ever looked up "get" in a good dictionary?) Of modern languages, Italian would seem to be the ideal choice for an international language of business, being even simpler than Spanish - only one verb "to be" and less colloquialisms. (Modern Dutch is regular, I'm told, but not as lyrical as Italian.) Even better would be the resurrection of the "rational language movements" from the early 20th century, Esperanto and Ido. Logically, their time should have come, with the modern emphasis on world commerce. But it looks like everyone else in the world will be stuck with English. They have my sincere sympathy.

My Urban Problems

csr

Pat and I both went to Kyoto on the second day and enjoyed many temples in the rain. It gave them a rather nice feeling. But again our time was very scheduled and we had to hurry on. The very worst aspect of this day was an American import, our box lunch provided by the ship: "Lunchable Tacos." This was the worst of USA fast food culture grafted onto the worst of hurry along Japanese. When I ask philosophical questions about how to nurture my aging self, I don't want it to be with the equivalent of "lunchables."

By day three Pat and I were ready to get off the buses. We decided to go on a mountain hike with a shipmate friend, Germaine, from the Colorado Rockies who also needed some encounter with nature. Our destination was the Nunobiki waterfalls. We should have hiked through the residential area to get there, but being used to trails in the mountains we (Pat) couldn't believe that was our "wilderness" trail, so we chose a dirt trail. Wrong choice. We climbed and climbed. No waterfall, but great views and some spectacular spiders, green and brown striped with flecks of yellow. Finally, Pat decided to backtrack, Germaine and I went down a different way. We later reconnected at the subway station and Pat said he had found the waterfalls - just a few blocks away. We should have taken the "path" which was just a street through a residential area. After a meal of fast food Japanese style, we hiked up to the falls. Here, I finally had time to sit and draw and think. And the falling water was refreshing to my citified spirit.

For this, our last night in Japan, Germaine and I decided to go to the public hot springs. These were indoor pools the color of rust which were hot beyond belief. We were the ones who had to save face - *American* face. All the women in the place were watching to see if we would (could?) go in. It took all my determination to step into that blistering water, but in I went, very carefully. After the first pool, the others were tame. The cool rinse was a delight.

Germaine and I took our time returning to the ship. We stopped to have tea with a family in kimonos, the only ones I saw in the country. It was a Saturday night and I had the feeling this was a special time for families in this part of the city. I bought a freshly steamed sweet bun on the street; I have no idea what it was, but it was delicious. As we walked around looking and sampling food, we could identify virtually nothing, but it was all displayed beautifully. For us it was a late return to the ship. Both Germaine and I felt pretty old as we hiked up the gangway at 10:30 pm and passed young students just going out for the evening.

Modeling the Experience of Aging

pjr

The Japanese have a special reverence for aging and the aged, so it was a natural place to reflect on my own "models" of the aging experience.

Numobiki falls

At Sea At Sixty

My old model of aging was a economics-type of "diminishing returns" model. What is one more year out of fifty or sixty? If you are fifty and you live another year, it is only 2 per cent more. You've pretty much seen it all, right? This is my third trip to Japan. Compare it to one of the faculty children at ten years old. Another year is 10 per cent of his total life, maybe 20 per cent of his really self-aware life, maybe 100 per cent of his reflective life. And he has never been to Japan, so it must mean more to him, fresh impressions, etc.

I had decided some years ago (about the age of forty) that this model is inadequate. That is not the way it feels at all, and I now prefer another model to reflect my experience. The key to the new model is "complexity," and a better, less-analytical sounding metaphor is that of "tapestry of life" or "mosaic of life." Sure, this is my third trip to Japan and I am sixty years old. Rather than being jaded, rather than being bored compared to a young one who is visiting for the first time, I have this more complex relationship with Japan. For example, on this trip Catharine and Germaine and I day-hiked in the mountains. In search of some well-known waterfalls, we were not finding any (dare I say "lost" ?) and, at an impasse on where to proceed, we decided to split up - they went on and I returned. (I found the waterfalls, by accident.) I am then reminded of my near fatal trek up Mount Fuji in 1978 with two guides who had worked on the Japanese translation of my first book (an applied math text). I then recall presenting a series of lectures in Tokyo, and remember being so impressed with the audience of ostensibly cold and up-tight Japanese professionals who broke into warm applause just because I opened my lecture by saying "good afternoon" or "hello" in Japanese. (*Kon nichi wa.*) Which then reminds me of another thread in my complex Japanese theme, Christmas of 1995 when Catharine and I were riding our bicycles not in Japan but in Australia, along the sea-side walkway in Sydney that would be the course for the 2000 Olympics cycling

Chapter 4 – Kobe and Japan

race, and we passed a crowd of 50 or 100 Japanese teenage girl tourists. I smiled as we went by, and called out my best *kon nichi wa*. They were thrilled, bubbled over with giggles and enthusiasm, ran after me, called out and begged me to stop and let them (surprise!) take my photograph with them, giggling more when I towered more than a foot over the delightful adolescents. Then I can remember December 1991, visiting friends who spent a year's sabbatical at Tohoku University in Sendai, Japan. I recall presenting a seminar to the engineering department, spending two nights in my friends' squashed Japanese apartment, bathing in a little square tub with a dipper for rinsing. Visiting a famous hot springs area with them and their Japanese colleague, with a near altercation with drunken Japanese young businessmen who were getting smart-aleck and insulting in the nude mixed-gender hot pool area, watching with satisfaction as another obnoxious drunk rolled off his perch into a dangerously hot pool and emerged wide-eyed and momentarily sobered. I can "compare and contrast" the port city of Kobe with the megalopolis of Tokyo and with the university community in Sendai. While all the Semester At Sea undergraduates were romanticizing the Japanese, I could better appreciate the clear but gentle counsel of two women SAS faculty members, one Japanese-born who lives in the states, that you could live for decades in Japan and speak, read and write perfect Japanese, and *never* be really accepted into Japanese society. You would always be a *gaigin*, that word that encapsulates so much of Japanese insularism, since it means both "foreigner" and "barbarian."

At sixty, I am not a blank tablet for impressions, because I already have a *relationship* with Japan, a personal history with the Japanese. My Japan experience is not one thread, however new and bright, but a multi-colored interlacing of old threads, recalling various periods of my life and career, summoning up my fond memories of valued friendships, renewing my former fascination with this unique and (to me) contradictory society. The Japan area of the tapestry of my life is richer and more complex than that of a young person.

Time, of course, will ultimately take its toll. Neural connections will fail, the complexity will become overwhelming, like an over-worked Baroque painting or too-intricate classical quartet. My will to face up to the complexity will fail. The colors of my multiple threads will fade. I do not expect life to continually become more interesting no matter how long I live. Not many people enjoy life in their 90's, and most lose interest much earlier. (Some in their 20's.) For me, life is still getting more interesting. I remember the bubbly young Mozart asking the Austrian King in *Amadeus*, "How many voices do you think I can sustain? Guess!" Guess how old I will be when the richness and complexity of life peaks out for me, when the complexity becomes so bewildering that I overdose, or just lose interest. Maybe sixty is already the peak, the optimum mixture of life's inherent complexity with remaining health, vitality, and functioning brain cells. If it is in fact "all downhill from here," I absolutely cannot complain. It has been fascinating, and will still retain interest for years, even if this is the peak.

Passing Thoughts

csr

One of the things which struck me on my first impression of Japan was what long hours the men usually put in with their office jobs. Being involved one way or another with company business from seven am until eleven pm is common. The corporation - employer is almost a part of one's identity or at least rates up there with family, maybe more.

This made me remember our own life style, which was decidedly atypical American. After graduate school (which had even longer work hours) we settled into a work schedule with very little of the typical American dependence on many hours spent in a car. Pat always worked within ten minutes of the office and the chil-

Chapter 4 – Kobe and Japan

dren walked to school. Within about seven years, Pat had a home based business and flexible work schedule, and I was teaching, which allowed the children to experience both parents as home parents and eliminated all of those office meetings and time spent commuting and carpooling. Most after school activities were accessible to our children with them providing their own transport, usually bicycles or mopeds. My mother had spent most of her maturing life in the car driving children here and there; I was very glad that I had found a way to avoid it.

Sayonara

csr

On Sunday we were told to be on board by 3:00 pm so we didn't leave the harbor area. There was a lot to see in a small area. We visited the Maritime Museum, had a light lunch and then saw the memorial for those who died in the 1995 earthquake. We were back on time and watched as our anchor was lifted and we slowly pulled away from land and were back on our watery home.

Chapter 5
The China Seas

Chapter 5 – The China Seas

Reflecting after Kobe

csr

The waters off the coast of Japan looked far different from the empty North Pacific, with many islands, many ships and boats.

The weather was pleasant and warm and it was a treat to watch flying fish and wonder what predators had chased them out of the water. In my marine biology class, students reported on what they had seen in Japan. It is clear from all our "wet market" experiences that Japanese like their fish sold alive . . . *fresh* is the criteria of value. It was exciting to see the fish flopping around and the excitement of buying and selling. No plastic wrapped and sealed products here.

Seas between ports were times of reflecting on what was experienced in the previous port. Japan struck me as very busy. The countryside, what little there was, may be more laid back, but certainly the coasts were bustling with businesses. The economy was in trouble (one estimate was that Japan had lost one half of its wealth in the 90's) which affected the entire Pacific Rim. The USA figures in all this because of corporate involvement in Japan. The economic entanglement of Pacific Rim countries, including the USA and Canada, will remain.

John, a senior passenger and friend of ours had an interesting conversation with an old Japanese friend of his regarding the question "Should Japan have an army again.?" The upshot of the discussion was that John's Japanese friend didn't think Japan should have an army and he expected the USA to protect Japan. John responded that while we currently have an agreement with Japan to protect it from aggressors, this might be reconsidered since the US is very involved in many places in the world. His Japanese friend thought the US should be "policeman to the world." When John spoke about parents in the US not wanting to lose children in such policing, the conversation drifted away.

Apologizing for Hiroshima

pjr

A popular side-trip for our stay in Kobe, Japan was an overnight to the War Memorial at Hiroshima. I do not have the stomach for this sort of thing. On a bicycle trip through Bavaria and Austria last summer with the Bicycle Adventure Club (a kind of co-op bike touring company whose trips we have enjoyed tremendously) we were invited to make a small side trip to Mauthausen, a WWII prison camp. Catharine and I declined to visit, but the information on Mauthausen was important and enlightening. It was primarily a working quarry, secondarily a death house, although some mass executions were performed there. It also provided the faintest salvage of pride in our fellow Christians during those times. Besides the Jews, Gypsies, homosexuals, and other enemies of the state, this was the final destination of those noble German soldiers who chose to die rather than carry out the Nazi orders. Traitors, they were, just like the second century Christians who were executed as traitors to the Roman Empire (and charged as atheists, too, by Roman standards). The martyred German soldiers numbered in the hundreds, not millions, but they should not be forgotten when Germany in the early 1940's is brought to mind. But I do not feel obliged to look at the photographs, the gas chambers, the chains. One of our bicycling group, a strong young woman, made it into the first exhibit room and almost fainted. To face something like that, it seems to me you either will be overwhelmed, or you will harden yourself, you will look with your eyes but withdraw. I did not buy the rationale of television news coverage 1960's and 70's showing the blood and gore of Vietnam as a prelude to family dinner, claiming that it would sensitize the nation to the horrors of war. Just the opposite, it de-sensitized us to all pain and suffering. Now we show it for entertainment, at all hours and on virtually all channels (except PBS).

Chapter 5 – The China Seas

Anyhow, we felt the same way about Hiroshima, but that, we think, is quite a different place. Some of the faculty managed to lay guilt trips on the undergraduates for Hiroshima, a remarkable achievement since these kids weren't even born before the Vietnam war, let alone WWII. (I was seven years old when "we" dropped the bomb on Hiroshima, so of course I can logically share in the guilt.) The undergraduates and many of the older people came back full of obvious but shallow moralizing. I heard one student say this was the first time she had been ashamed of being American. I am sympathetic, but I have a hard time leaving the issue alone.

Do you have to see the graphic evidence to be ashamed? Are you ashamed of being American, or just human? I have no problem with being ashamed of our human proclivity for war, but why *only* Hiroshima? How about Tokyo? The United States had fire-bombed Tokyo so mercilessly, with 100,000 deaths in a single raid (more than the 75,000 who died immediately in Hiroshima), that it was not even considered a worth-while target for the atomic bomb. Is it worse to die in a millisecond flash of nuclear energy, or to gasp out your last breath amidst magnesium fire bombs and your own burning homes? How about Dresden, Germany? The allies fire-bombed Dresden so intensely in one night that the heated rising air caused tornado-like fire funnels, affecting local weather. Does "Pearl Harbor" mean anything? It was not mentioned in the Core Course lectures. It was not mentioned at the Hiroshima War memorial, nor were the Japanese invasions of China, Burma, Korea, nor the Japanese atrocities in their prisoner of war camps. And why only mourn the "innocent women and children," as if every seventeen year old drafted into the Japanese or German armies was "guilty" of something other than ordinary human-ness. My own brother was in the U. S. Army Air Force in the Pacific area when the atomic bombs were dropped; perhaps he was one of the 100,000 U. S. military whose lives were saved by the use of the atomic bombs. How many *Japanese* lives were saved by the quick termination of the war?

In my Christian Brothers high school in the early 1950's, we read an excellent essay written by Monsignor Ronald Knox shortly after the war, titled "A Missed Opportunity." Close in time to the realities of World War II, he did not take the simplistic moralizing approach to Hiroshima and Nagasaki that is common today, but he did confront a real issue. His idea of the "missed opportunity" was that the U. S. could have avoided the deaths by simply demonstrating the weapon on some remote location. Once the Japanese saw the invincible destructive power, they would have surrendered.

It was a very persuasive and thought-provoking essay. It also provoked guilt of a creative kind, that is, not just some vague sentimental bad feeling, but the kind that could lead one to reconsider past actions and think differently about future options. Unfortunately, historical research since Knox's time has shown incontrovertibly that his good idea would not have worked. The bombing of Hiroshima itself, instead of some remote demonstration area, certainly demonstrated the destructive power forcibly, yet it was not enough to change the collective mind of the Japanese ruling military. They voted against surrender, conclusively, *after* Hiroshima. And after the second atomic bomb was dropped, on Nagasaki, they voted to surrender by only a small margin. It was not a missed opportunity, as Knox saw it.

But was there another opportunity? There was, but all the cheap moralizing, the indiscriminate guilt peddling, the sloppy sentimentalizing will not reveal it. There is a genuine moral issue involved, and a genuine structural flaw in U. S. policy that persists to this day. No one mentioned it in all their lectures. It is the longstanding U. S. tradition and policy of demanding "unconditional surrender" from its enemies in war. This, I believe, is the real issue at Hiroshima and Nagasaki. The historical evidence is that the Japanese military would have surrendered, even without the atomic

Chapter 5 – The China Seas

bombs, if the terms of surrender offered would have allowed them to retain their emperor. Ironically, the atomic bombs forced an unconditional surrender, but then General MacArthur allowed the Japanese to retain their emperor.

In the early 5th century, St. Augustine wrote in his *City of God* about conditions for a "just war." The work was often ridiculed by Catholic peace advocates during the anti-Vietnam war days just on the basis of its premise. As if there could ever be anything such as a "just war" to a pacifist. In fact, it deserves reading, or at least excerpts. We should do as well as St. Augustine wanted. He was very clear that taking a position of "unconditional surrender" was immoral. Always. By not allowing the ruling powers of the defeated armies to save face, by striking fear for the future of their progeny in the hearts of the enemy, by setting them completely at the mercy of their enemies, such a policy prolongs war past the point of reason, leading to almost total war of annihilation, increasing death and destruction for both sides. As it did, for example, in our War Between the States. Yet unconditional surrender is the proud tradition and policy of the United States since 1776. For me, this reflection leads to a genuine, non-sentimental, creative guilt. We should apologize for Hiroshima because we insisted upon unconditional surrender, which led to the necessity for using the bomb.

There are other remarkable inconsistencies in the American consciousness about nuclear weapons. For one thing, people still talk about Hiroshima as the standard for ultimate destruction. Sorry to say, later developments in thermonuclear weapons in the USSR and USA have completely overshadowed the old atomic bombs, almost as much as they had overshadowed their predecessor chemical explosive bombs. Their destructive power really is too much to handle mentally. In the other direction, relatively small-scale tactical nuclear weapons have been developed. You don't need a missile system to deliver these - a suitcase would work. We (humanity) are in luck on one aspect of physics. It turns out that it is easier to build a large nuclear bomb (not thermonuclear) than it is to build a small one. If the nuclear weapons had developed in destructiveness more gradually, from the one-ton chemical "blockbuster" bombs of WWII to tactical weapons like the 155mm Howitzer nuclear warhead, on up to Hiroshima-size bombs, people would have been less averse to using them, and then continually escalating the use. Undoubtedly, they would have been used in Korea, and probably in Vietnam, as Presidential candidate Barry Goldwater suggested, rationally but immorally. There would not be this strong distinction, this intimidating demarcation, between "conventional" and nuclear weapons. Humanity can thank God for this accident of physics.

It is remarkable and encouraging that the USA has been involved in three major wars since 1945, and has never used these weapons, nor even the tactical nuclear weapons that can be fired from unimposing field artillery. Neither did the old USSR. The world will soon see if the same restraint will be shown by the religious zealots of India, Pakistan, Israel, North Korea, and terrorists. The first decade of the new millennium could be the time. Even if the weapons are not fired, they will be used in threats, and already are being used as threats. The world wide policing actions of the USA will certainly be diminished as these countries hold the threat of random nuclear destruction.

There is an aspect of this specter that is grotesquely appropriate for any democracy. I think of it as the "nuclear crossbow" perspective. In 1968, I had just started employment at Sandia Laboratories in New Mexico, a nuclear weapons laboratory. I remember well a fellow graduate student at Notre Dame who blanched at the idea of working there. He was clear that he wanted the work done - the threat of nuclear war was real - but he did not want to do it. I accepted the responsibility, for a while, but the work and atmosphere became too much for me too, and I finally left. (It may be of interest to note that I encountered only one person in my stay at the lab

Chapter 5 – The China Seas

who was remotely close to the cartoon of a war monger. Everyone else was scared to hell of what they were doing.) I took my first trip to Washington, DC, and in free time I visited the Smithsonian. As a kid, I had enjoyed archery, and I now wandered about the exhibits of bows and crossbows. I came across a quote from a medieval Pope condemning the crossbow as "a weapon heinous to God and man," and imploring in the strongest emotional language that its use be eliminated in warfare. My initial reaction was to laugh. How "innocent," in the worst sense. Crossbows! What would that Pope think of machine guns, chemical and biological warfare, or nuclear weapons?

There seemed to be little connection between crossbows and nuclear weapons - or was there? Why such a reaction from the Pope about the crossbow? The warriors of that time already had plenty of death-dealing weaponry, now on display here at the Smithsonian - long bows, broad swords, rapiers, maces - all well designed to cause painful and bloody deaths. What was so different about the crossbow? The answer came back. I had known since the days of my youthful archery hobby that crossbows were *armor-piercing weapons*. The force of a longbow is limited by the strength of the archer, but a crossbow has a gearing system. It could not be fired as rapidly as a longbow, but even a physically weak soldier could crank up a crossbow, storing energy in the steel arms, and then release the heavy iron bolt to hurtle through the protective armor of a knight. That was the key. A crossbow soldier could easily dispatch a knight. Without the crossbow, the poor grunt foot soldier could kill other poor grunts on the other side, and knights could "honorably" engage other knights, but it was not easy for a foot soldier to dispatch a knight. The crossbow brought a kind of unwanted egalitarianism to the battlefield. Instead of being just a pawn in the hands of nobility, the foot soldier could bring the war home to the decision makers, the nobility. No wonder the Pope's moral sensibilities were offended!

And in our democratic states, who are the decision makers? Who sends the troops off to war now? The President, sure, but only after consulting with democratically elected representatives, and only after all of them consult the people through polls, press leaks, journalist essays, and all the techniques of modern political machinery. So if Saddam Hussein gets the bomb and a simple delivery system to reach our coast, maybe the people's decision on the next Gulf War will be somewhat tempered. The nuclear crossbow will bring home the war to us, perhaps even to the government center in Washington. We'll see how "intolerable" the enemy's actions are then.

Guilt and Personal Battles

csr

Assuming that war is used only in extraordinary circumstances, I have considered if any of these issues of guilt, war, and "just war" theory, have anything to do with my daily, ordinary, living? I think that they do because the decision to fight is a decision based on failed relationships of people, or countries in the case of war. Seeing so many war memorials around the world did make me think about personal issues of aggression, fighting, and guilt. I had to look at war memorials of my own; I had to look at conflict and guilt.

There is no way to live in relationship, whether as friend, family, lover, or life partner without disagreements and conflict, unless one party always "backs down." As a mental health counselor and minister, my observation of this behavior is that the danger of resentment building to explosive levels, or to the disintegration of self worth, is just about inevitable. So the question is *when* does one fight and *how*?

After sixty years I'm still working on this. I think I should fight when it is important; not just when I have a disagreement with another. This is one thing that may have improved over the years. Not

Chapter 5 – The China Seas

every disagreement, hurt, disappointment, emotional response to a situation warrants a "fight." As we used to say in Catholicism a long time ago, it must be "serious matter." This serious matter would include issues perceived as ones of deep personal integrity. If my sense of who I am (as good mother, wife, friend, church member, etc.) is at stake, then I must not just ignore it, but deal with the conflict.

How conflict occurs is in my hands to a great extent. Emotions just are there. They come. Tears leak out. But how to express strong emotions and how to express my thoughts about the issue at hand is my choice. One choice is to deal face to face as conflict arises, another is to deal through written communications (it is great to have an eraser or a PC so that I can change my words). And it is also possible to opt for silence and, sometimes, I think it is better to say that this is what I am choosing, rather than to just disappear. I won't go into a course on "How to Fight Fair" or "Conflict Management," but there are real tools out there to help us not go to war with each other for years - or for a life time.

Experiencing hurt and anger and saying all sorts of things in the heat of the moment leads to the question of guilt, just as war naturally brings up this question. There are moments just like that one in the fairy tale, when toads and frogs jumped out of the ugly sisters' mouths. Shouldn't I feel guilty about that? And about break-ups, and decisions which lead to no peace treaties in my life? A few years back guilt was a big mental health topic. Some therapists were for it, others against it. Looking back, I think this was misfocused. Guilt is just a feeling, and an important one. Without it, it is hard to be reflective about one's behavior; it is hard to change behavior. What is necessary, I think, is to decide what to do about guilt, rather than let it sit on top of one's (very) self, and dictate the rest of life.

Moving into old age I must look at those things about which I feel guilty. Have I "taken care of personal business?" Or am I putting flowers on my war memorials? Am I putting more energy into old business than new business? Have I determined what to let go and let be? Or am I dragging around ancient history (like many countries in the world) and allowing its presence to determine my future. With less time ahead of me in life, if I want to become a wise woman, then I will feel the guilts of the past, will address what is at war within, and set a new course.

Religion as Poetry, Religion as Politics

pjr

Semester At Sea offers a surprising range of religion courses. Traditionally, religion and language are the major descriptors of a culture, so this might be expected in a curriculum built around cross-cultural experience. Still, I was surprised at the range available. I took a comparative religions course, and Catharine sat in on an Early Christianity course and another on Islamic Civilization. Also offered were religions of the East, and others. There were Baha'i people on board, and I spent a lot of time in the first couple of weeks talking religion and related sociology with them. We would be visiting the Baha'i World Center in Haifa, Israel. So, as is often the case, I spent much time thinking about religions.

Religion is best treated as sincere poetry, not hard fact. That may sound like an old heresy, but like all the rest of old heresies, it has a lot of truth in it.

The old questions asked when I was a kid were "Why can't Lutherans and Catholics both be right?" The stock answer from my staunch Roman Catholic education (an excellent education, by the way) was straightforward. "There can be only one right answer to a question about God." This sounds good, but in fact, it does not even work for science. The scientists certainly felt the same way about the nature of light. The question was, "Does light consist of waves, or of particles?" A very clear question, it would seem. Dust is composed of particles, sound is a wave phenomenon; which ap-

Chapter 5 – The China Seas

plies to light? When a wave theory explained light behavior in some respects, providing incredibly precise and accurate predictions of experiments, the issue seemed settled. Then other types of experiments demanded a particle concept to explain and predict physical reality. Scientists decided to wait awhile for a definitive decision, until more data was in. They waited. In the meantime, when they had to build something, they just used whichever "nature" of light fit the reality at hand. In psychology, it is called cognitive dissonance - otherwise sane and rational people simultaneously holding mutually exclusive beliefs. The physicists could not resolve the question, so they finally adopted the terminology of "duality," the dual nature of light. In some situations it behaves as waves, in some as particles, no problem. It would not create a good impression with laymen to call it the "cognitive dissonance theory of light," would it? The younger physicists accepted it as a way of life, but I think the older ones were always a little embarrassed. It is not only a failure of the scientific method, but of the scientific pre-suppositions. There can be, and are two (at least, that we already know of) "right answers" about the nature of light. Are we religiously inclined people to claim that God is more easily understood than light? That human cultures, of which there are arguably no right answers but clearly are many reasonable stop-gap theories, are more accessible to feeble human intellects and soft science methods than the eternal? Our concepts of the nature of light at least can be tested - the concept predicts something, and we can then test the prediction against experience. But conceptions on the nature of God either cannot be tested systematically, or else they fail obviously, as when we say that God is good and therefore conclude that there could be no wars. The religious belief that everything that happens is God's will gives comfort to many, although it is frightening to those who think more about it. In any case, the belief or "model" has no predictive value. If it rains, if she dies, if we are invaded, it is God's will; if the sun shines, if she pulls through,

At Sea At Sixty

if they sign the peace accord, it is God's will. Some find comfort in this, but no one predicts what will happen. As claimed by Alan Watts, the late scholar of eastern religions, we should not even use the word "God" until we recognize that we are speaking metaphorically rather than metaphysically, in which case he preferred the non-theistic term "Supreme Identity." So if we admit that we cannot grasp the nature of light, and therefore perhaps may be forgiven for not being able to grasp the nature of the Supreme Identity, and recognize that we are using metaphors, can we logically say the following? "There can be only one right *metaphor* to a question about God."

The point is, we cannot figure it out. Re-reading Thomas Merton's "The Way of Chuang Tzu" for the hundredth time felt so appropriate as we crossed the Bering Sea trench in the North Pacific, over 20,000 feet deep. Old Chuang Tzu, maybe 300 years before Christ, is confronted by an erstwhile student monk who keeps chasing his own tail, working himself into a lather of philosophical confusion. (I can relate to this.) Chuang Tzu advises him to calm down, and as we might say today, set more realistic goals and expectations for himself. "You are like a man out at sea in a rowboat, trying to measure the depth of the ocean, but you only have a six-foot long measuring stick." Great image. I spent a 35 year career working on the Navier-Stokes equations of fluid dynamics, and actually reached the point of understanding them quite a bit, except that just two years ago a new and very lengthy paper was published that shed for me a whole new light on their nature. I do not fully understand the paper, but I think I might if I worked diligently at it, and first found some help with the mathematics involved. Maxwell's four equations of electromagnetics were developed in the 19th century. I think I understand one equation at a time, and maybe two, but I cannot gestalt the entire system of four equations at one time. So I am supposed to figure out what is *the* right answer

Chapter 5 – The China Seas

about God? Sure, and then I will measure the depth of the North Pacific Trench with a double-length yard stick.

If you persist in reasoning about what cannot be understood, you will be destroyed by the very thing you seek.

Chuang Tzu, on the other hand, says that the Tao (sort of the Divine Will without a Divine Being) is *like* a grandmother. I appreciate this. Jesus said that God is *like* a mother hen taking care of its chicks. A helpful and comforting image, which fortunately was communicated as a simile instead of a metaphor as was the concept of God the Father, otherwise the pope would be insisting that only chickens could be ordained as priests. The religiously oppressed people of the world should unite under the banner "Down with Metaphors, Up with Similes." Anyone would be willing to kill for a metaphor, as humanity has done for ages, but a simile ? - perhaps not.

I use similes and metaphors all the time, even in science and mathematics. But you can't fall in love with your simile. According to St. Matthew, Jesus always taught in parables, he never taught without parables. Get it? *Parables!* Duh.

On a related but extremely important subject, I have learned after 35 years of marriage that I must not use similes to argue my point in a marital disagreement. That is a big mistake, leading to an argument about the applicability of the simile to the subject at hand, and leaving the original untouched, thus doubling the disagreement. I once caught myself starting to argue the appropriateness of my simile by explaining it with - guess! It was a true moment of Zen enlightenment, and I have not used a simile in marital disagreements since.

In the first meeting of our class on Varieties of Religious Traditions, Professor Bill Smith asked for definitions of religion. Of the eight or so offered, no one mentioned God. This is a good sign,

I think, a sign of intellectual humility and of caution. The word carries too much baggage with it to use straight away to study religions comparatively. (Besides, some of the most important religions are non-theistic.) But if you like to pray, the "Supreme Identity" is a little chilling and antiseptic. Then you use "God" or Father or Mother.

When the social scientists ask the Japanese for their religious affiliations, they find 96 per cent are Shinto (an old animistic religion), 76 per cent are Buddhist, and 13 per cent are Christians and others. Is there something wrong with these numbers? A lot of people are claiming adherence to two or three religions (although neither is "practiced" very much in Japan). So what if the Japanese use more than one analogy? Big deal. I like - in fact, I love - the analogies, the poetry of Taoism. Appropriately, my favorite religious book is a rendering of Chuang Tzu by Thomas Merton, an Anglican intellectual who converted to Roman Catholicism and studied Zen and other eastern religions. Intensely analytical and highly educated, he might be expected to be above the simple metaphors of Taoism but he said he enjoyed writing that book more than any other (and he wrote much - hardly had an unpublished thought).

All this is not to say that all analogies / metaphors / religions are equally valuable or appealing or ennobling. Some are degrading and pernicious, leading to human sacrifice, crusades, slavery. But even the worst have some worthy elements, I think. But then, "worst" is a dangerous word, begging for a "best," and implying a hierarchy, a completely ordered set. Religion A is better than religion B, aggregate of metaphors X is better than aggregate of metaphors Y, just as 99 is greater than 98 which is greater than 97. . . Nonsense. We can't even rank college football teams in an ordered set. In 1993, Florida State was Number One, Notre Dame was Number Two, according to the Associated Press poll. Both lost only one game. But Florida State lost to Notre Dame! By ten

Chapter 5 – The China Seas

points! Somebody explain that one to me before I try ranking the Methodist religion compared to the Quaker religion.

Merton, just before his bizarre death by accidental electrocution, finally got it, I think. Reading his strange "Asian Journal" collected by his colleagues posthumously, struggling through his wordy, convoluted intellectualizing replete with footnotes and obscure literary / philosophical references, you find him at last confronted with the non-verbal reality of the great reclining Buddha in Sri Lanka. Merton can't even write about it in his journal for several days - there is a gap in his compulsive intellectual jabber. Then he describes his experience of the reclining Buddha, "accepting everything, rejecting nothing." Another few days, a flash of electrons, and his light is out.

Touring religious sites in Kyoto, it was good for us (Catharine and I) to see the temples and shrines with their charlatanism and money making, and to read about Taoism and Buddhism being co-opted. An article from *Archeology* magazine (Sept.-Oct. 1996, pp. 60-65) in the Core Course reader makes a convincing case for the politicization of Buddhism at the "Cloud Hill" site in China, 1500 years ago, exalting imperial authority by equating (in sculpture) the emperor with the Buddha. Merton himself thought that later Taoism was a "popular, degenerate amalgam of superstition, alchemy, magic, and health culture," no relation to the sixth to third century B.C.E. classic Taoism of Lao Tzu and Chuang Tzu. It is good for Catharine and I, because we see that the worst of our own religious tradition is perhaps no worse than the worst of others.

I guess I am still as much Christian as Taoist, and I am glad of it. I believe in practically all that Jesus said and did. (And if the Inquisition ever put me on the rack in the basement of the Vatican, I'd believe anything they wanted me to believe.) Maybe the only honest alternative is to skim the cream off each one; maybe I should start my own church, the "Church of the Holy Skimmers."

•

Core Matters

csr

Issues of treaties, wars, both past and present, were continual topics as we traveled. The central course of the Semester At Sea was called the Core Course and it was mandatory for all students, staff, and senior passengers. Before we arrived in each port we were given academic information about history, geography, business and cultures. The Core Course varied quite a bit in amount covered (which was greatest before Japan) and the quality of presentations varied also. If they weren't as well done as we expected, that generated conversations as beneficial as if we had had a good Core. The was true especially among faculty and senior passengers. What I noted was that there seemed to be a selective memory about Japan and her history and policies. Presentations were very favorable; there was more negative history presented before China. All this reinforced my belief that all history is interpretation and is influenced by the present. There is no such thing as objective historical writings. At best there can be attempts at balance, but in the long run who edits determines a great deal. This is evident from my study of Hebrew and Christian scriptures. It was evident thousands of years ago, as well as today.

As we approached the passage between Taiwan and mainland China we encountered our third typhoon, Yani. This one was not as severe as the other two and only lasted a day, but it did slow us down so that we were late arriving into Hong Kong.

The day after the storm was Yom Kippur and my friend Loreen and I went to the services which were well attended by students. The ones leading the services were sensitive to the different Jewish traditions. The prayers of repentance were powerful; this is one way of dealing with guilt. Most of all I was impressed by the devotion of the students. These devotions and others on the ship by Christians and Muslims attested to a relevance of religion which I found positive.

Chapter 5 – The China Seas

We entered Hong Kong harbor on a warm and pleasant day. The blue green waters were full of ships and boats of fishermen and families on holiday. It was the birthday of Communist China as well as the ancient Moon Festival so there was a festive air.

The harbor was surrounded by very tall and modern buildings. Large neon signs announce the important corporations in the world economy and Hong Kong's economy. My most lasting impression of the harbor was that of a changing reality. Dredges were moving earth at a great rate. New islands are being built, channels are always being dredged. Tunnels and bridges connect Kowloon, Hong Kong Island and the New Territories. True, the capitol of the Peoples Republic of China is far to the north in Beijing, but when you are in the harbor it is clear that the center of commerce is still here in the south. Here China not only meets the rest of the world, but deals with it . . . in every sense of the word.

Chapter 6
Hong Kong and China

At Sea At Sixty

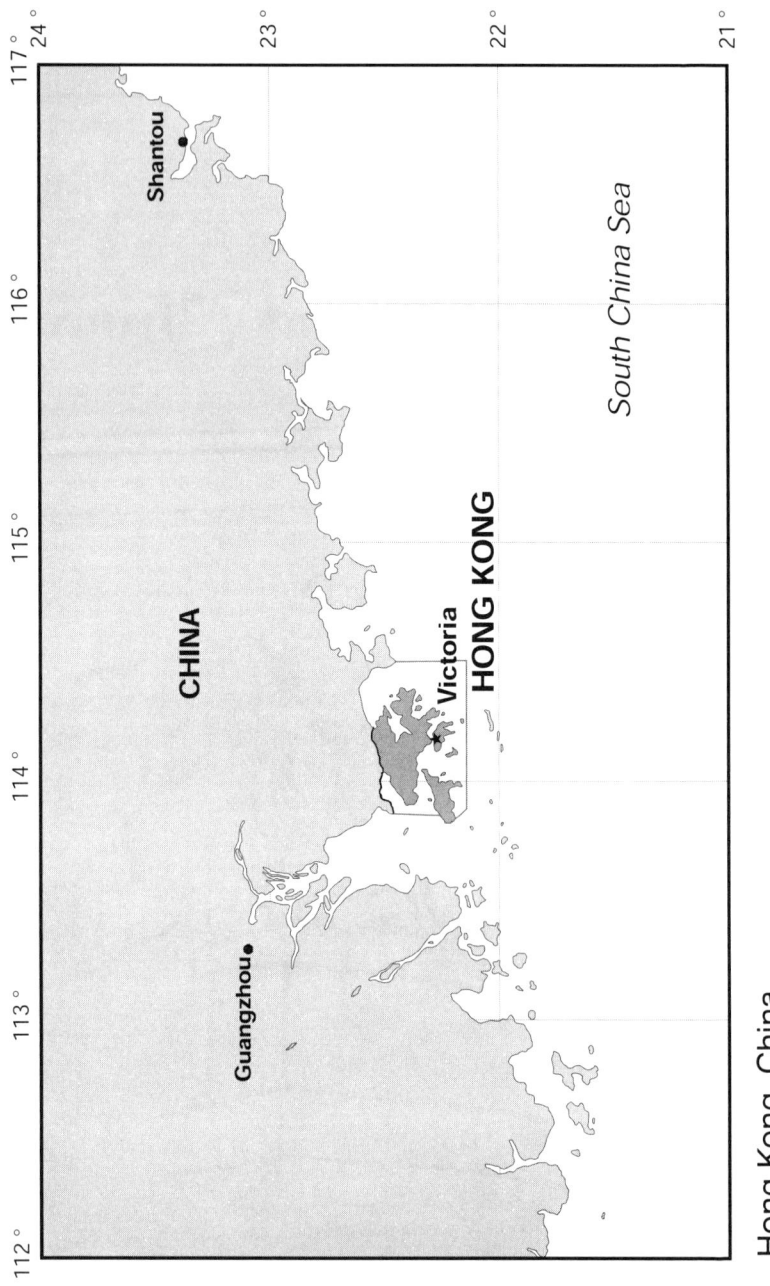

Hong Kong, China
Latitude 22.2°N Longitude 114.1°N

Chapter 6 – Hong Kong and China

Land of Many Dragons

csr

Having arrived six and a half hours late into Hong Kong, we were very glad we had not booked ahead for flights to Beijing. There was a whole lot of commotion for those who had: changed flights, rushing for buses, etc. Instead of all this, we went with friends to explore an area near the port and hopefully find a sculpture park in Kowloon Park. Find it we did and it was a very good display of some impressive pieces. The whole park was a treat and full of families dressed up and having picnics. We liked all but a few of the twenty or so sculptures, remarkable in these days of junk passing as art.

We found a restaurant (tip: in Hong Kong, look *up*stairs for restaurants) and had to deal with a *real* Chinese menu. I passed on "wings and web" (duck wings and feet) and eel, slugs, sea cucumbers and welk. Instead we ordered sweet/sour chicken, crabmeat "balls," and scallops and taro. The latter was deep fried and strange to our Western tastes; it was rather like wallpaper paste. Dessert had the taro in a sweet bread form (not much better) and we sampled "sweet white fungus." This is very hard to describe. The fungus is crinkley and white and floats in a sweet soup. There was very little taste, but it did have texture.

Food is such an important part of a culture. In China I enjoyed the rice, vegetables and meats, but had a hard time knowing what it was I was eating . . . just knew a general category. It is probably a good thing that I didn't know and that we generally kept pretty close to the tourists areas. Like most foreigners I enjoyed the *dim sum* very much; it was both interesting and tasty. When I went to the markets I was slack-jawed at the creepies, crawlies, and slimies. The experience made me wonder what would lead someone from this part of the world to say "Yuck." One object I thought was a lizard fan turned out to be not for fanning but a dried lizard "for eating, madam" and produced the special quality of longevity. I for one would prefer to live a little shorter life.

When we came outside from our dinner we found all the streets closed off and throngs of people moving towards the port to see the fireworks display in honor of the Communist holiday. How lucky it was that we were docked right next to the place where the fireworks boats anchored. In fact all we had to do was step out of our cabin and onto the deck and had the best seats for the show. And what a show it was! The Chinese invented and continue to develop fireworks. My favorite display consisted of a huge burst that changed into little lanterns that floated down from the sky and were extinguished in the water. It was loud, noisy, breathtakingly expensive, and a little intimidating. But it was all that fireworks should be.

The next day was a rather typical tourist day in Hong Kong. With another senior passenger and friend, Geraldine, we first took a taxi to Hong Kong Island looking for groups of people doing T'ai Chi, since I practice a form of it (Tai Chi Chih). We had no luck in this since Pat could not be understood saying "Hong Kong University" and I could not be understood saying "T'ai Chi." I didn't expect my Chinese to be understood, but was surprised that we couldn't get these few words in an intelligible form to the taxi driver. Next we rode the famous tram up Victoria Peak and walked around. I think because of all the pesticides used there were not many insects, hence very few birds along the paved paths. Pat went looking for an Internet Cafe and I went shopping at Stanley Market. I bought silk pajamas for our daughters and myself. What a luxurious treat! It turns out that these were the best bargains of the whole trip around the world. And the quality was very good and the sales people very helpful and courteous. When we were in the People's Republic of China in high tourist areas, this was not the case, at least not in stall or street buying. There we found very aggressive merchants and felt unable to think about a purchase; con-

Chapter 6 – Hong Kong and China

sequently we didn't buy. I don't know if this is a cultural difference, or the result of being a tourist mark. But I do know that I don't like being what I could only call cheated and harassed. We experienced this in many of the countries we visited. How we looked ("Western") meant dollar signs. To sellers in developing countries, we were rich. And by their standards we surely were. But this intellectual understanding didn't go very far in making us feel comfortable with this "don't take your time" behavior. It was especially difficult to deal with when the sellers were children.

Ferrying In Hong Kong

pjr

I enjoy just about anything on water, and Hong Kong's famous Star Ferry was no exception. The Star Ferry, familiar (we are told) to James Bond movie fans, connects Hong Kong Island proper to the Kowloon Peninsula, and the fleet of old Star Ferry ships are in perpetual motion, bringing commuters and tourists back and forth across the busy harbor, dodging ocean liners, freighters, small pleasure craft, fishing sampans, and other ferries. There was even more commotion at the Aberdeen Bay area, originally a secluded harbor providing shelter from typhoons, but for years now a permanent residential area, a floating suburb of live-aboard sampans, water taxis and outrageously ornate restaurants.

Both the Star Ferry and the Aberdeen Bay area will be disappearing soon. The Star Ferry will be replaced by a bridge, and the Aberdeen bay area will be back-filled and topped by high-rise apartments. We feel privileged to have experienced both. The progress is dehumanizing, but yesterday's inhuman technology always becomes today's nostalgia. People get dewy-eyed over steam locomotives, the good old days. I love them myself. Our good friend and good neighbor, Bob Anderson, is a railroad fan to the point of major avocation - history and photography. He tells us that railroad professionals refer to fans as "foamers," as in "foaming at the mouth." Have you ever ridden a steam train? They are filthy, noisy, air polluting, spewing cinders all over the place. But we have seen some of the greatest scenery in the world on old steam trains. Like Colorado's Durango to Silverton train, where we used to race the train on bicycles over two mountain passes in the Iron Horse Bicycle Classic, then take the train back to Durango. But then McDonalds took over the race operation, the roadies gave way to gnarly mountain bikers, and the rest stops ran out of bananas. Now that is true nostalgia - old Italian road bikes. Graceful, light, with dignified musical names like De Rosa, Cinelli, Campagnola. Made with steel, not carbon fiber and aluminum and titanium. Steel is real. We raced the real steam locomotive narrow gauge train on our real steel racing bikes almost two miles above sea level over Coal Bank Pass. There is a real name for you - who would brag about climbing a bike over something called "Diesel Pump Pass"?

But I don't think the American Indians saw the steam engine as the good old human scale technology. Those steel rails nailed to creosote hardwood ties were hard to dislodge, and the trains brought buffalo killers (not "hunters" at all, they shot from windows at animals easier to hit than the neighbor's dog) whose inhuman long rifle technology crushed the Indian's stone age weapons. And the buffalo killers were followed by farmers who treated Mother Earth like a pimp treats his whore, and these are the same "small family farms" whose technological life style we now sentimentalize in contrast to big agribusiness with its laser-aligned broccoli rows and high finance. In Hong Kong Harbor, I'm sure the noisy, rattling, diesel-smoke-belching Star Ferry, paying minimal wages to hired hands, looked like the apparition of death itself to the sampan captains who lived independently on their silent, graceful craft they had built by their own hands from living vegetation and coaxed and rowed with intimacy through breeze and current. But to us, the Star Ferry and its motley passengers looks and feels quaint and human, compared to the planned commuter bridge be-

Chapter 6 – Hong Kong and China

tween Kowloon Peninsula and Hong Kong Island. And Aberdeen, a safe typhoon shelter with its dazzling swirl of family living room and fishing boats, its small ferries and water taxis, its ornamented floating restaurants, surely looks better than the prospect of land fill and yet another concrete and steel high rise.

I was here in Hong Kong in 1991, after the transfer back to the People's Republic of China had been announced and scheduled for 1997. I was surprised that the magnates of Hong Kong were building like there was no tomorrow. I realized that the very wealthy would not be strongly impacted by the take-over of a communist government, because they all had their "ace in the hole," as the old song put it. For years, the wealthy of Hong Kong had been moving assets out of the city-state, creating wealthy expatriate communities in the Pacific Northwest coast of America, from Seattle to Vancouver, driving up real estate prices and driving out the "natives" from the market. They would certainly lose wealth in the takeover, as measured by numbers in their net-worth statements, but their lifestyle would not be radically affected no matter how pure their new communist masters were. Besides, the PRC needed Hong Kong to teach it how to play the international money game. At the other end of the scale, poor people are not impacted that much by a change in economy and government, unless it involves true madmen, as in North Korea. But the middle class, like the engineering and mathematics people at my meetings, had plenty of worries. They had something to lose, but not enough to keep one foot out the door, like the wealthy. So far on this 1998 visit, it did not seem that the PRC intended to install any draconian measures, and middle class life was going on. However, the crash of the Hong Kong stock market earlier in the year was clearly traceable to the PRC meddling and deterioration of accounting standards and market rigging. The reversion of the island city-state of Macau to PRC is yet to come, in 1999. I had also visited Macau in 1991. A small island, full of the history of pirates, the black ships, Jesuit influence in the Orient, it was a pretty weird place. A colleague and I had a great visit to a Buddhist temple there, full of incense and icons. The most impressive and ostentatiously wealthy building in Macau in 1991 was the Bank of China office. It was clear then that "Red" China knew where to get help with international money transactions - go to the crooks. Macau has been a den of thieves forever. We Semester At Sea people were warned by the U. S. Consulate to not visit Macau because of problems with the "Triads," the Macau equivalent of Mafia families. The week before we arrived in Hong Kong, there were gang murders, and more occurred during our stay. It reminded me of a T-shirt I had seen on a Central American archeological dig the first time I had been in Belize in 1987. "Rainy days and automatic weapons just get me down." The PRC needs Hong Kong, but Macau needs the PRC, to clean it up, as they did the mainland port city of Shanghai.

Hong Kong is a very easy city to get around in, with excellent subways, ferries, and numerous taxis. There are plentiful excellent restaurants and shops, but our experience was not totally pleasant. The people were not exactly rude but surely not gracious; they were hurried, intense. The one exception was our wonderful guide (the best of the entire round-the-world voyage), Jesse, but she turns out to be not a native of Hong Kong but Malaysian by birth. Her graciousness, so appealing to us, earns her an epithet from her Hong Kong friends, who call her a "banana" - yellow on the outside, white on the inside.

Jesse was our guide for the side-trip from Hong Kong into the PRC. She warned us about the other side - about the importance of saving face, the rapidly changing situation, and verified what I had guessed - there are new rules every trip she makes. (She only goes into the PRC a couple of times a year.) Hong Kong became part of the PRC on July 1, 1997, fifteen months before we arrived, but the changeover is far from complete, and presents surprises. Like, if it is all one country, why did we have to exchange money from Hong

Chapter 6 – Hong Kong and China

Kong dollars to real "Chinese" money (yuan)? And why did we have to go through *immigration* lines between Hong Kong and Guilin? And why did we need a second guide who took over in Guilin, while our Hong Kong guide went along for the ride, and to shepherd us back through immigration to get back to Hong Kong? One country - it is, but it isn't. As we expected, it is not like traveling from California to Nevada, but it even seemed more like a border crossing than traveling from the US to Canada.

Our guide on the Red China side was one cool character. She was poised, and presented the "party line" faultlessly but was obviously nobody's fool herself. Everyone on the trip was amazed to find out later she has never been out of China. Some dismissed her English language facility once we found out that she was taught by an American living in China, but I know better - I've known Chinese engineers and mathematicians who lived *decades* in the US and didn't speak anywhere near as well as our guide. I could not understand them, nor they me. The partial differential equations were still there, but math needs a few words now and then, maybe even a sentence or two. This did not prevent them from teaching hapless US students. No wonder our graduate schools are heavily populated by foreign nationals - once they get in, they drive out the locals (us) from frustration. In science, math and engineering, many graduate schools are 90 per cent foreign born. Some ten years ago, I visited a consultant at U.C. Berkeley, and I congratulated him on having one student who was obviously a native English speaker. Yes, he said, it was great - the lad was from Ireland! (The professor himself was a WWII escapee from Poland.) Also, the foreign graduate students are willing to put up with more crap and unfairness from advisors than we are. (There are a few other things keeping young America from the discipline of graduate education, such as sex, drugs, and rock'n'roll.) On a cycling trip in Austria the previous summer, I had noted again that people tend to reach a "personality plateau" on language skills. One reaches a certain point of being understood, then one "digs in" on accent and even grammar, as if "passing" for a native speaker would involve a threat to one's identity, a surrender of one's perceived self-ness. As for the problem of US graduate school students and faculty, it would be preferable to have native US students better represented. One real and frequent problem with foreign born faculty is their refusal to embrace American tolerance and equal opportunity ethics. But overall, the problem of foreign-born faculty domination does not appear critical to me. I have much more in common, in interests and values, with technical graduate students and faculty from anywhere in the world, any political inclination, race or religion or lack thereof, than I do with "real Americans" standing on a corner listening to rap music on a boom box.

My feelings about this common academic culture had already crystallized in 1991 when a colleague and I visited the newly opened Hong Kong University of Science and Technology. This very impressive, modern and obviously expensive campus had been built during the uncertainty of the PRC takeover, a brave act that for me put to shame the half-hearted commitments to higher education in the US. That first year, Hong Kong UST only had 500 or so students, but they were expecting to reach 30,000 in a few years. The University had been advertising for faculty in US professional newsletters for several years, and their generous salaries and benefits had attracted some excellent people, usually Chinese or Chinese-Americans or other hyphenated Chinese. The cultural ties of Chinese world wide go far beyond modern national allegiances, even prompting one international financial analyst to refer to them as the "invisible nation." I would never be accepted into this club, yet again I feel more in common with them than with many of my fellow Americans. I admire their commitment to higher education, as witnessed by the massive investment in Hong Kong UST, and their long held cultural values of science and arts. I can imagine the founders of the United States, intellectuals like

Chapter 6 – Hong Kong and China

Jefferson, Hamilton, Franklin, and Madison, feeling closer to these world-wide Chinese cultural values than to the present day celebrity-worshipping, royalty-fawning, anti-intellectual mainstream American culture. If the Chinese culture proves to be the inheritor of world intellectual leadership in the 21st century, they deserve it.

A Work of Art

csr

In the evening of our second day in Hong Kong, we enjoyed dinner on board ship and packed for our early morning flight to Guilin, about 500 kilometers (300 miles) northwest of Hong Kong, in the province of Giangxi. For this trip we had a tour guide who turned out to be our favorite of the whole voyage. Jesse was informative, answered any questions in a straight forward manner, and knew how to get things done, yet was very sensitive to local guides and their needs to be the knowledgeable ones.

Guilin had been an image in my head ever since I first saw Chinese brush paintings. I had thought that the paintings were very stylized; I didn't think the mountains could really look like that. They do. They are gumdrop shaped mountains of limestone which rise up from the Li River for miles and miles. Our tour was a four and a half hour one on a boat that traveled slowly down the River. I was surprised to be informed that eight million Chinese visit this area each year, with an additional four hundred thousand foreigners. Our huge lunch including soup, chicken, rice, tofu and delicious onions and sprouts was made special by sharing it with a couple and their child who were from Taiwan. It made me wonder if they are counted as "foreigners" or Chinese?

As we traveled on the river we saw fishermen and their cormorants. It made me think of *The Story of Ping* which I had read as a child and used to read to our children. It tells the tale of a little yellow duck who ends up with a family of fishermen. They put a ring around the large bird's neck and then when the bird dives and catches a fish, the fisherman takes it from him. No need for tackle and bait. The only reward the cormorants get are the small fish which slip past the ring. I looked forward to reading this story to our granddaughter when we returned home from our travels. She wasn't interested. The illustrations and stories of the past just didn't have the same appeal to her. You'd think I'd just leave this alone. No. I sat my husband down and read it to him. He was a good audience.

The five hour, 70 kilometer (40 mile) bus trip from the river back to Guilin was another lesson in patience. For some reason, dealing with country roads in China elicited more patience from me than long rides in modern Japan. There were so very many interesting things to see: string sacks on top of a bus holding live ducks quacking away, pink pigs on top of trucks and bicycles and people, people, people. Walking, riding all sorts of contrivances, tearing down houses, rebuilding, groups socializing. On the long trip I also enjoyed getting to know some Semester At Sea students better. I was impressed with their enthusiasm. They freely shared insights and opinions that revealed to me their life experiences so different from my own. They made me feel hopeful about the future.

The sunset was a huge orange ball, very beautiful, but the result of pollution, I'm afraid. This was one of many paradoxes. I can't say the sun wasn't beautiful; neither can I deny the terrible pollution we saw in China. There is a similar difficulty with the beautiful children I saw in very over populated countries. Always questions, with many difficult answers. Answers coming from me who overpopulated also (five children). I wonder if my view point now is as off-base as my image of myself as an eighth grader going door to door in Texas in the early fifties getting signatures on a petition to keep China out of the United Nations. Am I the same person, just much older, thinking I know an answer for people in such a different culture? Or am I someone very concerned about the future of the planet? Am I willing to make changes in my life, appropriate to my non-child bearing age, that could make a planetary difference? What would those changes be? These were questions to be considered on the long voyage and in the months to come.

We were back in Guilin in time to see a cultural dance performance. The dances were to represent many of the ethnic minorities in China. (The Giangxi province, in which Guilin is located, is home to many ethnic minorities.) The dancing, music and costuming were enjoyable and very colorful. What was puzzling was the commentary. None of the dancers were from the regions being portrayed and yet the speaker was telling us that all these minorities are appreciated by the ethnic majority Han and all get along and intermarry. All I could think of were the "Free Tibet" and "Free Mongolia" protesters who demonstrated when Chinese officials visited the US recently. My impression of the PRC was that there is a well articulated party line evident in this dance show, and in the English language newspapers and magazines, but there is something happening under the surface. That something is dissatisfaction with current Chinese policies that ignore cultural diversity and human rights problems. I wonder if the PRC can keep a lid on these ethnic problems. Will China experience ethnic wars such as those now dominating in Africa, India and the Balkans?

Cruising The Li River

pjr

Most of the Semester At Sea people took the popular side trip to the pollution monster Beijing (one of the world's last places to experience old-style industrial pollution - not wimpy photochemical smog, but raw diesel fumes and coal dust), and a quick but worthwhile experience of the Great Wall. We chose instead to fly to Guilin, China, about 500 kilometers (300 miles) northwest from Hong Kong, for a river trip.

At Sea At Sixty

Guilin is a newly expanded city, obviously built by outside money - new airport, new roads, new hotels with familiar names like Holiday Inn, etc. The big attraction is not the city, but the river. The Li River, from Guilin to Yangshuo, must be one of the most photogenic thirty miles on earth. Flowing through classic Karst formations of limestone hills threaded with caves, the countryside is famous for its "gumdrop" hills, once thought by westerners to be a largely mythical stylized form of classic Chinese water colors, now recognized to be quite literal representations of this unique valley.

When we arrived by bus at the departure dock for our river trip, we were disappointed by the crowds and noise. I was fantasizing something of a wilderness experience, but these are large (though shallow draft) boats, carrying perhaps fifty passengers, and the boats are stacked alongside one another at the docks. The boats are noisy, diesel belching, and old. Then I thought, well, we will spread out on the river once underway. Not so, there were always boats nearby - usually we could see three or four ahead of us at every stretch of the river. But it was not a disappointment for me. I got into the scene. Other than wilderness areas, rivers are usually locales for hustle and bustle, commerce and commotion, like the Mississippi of Mark Twain.

The hundreds of tourist boats on the river came in various sizes, vintages, and conditions of disrepair. A Semester At Sea faculty member who taught business courses asked our PRC guide how many companies ran tourist boats. Without cracking a smile, she said definitively, "One." The government owns the whole operation.

I took a lot of video films on this trip, and thoroughly enjoyed it. I am new to using video cameras (other than at racquetball tournaments), and I found to my surprise that taking the videos did not interfere with the travel experience for me. I find still photography so annoying, so interfering, that I often go days on a trip without

Chapter 6 – Hong Kong and China

taking any shots at all. The decision of what and when to shoot, how to frame the photo, evaluating light and shadow contrasts, etc. distracts me from "being there." But the video camera flows, and is forgiving. Zooming in and out focuses the attention, and lets you present both the particular focus and the context in the same swoop, nothing at all like having a wide angle still photo presented next to a telescopic lens shot. And the electronics are so forgiving of light conditions that you don't think about anything but looking. People wave and smile, there is *action* in video. And video is made for river trips, especially for the Li River. You just point and look and shoot anywhere, swing around one side or the other, or just hold it steady and let the boat and bends in the river pan for you, and you look like a cinematic genius.

The river trip lasted about five hours. After much shooting outside, I finally went inside to lunch, not bored with filming or looking, but confident that I could not possibly take it all in, with or without the camera, knowing that any time I could look up from my food and friends and new acquaintances, and it would be there, the hills and the water buffalo and swimming children and fishermen and Chinese tourists on all kinds of boats. I spent an hour at lunch inside, hardly looking outside, enjoying good conversation and an elaborate multi-course meal. Slurping our noodles with a young Taiwanese tourist family, we did not share much language, but it was clear that he was worried about the PRC. I drank good Chinese beer (say what you will about commies, they make a decent beer) and I could not possibly pass up a complimentary glass of wine poured from a two-gallon jug containing a snake. This was not some token worm hiding at the bottom of a bottle of Mexican Tequila - this was a *big snake*, coiled four or five times around the inside of the jug. I remember my first graduate school days in the early 1960's when our department head and founder, a remarkable character named F. N. M. Brown, told me about his years in China in the 1930's. In those non-politically-correct years of the early

At Sea At Sixty

sixties, he was clear that Chinese men "will do absolutely anything for an aphrodisiac." Nice of that old man (my age now) to share that with a young grad student. When you read about any venerable Chinese folk medicine or herb that says "vitality" or just plain health, translate the euphemism. This aphrodisiac-lust plus Asian superstition creates environmental disaster. Shark fins, sea horses, rhino horns. Sympathetic magic. Big snakes. Get the imagery? Hard-on like a tent peg. Why else would anyone eat the animal called a sea cucumber, except that it is big and tubular? On a moonlight lagoon float trip in Belize, an old woman high on marijuana (not my wife - but she was there, too) eagerly confided to me that she had seen jaguar penis for sale in the night market in Hong Kong. Thanks just the same, I think I will pass, but I would prefer even this to a sea cucumber. It is all anus, a lazy, barely alive seafloor slow-motion vacuum cleaner, practically brainless, mostly soft and immobile, a dirty bottom dweller. Hmm. Perhaps one of the greatest environmental boons will turn out to be the invention of Viagra.

The trip back from Yangshuo to Guilin was by bus, and the combination of a major PRC holiday with construction zones turned a 70 kilometer (40 mile) bus ride into a sweaty, noisy five hour ride, with neither food nor restroom stops. There was plenty to complain about, but strangely enough, as we finally creaked out of the bus back in Guilin, Adrian, a woman student whose company we immensely enjoyed on the bus, observed that miserable bus ride was the best part of the trip to China. I was surprised to find myself in agreement, at least from the viewpoint of experiencing a bit of the "real" China versus the tourism. We had moved slowly and unobtrusively through many villages, had a look at village life and traffic and construction problems. I had particularly noted a construction crew tearing up an old stretch of highway concrete that had deteriorated: about twenty not-young men in a line with pick-axes, mostly immobile, never more than one or two

Chapter 6 – Hong Kong and China

with their tools in use at one time. There were large buildings that had been built too close the roadway, now being widened, so the buildings were being moved. Traffic was so slow, even completely stopped for minutes on end, that some of the women students were able to flirt with local guys on motorbikes. One local offered a woman a ride on the motorbike through the traffic jam - I would have been tempted. A high truck behind us struck an overhanging tree limb, breaking it so it dangled into the road behind us, further blocking traffic. A small crowd formed and a young man managed to climb up the tree, and after five minutes or so, snapped it free. We were still there to cheer him, since the bus hadn't budged more than a twenty yards during it all. As the sun set, people on motorbikes and on foot were headed into a village for a dance. We passed some, but then the bus stopped again, and we were re-passed. The walkers made it into the village before we did.

Capitalist Hustle in Communist China

pjr

The obvious impression of any American who has dealt with Russian or Chinese people since the thaw in the Cold War is that they really do not understand about capitalism or a free market mentality. They get the idea about taking in the money, all right, but they do not get the idea about *providing* something, such as goods and services. The hustle at the end of our Li River trip from Guilin to Yangshuo was extreme.

The return trip to Guilin was to be by bus, and we were to board just outside an area of hundreds of vendors' stalls. With some time allotted for shopping, we walked around for about half an hour. The sales pressure was an assault. People shoving things in your face, shouting at you, *arguing* that you should buy their trinkets, hats, paintings, T-shirts. The delicious irony was the sale of T-shirts emblazoned with Mao Tse-Tung's benignly dictatorial

At Sea At Sixty

face. I hope the old murderer is spinning in his grave as his people do the capitalist hustle.

These market places, like the others we would visit on our world journey, are terrible places to enjoy shopping. There are beautiful items, to be sure, but you cannot enjoy looking at them because of the hustle. Just walk past a stall looking straight ahead, and you are accosted. Glance at something in a stall, and the owner acts like you have signed a contract in triplicate. If you ask the price, the owner acts as if you have promised to buy with your first-born as guarantee as soon as the bargaining gets down to a third or less of the first offer. I know the liberal apologists will immediately claim that I am insensitive to the poverty of the people, but poverty is not the factor; it is greed and rudeness, unmitigated by an understanding of how Americans shop. For example, I have shopped and bargained and purchased jewelry and art and other items from poor and economically middle class Native Americans at feast day dances at Pueblos in New Mexico and reservations in Arizona. I never felt hustled, hurried, or pressured, and I knew I could freely discuss and admire jewelry, pottery, or paintings with the artists without them assuming that I was therefore obliged to buy. (I do know to avoid asking prices in rural areas in Central and South America unless I am serious about buying, to avoid hurt feelings and the embarrassment of people reducing their prices to undignified, unjust levels.)

I did find an exception at Yangshuo. Just off the main vendor street, the pace was noticeably more quiet, although there was still pressure. At an open shop full of classic design watercolor scrolls, the thirty-ish woman proprietress was polite and pleasant, and gave me some room and time to look. Only when I admired two scroll paintings did she say that her husband was the artist. I expressed interest, and continued to window shop at another area and asked the price of another painting, and did her husband paint this one also? No, only the paintings in one small area. I wanted to buy one

Chapter 6 – Hong Kong and China

of his, so I went back to that area, and inquired the price of each of two of his scrolls, which was 35 yuan. At this point Catharine came up to me to ask for more yuan. She had been happily bargaining in the middle of the street, a few stalls down from mine, with a four-foot high septuagenarian munchkin, a glowing smiling hunchback woman who had sold Catharine on a stone carving. (It turned out to be plaster.) As I turned to leave my stall to give Catharine the money, the proprietress jumped a little and perhaps was about to resort to more aggressive bargaining with me when I turned back to her and assured her that I would be right back, that "I will buy one of your husband's paintings, I will." She looked a little surprised, since we had not bargained, but she gracefully trusted me. I returned after a few minutes of chuckling with Catharine and the munchkin, and resumed my enjoyable perusal, appreciative of the time and room. I decided on the painting, asked her to wrap it up, and said "30 yuan, that is OK, isn't it?" She was slightly surprised, and said of course. My objective was not to chisel down the local artist to the minimum price, but to just let them know that I knew the rules - a nominal bargaining, lest the word spread that Americans are easy marks. At this point her husband appeared with a beautiful baby on his arm. As the woman boxed my scroll painting, I told her I knew how it was to be married to an artist - she smiled faintly, glanced sideways towards her man, and she and I shared an insight across cultures.

    This couple were far from wealthy, although clearly well educated, and did not display the all-out aggressive greed of most of China and most of the world. The most extreme example of the blatant greed and hustle occurred back in Guilin at an expensive gift shop. Just before our tour bus headed back to the Guilin airport for our flight back to Hong Kong, we enjoyed a huge family-style lunch at a new restaurant and gift shop area. We exited the restaurant through the gift shop (good capitalist design there) and as we were waiting for all our group to assemble, I decided to get rid of

At Sea At Sixty

the last few yuan I had, since it would be a pain to exchange them back to Hong Kong dollars, thence to US dollars or Malaysian ringits or whatever. So I started cruising the display shelves for anything - candy, nuts, cards, drinks, calendars, literally *anything* to get rid of the yuan.

I was immediately confronted by a well-dressed young woman sales clerk who almost ran to the display shelf, grabbed something totally at random, shoved it in my face, and ordered "Buy this!" My first reaction was to say "Why?," or perhaps "Why would you possibly think I could be remotely interested, since I did not look at it and don't even know what it is? And I doubt you do." But she did not speak English well enough to argue or debate sales manners, so I just turned away. Undaunted, I walked to another display shelf. Again, before I could so much as focus on what the boxes contained, another budding capitalist sales clerk grabbed an item at random, shoved it in my face, and demanded "Here, buy this!" One more attempt, and I was indeed daunted. I quit, walked outside, and took my yuan back to Hong Kong. These people could not sell bread in a famine. They think capitalism and free enterprise give a license to assault. By contrast, the merchants of Hong Kong are capitalists *par excellence*, and though they are brusque and might even be considered somewhat rude at times, they are models of decorum and civility compared to the budding free-enterprise converts from communism.

Guilin also provided our first encounter with maimed beggars, who gratuitously pointed out to us their own infirmities and missing body parts. However, their approach was not obnoxious, and I would prefer their hustle to the "capitalists" of Communist China.

We were also taken to a small lake (really a wide spot in the Li River) in downtown Guilin and were directed to the "Elephant Rock." No, it does not look much like an elephant at all, but there is a poorly rendered plaster elephant statue near the shore, and couples take their photographs there. The Chinese are tiresome and

Chapter 6 – Hong Kong and China

banal in their insistence on naming natural shapes, more so than place-namers in our Grand Canyon, I think. On the Li River trip, it was one after another of things like "Sleeping Boy Rock" or "Two Fisherman" or "Five Tigers Catch a Goat." Corny and distracting, it detracts from my enjoyment of the scenery - rather like being hustled again. "See the fish? See it?" No, I don't - I could, but I just want to see the rock. May I, please?

Isn't it strange how *shapes* have the power to move us so? The description of the Li River trip in our Semester At Sea Field Program used the words "strangely-shaped," "shrouded in mist," "stone forest," "haunting atmosphere," "fairy-like," "classical Chinese painting." All accurate, I could not agree more, and the experience was deeply moving. Yet how strange that I and others would be so moved. These are just shapes, formed randomly by well understood physical and chemical processes. The people on our trip are well educated, and we seniors might be excused for being jaded after five to seven decades of living and traveling. Yet we glide around a curve in the river, there stands a minor variation of calcium carbonate dissolution, perhaps a tower shape, and everybody lets out a collective "Oooh!" My own "Oooh" is often the first and loudest. Queer, but an undeniably real power.

Also on our last day in Guilin, we had a trip to the justly famous "Reed Flute Cave," a gorgeous limestone cave with unique formations and a poignant history. First discovered in the Tang Dynasty (618-907 P.E.), this is the cave described by the old woman in the book (and film) "The Joy Luck Club," where the villagers hid from Japanese bombs during WWII. Unfortunately, the presentation of the cave is just about the worst we have seen in the world for a site of natural beauty. There were long lines to enter (it was a major PRC holiday weekend when we were there), trashed out grounds, smelly restrooms, junk shops. Then, inside the cave, it was clear that the limestone formations are deteriorating with the passage of so many visitors, cigarette smoke, and invading diesel bus fumes. The crowds were noisy. The worst aspect was the lighting. Single fluorescent bulbs were placed randomly, not even aligned any particular way, not hidden from view to illuminate the formations, but right in the main view. What you mainly see is fluorescent light bulbs, with a little limestone formation in the background. To add zest, the lights are multi-colored! The wiring consists of long extension cords, also clearly visible in random coils and tangles. One "highlight" is a photography portrait stall, set up well inside the cave, with little floodlights so you can have your photo taken in front of a fine "bridal veil" formation which I'm sure had been beautiful before the photography stall was put in. I was startled when I came upon it, and more so when the aggressive (even by Chinese standards) woman fixed me with a stare, charged out at me, and shouted "Take your picture here!" She was equally startled when I charged her and shouted "No!" in her face. She understood. At the farthest reaches of the cave, there was a moment of semi-silence, a hint of peace, and a few seconds to take in the beauty. And in the huge main room, where the villagers hid from the bombing raids in the late 1930's, we could imagine their experience. But overall, the Reed Flute Cave was an angry encounter for us.

Another aspect of budding capitalism in PRC is the press. The English language *China News* and *South China News* are just about what you would expect. A touch of mild, controlled "controversy" - as if anyone could really say what they mean about the government, which basically *is* the country. Essentially, these publications are company newsletters, "house organs" that are about as objective and controversial as IBM or General Motors magazines. For example, there is an article about reforestation. They are going to fix the forests, you see. They are retraining lumberjacks to plant trees, and the forests will be back in three years. Well, that is a relief to know, isn't it? The paper made no mention in the article about the cataclysmic flooding this year of the Yellow River,

Chapter 6 – Hong Kong and China

which everyone knows is caused not just by variations in natural weather patterns, but by the massive deforestation in the watershed of the river. It is too late! "Reforestation" is a lie, in China or in Washington and Oregon. The forest is gone for good. We may plant trees, but the lumber companies in our Pacific Northwest (many owned by the wood-crazed Japanese) will never let the area become a full forest ecosystem, which would take hundreds of years, even millennia to re-grow a rain forest.

Our sense is that the Chinese of the PRC are masters of tokenism. They give the English readers (who are hopefully here to invest) what they want to know. I would not trust one word of it. Consider the *Beijing Review*, "A Chinese Weekly of News and Views," with that "Views" in the plural, as though there could be more than one viewpoint expressed in print. According to the *Beijing Review*, the way to handle the flooding disaster is simple; you declare it to be a victory! "The leaders of the Communist Party of China and the Chinese government have called on the governments and people of flood-stricken areas to start resuming production as early as possible after the decisive victory in the two-month campaign to halt rampaging flooding." *Decisive victory?!* In case you doubt who cracks the whip over whom, "The reconstruction should be based on self-reliance of the local people and government, in addition to state support, . . ." These guys are definitely communists, not socialists. Also, it is sad to see how they have betrayed the communist traditional leadership in gender egalitarianism, as in this quote from an article entitled "Women's Books Become Increasingly Popular." "Psychologists believe that women's unique physical and psychological character, as well as social status, determine their relatively narrow reading interests."

But it is fun to read the back pages of the *Beijing Review*, with advertisements for modern adaptations of traditional Chinese herbal cure-alls. You would think with all these ancient cures and esoteric holistic medical practices that the Chinese would never get sick. In fact, their cancer and other disease rates are high, and life expectancy is short, compared to those who use our increasingly demonized Western medicine. But that does not prevent their advertisements from looking like something from a Santa Fe alternative newspaper. Probably the only reason for the Chinese herbalist nonsense is that the audience for the *Beijing Review* is American. It reminds me of the First Rule of Consulting in Science and Engineering: *Live out of town*. Exotic cures work only if they *are* exotic, that is, from far-away places. If the Chinese locals were reading this sorry excuse for a newspaper, they would have ads for services from Santa Fe, like astrology or numerology or channeling or my all-time favorite, counseling services from an American "Psychic Intuitive Animal Communicator." (Could I make that up?) On the other hand, certain types of Santa Feans are well known for believing anything and everything - I doubt that even the superstitious Chinese are *that* gullible. Of course, we Western scientific types can be too skeptical and supercilious at times, as in the deep suspicion of acupuncture when it was first introduced to the West. But the beauty of the scientific method is that it allows for even surprising techniques like acupuncture to be proven, which it has, and herbal medicines to be rationally evaluated, some with positive qualities. This often mis-named "Western" methodology is of course not unique to the west, but is well known in China and the rest of Asia as well. True Chinese medicine, like Chinese physics and Chinese mathematics, is not all folk wisdom and hearsay, but the latter packs the anti-establishment appeal in places like Santa Fe.

Chapter 6 – Hong Kong and China

Hong Kong Farewell – Auf Wiedersehen

csr

Our brief five day stay in China ended on a rather funny note. Right next to our ship, an outdoor *Octoberfest* was in full swing on the roof of the parking garage of the posh HongKong Hotel. Sponsored by several German firms with offices here, including BMW and Mercedes dealers who have major sales to wealthy Hong Kong business people, the "German Bierfest" offered Lowenbrau on tap, sauerkraut, bratwurst, an imported oom-pah-pah band, and Chinese waiters in leiderhosen. Well, it wasn't what the faculty thought of as an authentic *traditional* Chinese experience, but it was an authentic *modern* experience of this singular Chinese city. Hong Kong is a major international business center; I wouldn't blink an eye at this in Los Angeles or New York, and Pat and I enjoyed it.

pjr

I had a satisfying moment at the Hong Kong bierfest. In July of the previous summer, Catharine and I had bicycled from Munich to Vienna with the Bicycle Adventure Club. In preparation for this trip, we had studied some tourist German and I had listened to all of a thirty lesson set of tapes. In Germany and Austria, I did not really get to use much of what little I knew, which was disappointing. Now, here I was in Hong Kong, at a German Bierfest with lots of Germans. After we paid our entrance fee, which included a complimentary beer mug and one fill up, I went looking for the food. I walked up to a line for desserts, and in a flash my minuscule German language facility returned. I said to a guy at the end of the line, *Entschuldigen Sie*, which means (I think) "Excuse me," and he understood! He thought I wanted to cut into the line in front of him, but I just wanted his attention. As he motioned me forward, I waved him off, and said, *Entschuldigen Sie, Wo ist die Bratwurst ?*, which means, I hoped, "Excuse me, where is the bratwurst?" From his answer, it was clear that he understood me again! Of course, I could not understand a word he said in response, but luckily he motioned in a general direction, I said *Dankeschoen* (I hope I did - maybe I said *Gracias*), followed his gesture, and there, sure enough, was the bratwurst and the rest of the meal. One of life's little victories. On the defeat side, Catharine and I both came down with diarrhea the next morning. Perhaps we should have stuck with chicken feet and sweet white fungus in Hong Kong.

Despite the international and cosmopolitan attractions of Hong Kong, we and all the students made it back to the ship on time for our night time departure. With all its giant neon signs, Hong Kong was one very spectacular harbor to leave at night. We were impressed here, as well as all our other ports, by how very different it is to arrive at or leave a city by ship, compared to an airplane. Views from the air can be impressive, but ship entry or exit is an

Chapter 6 – Hong Kong and China

event, an excursion in itself, going to the historic heart of a city. Not some late add-on an hour's ride away like a typical airport, our ship entries and exits were usually highlights of the visit. The pleasure was doubled by being in the company of shipmates who thought it worth an hour or so to relish an experience such as watching Hong Kong's lights fade into the horizon.

Chapter 7
South China Sea

Chapter 7 – South China Sea

Conversations, Reflections, and Diversity

csr

We continued to sail in the South China Sea for only three days, but still there was time for conversation and reflection among those of us on the *SS Universe Explorer*.

What seemed clear, and became more clear as the days rolled by, was that each one was having a different Semester At Sea. I doubt that any two itineraries were identical, but even if they were, the experiences would have varied greatly. Physically, academically, emotionally, socially, and spiritually, because of ages, backgrounds, interests, and past travel experiences we were having dissimilar experiences of the one hundred days. We shared the commonality of being on the *SS Universe Explorer* in the Fall of 1998, but that doesn't tell the tale. Some participants saw a port as place to shop, or party, find a McDonalds, go on a tour or take off on their own. Just between Pat and me there was a difference in perception and involvement in the cultures. Noticing the differences among us has hopefully impressed me with how limited is my own experience of anything and anyone. It was a good exercise in "don't universalize the particular."

All this diversity made for great conversations and exchanges of information late at night, before sailing, in the laundry and the cafeteria. I was really stimulated by this. Before we began I wondered what can you see and do in just five days? I found the answer to be not much, and quite a lot . . . all at the same time.

The faculty made efforts early on in the voyage to distinguish us as *travelers* rather than mere *tourists*. Now, after two ports, I began to reconsider this distinction. In his book *A Pirate Looks at Fifty*, musician Jimmy Buffet identified predictability (of accommodations, food, itinerary) as the primary need of a tourist, contrasted to a traveler. I found his distinction appealing. Although I would like to fancy myself somehow more than a tourist, I have to admit that until you live in a place for some time, you remain, to locals and yourself, a "tourist." On the ship, we were encouraged to "be flexible" and to explore ports and plan unique itineraries (which were less predictable) than the "average" tourist who flies in and stays at Holiday Inns. At the same time, let's face it, we *were* tourists. I don't see this as negative. It implies that you are curious about places away from your country (or county, for some of our less-traveled students). It can mean either that you are open to "otherness," or that you are critical of what you see.

I think that I, and most Semester At Sea people, were informed and flexible tourists. That is the most that I expect of myself as an aging, retired woman from North America, specifically the southwestern part of the USA. I bring with me my own history, art, ministry, and mothering. I come with my values. Again, I don't see this as negative. It is my reality. If I try to "go native" in ten ports then I'm headed for unhealthy mental flip-flopping and, importantly, I am denying my own reality every bit as much as the tourist who finds fault with foreign cultures because they aren't the same as his or her own, even in the details of what is eaten or worn. Thomas Merton's rendition of Chuang Tzu's "The Pivot" puts it this way. "If I begin by looking at anything from the viewpoint of the 'Not-I', then I do not really *see* it, since it is 'not I' that sees it. If I begin from where I am and see it as I see it, then it may also become possible for me to see it as another sees it." My goal on this voyage was to be observant, note differences, and be in touch with what values of mine need questioning, change, or a renewed reinforcement.

As we passed through South China Sea we, students, faculty, and seniors, talked a lot about what we had observed in China. Those who went north to Beijing and Xian had the opportunity to see Tiananmen Square and the Emperor's Palace, the Great Wall, and quite a bit of traffic, heavy pollution and crowding. Those of us who stayed further south shared a common discomfort in regard to street sellers and transportation problems. Most of my reflection

Chapter 7 – South China Sea

focused on Hong Kong and its relationship to the People's Republic of China. Since the recent inclusion of Hong Kong it seems to me that either there is an identity crisis - if you are a capitalist and financially involved in Hong Kong - or there is one China which is solving all problems from finance to pollution to population.

"China is one big happy family" is the party line. It was articulated several times both in Hong Kong and in the Guilin area. I would say it *is* like a family and my experience of that means that there are many different understandings of what that means. And how it functions. Confusion, contradictions, expectations, comfort and disappointment are part of the reality. Nothing ever gets "worked out" permanently. As in modern families, the issue of "Who's in charge?" is a real one for this family of 1.2 billion very diverse souls.

Chapter 8
Ho Chi Minh City (Saigon) and Vietnam

At Sea At Sixty

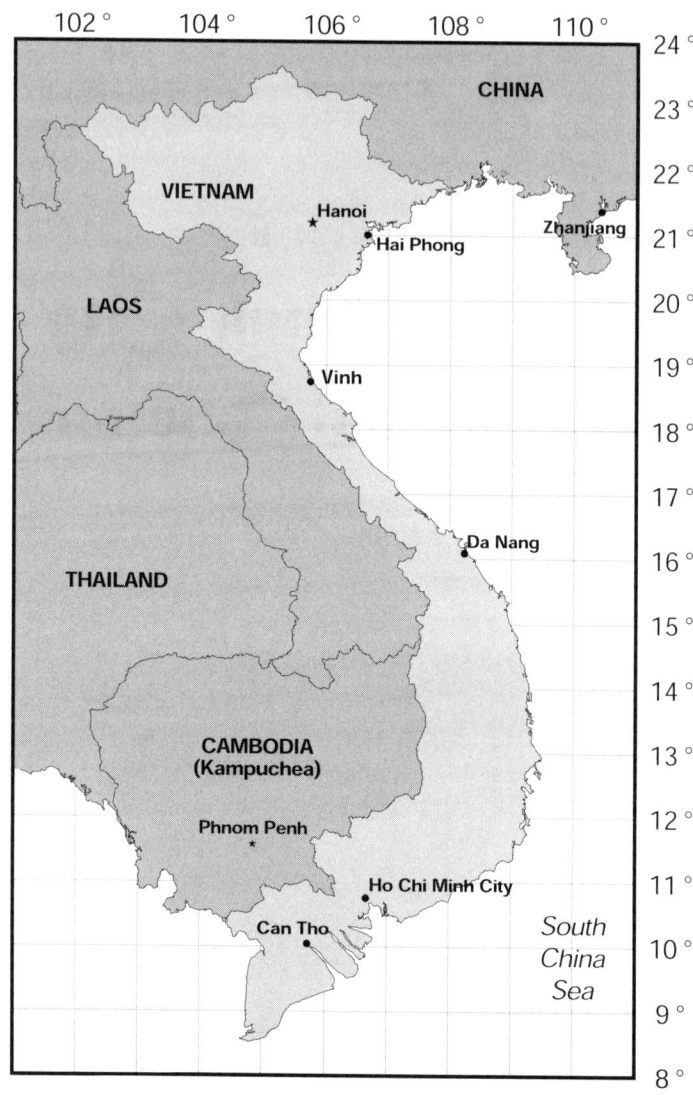

Ho Chi Minh City, Vietnam
Latitude 10.5°N Longitude 106.4°E

Chapter 8 – Ho Chi Minh City (Saigon) and Vietnam

"Madame, Madame, Postcards"

csr

The captain told us that the most challenging part of the voyage navigationally was not the typhoons, but rather negotiating the Saigon River. It is very shallow (it is necessary to navigate the river only during high tide) and it changes its channel often. Here we really needed the services of the local pilot who came aboard.

The Saigon River is brown because of rains, silt, and clear cutting. And it is full of trash. There is heavy traffic all the way up to the port of Ho Chi Minh City, or Saigon as most still call it. This activity is an indication of the growing importance of Vietnam in the world market. In fact, this is one of the lasting impressions I had of the country. It is economically on the move. It was curious to hear so much talk of infrastructure and markets in a communist country.

As we approached Vietnam I marveled that, for the third time on this journey, we were entering the territory of a (hot or cold war) former enemy of the USA. I was in grade school when we entered WWII and the war against Japan. Relatives fought in this war, friends and loved ones died or were left with scars. From grade school until very recently Communist China - the emphasis here was always on *communist* - was an enemy or at least a dangerous rival of democratic principles. And I was a parent of small children during the horror of Vietnam. My brother was a conscientious objector. In one way other another, I think that Americans have never been the same in their relation to wars on foreign soil after Vietnam.

There was decidedly something strange about disembarking in Vietnam with all our recent history. It was here that the age differences among shipmates were most significant. The students hadn't even been born at the time of the Vietnam war. Senior passengers, on the other hand, had memories of it and other wars of our lives: World War II and Korea. I found out that it is very difficult to communicate the reality of living with war (albeit not on American soil) as a daily occurrence; war movies and books can only go so far. Having friends and relatives die and be permanently damaged and having received a steady diet of destruction for years is impossible for young people to imagine.

And yet, here we were. Dollar signs disembarking to bolster this third Asian economy. Contemporaries in each country we visited have had strong, usually negative, images and experiences of Americans. Some had been defeated, some victorious. What are the older generation thinking now? What are the young people thinking? Is what happened twenty-five or fifty years ago as important to them as the latest in fashion, movies, electronics, or investments? Our young undergraduates usually met other young people in these countries. My impression is that they sometimes spoke of ideas and history but never were as burdened with the past as those of us who were older. They were free to just enjoy the present. This is not the reality or luxury of the older generation. We have the burden of the past and past mistakes. In pre-port briefings we were urged to "put the war behind us" yet many of the side-trips offered focused on the war: the Cu-Chi tunnels, war museums, even a firing range experience where tourists (in this case, American students) paid a dollar a bullet to fire "real guns just like those used in the war." Hearing about this really upset me; it made me nauseous. I think I was ashamed on hearing this just as the student who had said she was ashamed to be an American after seeing the war museum in Hiroshima. But there, no one there was offering an experience of "dropping the bomb" for a price.

This issue of remembering past wars by memorials and writings and speeches is an important one considered in every age. Is it possible to put civil wars behind us, or genocides, or revolutions? Should one? Should a nation? How can a nation remember so that lessons are learned, and yet not be dominated by the past? I think it is not an either/or situation" but one of balance. I see some nations

Chapter 8 – Ho Chi Minh City (Saigon) and Vietnam

(and individuals) locked into the past and dealing with old, terrible issues, and others moving on with not much attention to what happened or why. Both approaches can lack wisdom, but if one errs in the balancing, I think it better to err on the side of letting go, or forgetting. Surely, forgiving is called for. I think forgiving past offenses, wrongs, mistakes (I'm comfortable calling them "sins") is the balance which does not deny the reality of the past but does not let it dominate the present. We have to figure out whether to live *in* the past, or move forward looking for forgiveness, or extending it as the case may be. You can't live for sixty years without making regrettable mistakes, mistakes which hurt others and yourself. Countries and religions also make terrible mistakes. All need to say *mea culpa* and make amends when possible. All need to be in pursuit of justice and truth, but all need to know their limitations.

That is where trouble arises: when each differing entity seeks absolute justice in terms of their own sense of right and wrong. Often to achieve this is not possible; there are real conflicts of culture, religion, class. So instead of bringing about relative justice (and maybe some sort of peace), each party hangs on to their truth and sense of righteousness. The people of the earth are not well served by this.

As the old song of the sixties says "When will we ever learn, when will we ever learn?"

The World Heritage Site of Halong Bay

csr

Ho Chi Minh City (HCMC) was bustling with traffic in all directions and with all sorts of vehicles, both human, animal, and machine driven. I had a hard time crossing any street. The rule was "Don't make eye contact with drivers!" I found this very difficult to do so I relied on others more experienced than I in dealing with such matters.

The day after we arrived we joined a tour north to Hanoi and Halong Bay. This was one of my favorite adventures of all the countries we visited.

We flew to Hanoi, which means "dragon descending," and boarded a bus for Halong Bay, which means "dragon ascending." This trip of 150 miles took all day, and included two bus ferry rides, rice fields, many beautiful water buffalo, and lovely children as well as aggressive ones. Even roads that were divided had bicycles, people, burros and people coming towards us. I was amazed to see a bicycle coming towards us with a platform holding three huge, very pink, slaughtered hogs. The man must have had close to a thousand pounds to pedal. He couldn't have weighed more than 110 pounds himself.

It is common practice in Vietnam to lay out the rice stalks on the roadway and have the traffic run over it to begin the thrashing process. As in most poor countries I have visited, I noticed that the country people look healthier than the city folks. The water buffalo looked healthiest of all; they are considered a "friend of the family" and are well cared for. Adjacent to the rice fields were fish ponds for raising commercial fish. I was delighted to see a whole family of ducklings crossing in front of our bus. It reminded me of *Make Way for Ducklings!* . . . how many times I read that story to wiggling youngsters. Our guide said that there were many ducks on the road and going to market because it is the duckling time, or the time between harvests. This particular year the harvest had been late in the north because four months of floods had delayed planting. In the south it was close to harvest time, and we were told a great time for "rice mice" which are considered very good eating. Our friend Loreen from western Canada amazed me with her quick response to the question by her driver, "Do you like mice?" She admits to being "quite taken aback," really speechless. But she managed to say, "Do *you* like mice?" and was given an enthusiastic reply. To me this was culturally sensitive and I admired her ability

Chapter 8 – Ho Chi Minh City (Saigon) and Vietnam

to focus on his sincere question rather than her own horror. Vietnamese markets offer items unthinkable to our Western taste: monkey, snake, dog, mice and parts of animals which don't even make it into hot dogs in the US. On the very delicious and attractive side were huge prawns which are fresh water farmed and grow to about eight inches. Dragonfruit is about the prettiest fruit I've ever seen - bright pink with green spiky scales. On the inside, it is very white with many tiny black seeds. It is very refreshing. Lots of mangos, bananas and pineapples. Fruits are both plentiful and inexpensive.

We had a very positive experience when the bus stopped for us to take pictures of the rice paddies and water buffaloes. Children gathered around, very excited about us and our cameras, especially the video cameras which projected images on a little screen. These children, and the ones I met later in the Dalit village in India were highlights of the trip for me. Very fresh and natural, the weren't asking for anything. They were just curious, which is what I like children to be - adults also.

The next day we went on a terrific boat trip in Halong Bay. It is easy to see why it has been designated a World Heritage Site. There are about one thousand islands in the bay looking very much like the formations along the Li River in China. In fact they are the same geologic formation, karst, which is a type of eroded limestone. (Thank the Creator God for the blessing of limestone; in modern ritual, $CaCO3$ should be worshipped like the Pythagorean geometry formulas were in ancient Greece.)

I was very glad to have time to paint and let my imagination wander to past times of pirates and intrigue. There is probably a fair amount of that still going on. The trip had more pirate concerns than I had expected, here in Vietnam, in Malaysia, and while passing the Barbary Coast. Once in awhile there will be news items about piracy that reach the American press. It is a very real problem for those who earn their livings at sea. We tend to think it is something from the 19th century. The pirates today have fast boats and are well armed.

The water was very warm and green because of the high nutrient content. I'd guess the water temperature was about 89F. We literally dove in from the ship and it felt very good to be swimming. We splashed and played, young and old. It was great fun.

We tied up to an island and went into a cave. It was rather small (by Carlsbad Cavern standards) but beautiful with lovely stalactites and stalagmites. After a real seafood feast we motored back to shore and boarded our bus for a five hour trip back to Hanoi by a slightly shorter route.

Hanoi had a very different look and feel from Ho Chi Minh City. There were more trees and parks and wider streets with less

Chapter 8 – Ho Chi Minh City (Saigon) and Vietnam

congestion . . . or so it seems. Two treats awaited us - the Water Puppet Show and the Four Seasons of Hanoi Restaurant.

Water puppetry is part of the culture of Vietnam and I think it is unique to it, I surely had never heard of it. It developed many hundreds of years ago in the flooded rice fields. The performance in the theater was more impressive than the taste of a water show we had in HCMC on their city tour. The announcer spoke in French, English and Vietnamese and gave us a good introduction to the music and the instruments as well as the story portrayed by the colorful and dynamic puppets. I think I expected remnants of the French in south Vietnam, but their presence for a few generations seemed even more intact in the north. "Uncle Ho" did not tear down the French colonial buildings or fill in the parks. In fact, the opera house has been restored and Italian and French operas are performed there.

We were so impressed with the music and the sound of the one string instrument called the *dan bau* that we bought tapes. The *dan bau* produces different tones on its single string when the tension is changed by the artist's left hand as she plucks with her right hand. The effect is often a sliding tone, somewhat like a steel guitar, but beautifully clear.

Our meal at the Seasons of Hanoi was magnificent, one of the best meals I've ever had. We were seated upstairs in an old home which would have fit in comfortably in the French Quarter in New Orleans. The many dishes were carefully prepared with quality ingredients and delicate seasonings. The presentation was a work of art. What more is there in cuisine? Very oriental, and at the same time, very French.

Before our flight back to HCMC we had time to see some of the sites in Hanoi, which was the headquarters of Ho Chi Minh and the North Vietnamese. I didn't expect to be impressed with Ho's residence, but I was. It was very simple and had a sensitivity to its natural surroundings. How strange it seemed to be on a tour of Hanoi, led by a guide who was probably the son of a Viet Cong. Now he was making a living guiding French and English speaking tours. The world is an amazing place and history is sometimes more forgiving than I had ever imagined. The war zones of our younger years have now become the tourist destinations of the retired. That is a hopeful sign to me.

One of our stops was a ninth century university, one of several I have seen in my lifetime that is designated "the oldest university in the world." In any case, it was old and had tablets with the names of those who had passed examinations. If you lived dishonorably, your name was taken from the stone. I cannot imagine any university taking away my degree or any one's degree, based on how one lived after graduation. They had the power to erase a graduate from history! This connection between what is learned and how it is put into practice is something to think about.

We arrived back in HCMC in time to see part of the 300th anniversary celebration of the founding of Saigon. The most amazing part was that our bus drove right through the parade. Most people, locals and tourists, still use the name Saigon although it is no longer its official name.

The next day I discovered a part of me I hadn't known before. I headed off with my friend Geraldine to the post office. I started out adventurous but quickly found I just wasn't up for the aggression of the city. We decided to go into the very elaborate and western Rex Hotel to get our stamps and mail our letters. We decided to have pastry and coffee. It was a welcome respite from the noise and hassle outside. We just hid out there. The adventurous spirit had flown and was replaced by the Catharine-who-loves-quiet-and-beauty. I found out I have a hiding side. I decided that was OK.

We sailed that evening. My feelings were mixed about Vietnam. I look back and think it was the most hopeful place we visited. I'd love to see it in about ten years. I think it will be more prosperous, and prosperous its own way. Yes, it will make a deal

Chapter 8 – Ho Chi Minh City (Saigon) and Vietnam

with Japan, China, Australia, the US, all the other countries who want to trade or send tourists, but the style of dealing with others felt different from business in the other Asian areas I have visited. It's difficult to put my finger on it; surely the attitude of hard work is involved, but also there seems to be a forthrightness and trust missing in other countries. Many of our shipmates, including faculty, had similar feelings and high praise for Vietnam. Maybe part of the picture is that they have not been a dominating power in their own right for 1200 years. They come more from a history of one down rather than one up.

I'll just have to wonder about this.

The Bottom

pjr

I enjoyed Vietnam immensely, and I admire the Vietnamese. It is true, they genuinely like us - not just the hustlers, but most everyone we met - and vice versa.

As much as I loved the Vietnamese, I must say that the only truly disgusting thing I saw on the entire world voyage occurred in Ho Chi Minh City. A woman beggar thrust an infant in my face and asked for money for the baby, perhaps a year old. The child looked *terrible*, immobile, with open but de-focused eyes. I was startled and frightened, and then remembered a *PBS Frontline* documentary on these professional beggars of Saigon. To make the babies appear to be at death's door, the beggars drug them. Paregoric, with *opium* - very effective. Later, a fellow senior passenger reminded me that Saigon businesses *rent out* the drugged babies to the professional women beggars. If you give them money, you encourage the practice. Supply and Demand. This is my candidate for the bottom of human nature.

Puzzling Out Vietnam

pjr

"The Vietnamese like Americans." Yeah, right. But everybody says it. Our friend Marvel and her parents and the Semester At Sea Dean, Dr. Jill Wright, all said it was their favorite country, their favorite people, and that the Vietnamese love us.

The Vietnamese economy is in shreds, after years of war and ill-conceived communist rule, but it is clear to all of us that these people will make it. They work, they are not bound to their past. They got over the war, and everything else. One key point in this puzzle that is virtually always overlooked is that "they" did not *all* win. Some of them *lost* - namely, those whom we Americans backed. Not all of them were able to leave the country. In pursuit of this fascinating puzzle, I offer the following list, gleaned from my own observations and imaginings, as well as several of our shipmates. The list may be semi-humorous, but I mean every word.

The Top Ten Possible Reasons
Why Vietnamese Love Americans

10. The Vietnamese are just nice people.
9. They want our tourist money.
8. They haven't seen anyone but Communist bureaucrats for all their lives, so anyone else looks good.
7. They have a more realistic attitude towards war as a fact of life - nothing personal, just war.
6. We are the world's biggest pushovers for beggars.
5. We are the world's biggest pushovers for hawkers.
4. As one Vietnamese actually said, compared to other people who occupied their land (Chinese, French), the Americans were not there to *take* anything.
3. We lost.
2. They won.

Chapter 8 – Ho Chi Minh City (Saigon) and Vietnam

1. Although most Americans love to criticize themselves, we are, generally speaking, a generous, cheerful, patient, fun-loving, tolerant, and thus lovable people.

   As for our feelings as Americans towards Vietnam - well, you've gotta love a country that calls its currency the "dong."

Chapter 9
More South China Sea and The Straits of Malacca

Chapter 9 – More South China Sea and The Straits of Malacca

Calm Water, Unsettled Thoughts

csr

The long journey back down the twisting Saigon River brought us once more into the South China Sea. The first thing we had to do was deal with a massive amount of crustaceans picked up in the cold Alaskan waters during summer cruising. These organisms impaired the functioning of the engines because they had grown so much in the warm China seas. We stopped for several hours while some were blown out, but major clean up work would have to be done in port in Malaysia. After this problem was dealt with, the air-conditioners functioned better and the swimming pool was opened. I understand that barnacle problem is a common occurrence when ships use this route.

Questions of war still invade my thoughts. I ask myself: for what am I willing to die? For what am I willing for others to die?

- I think of my grandfather and his war, the War Between the States, 1860-65.
- I think of "The Troubles" in Northern Ireland and the very recent vote in Northern Ireland and the Republic of Ireland to say "yes" to a compromise. (We happened to be there at the time on a bicycle trip.)
- I think of Germany and Austria letting go of being wrong and guilty, and living now with a consciousness of their capacity for evil and war.
- I think of Japan letting go of divinity and power and in the process finding a new way of living in the world community.
- I think of China and Mao, Vietnam and Ho Chi Min. What has come about in those two countries isn't what their leaders originally envisioned. They must be turning over in their glass caskets. All those people died for "the cause." Now what has happened? More of the ideas of their enemies have been incorporated than they ever could have thought possible. Now communist guides talk about investments and infrastructures. That

is a big "wow." Where does war get you if your ideas and ideals can be co-opted so quickly?

I propose a new question: For what am I willing to *live*? I'm willing to live, and change how I live, for beauty, for smiles, for sharing, for friendship, for the small moments, rather than grand ideas. I am willing to live more justly so that justice may flourish. I'm not willing to die for justice. I don't think dying can give birth to justice. Living justly has a better chance of bringing it about. The phrase "live and let live" has a particular meaning to me after Japan, China, and Vietnam. Propaganda, finger pointing and breast beating usually don't achieve the goal of furthering life. Yes, speak what I believe is truth, live it and analyze it, and know that there are many truths and differing ways of living it. Feel guilt when I, or my country fails, but don't become immobilized by it.

Such unsettled thoughts were shared onboard our ship. After each port we had evenings of reflections, with students, senior passengers, faculty and staff participating. The evening of reflection after Vietnam was impressive. Thoughts and feelings were expressed in song, wordless music, and many stories. Some students were very sad, others overwhelmed. One of the professors asked what did the Communist victory achieve? He noted that the life of the farmers and fishermen was much the same before and after the war, before and after the thousand year rule of China. The life of the rulers and wealthy has changed somewhat. Was it worth the price in human life? In the US we pretty much acknowledge that the Vietnam War wasn't worth the price . . . and wouldn't have been even if we had "won."

Preparing for an Islamic Country

csr

But now it was time to begin to let go of that port of Vietnam and its experiences. Time to prepare for the Islamic Federation of

Chapter 9 – More South China Sea and The Straits of Malacca

Malaysia. This is a rather new (1957), "made up" country of sixty percent Muslim, mostly Malay and Tamil, thirty percent Chinese, and ten percent "other." The majority struggle for education and power, the *minority* Chinese control the economy. Not a simple situation. In the US we are more accustomed to a minority demanding human and civil rights. The current head of government is the focus of many scandals, the former Finance Minister is on trial. The only thing that seems to unite the people is their fervent desire not to have the bloodshed of their neighbor Indonesia. How to do this was not clear to me; I don't think it is clear to Malaysians.

In my Islamic Civilization class my consciousness was raised by information I had not previously absorbed, like the fact that only 15 per cent of the world's Muslims are Arabs, and that of the top eight Muslim countries, only Egypt is Arab. Indonesia has the largest Muslim population, followed by India, then Pakistan, Egypt, Iran and Turkey, none of which except Egypt are predominantly Arab. I had to think about the fact that as Islam moved East through India to China its converts were sailors and merchants - not people from the lowest castes. Peasants and even Dalit ("Untouchables") clung to Hinduism not wanting (or knowing how?) to break from Tradition, even if it meant being treated badly. I must confess that this is difficult for me to understand; I would have thought that the egalitarian beliefs of Islam would have appealed to the lower caste people. Historically, it didn't happen. Today it is still a difficult situation.

During the Core Course in mid-October we passed by the southern tip of Malaysia and came within one degree of the equator. The waters were about 86° F. As we passed Singapore, we entered the Straits of Malacca. This body of water has had the greatest amount of ship traffic in the world since it is the primary and shortest route between the Pacific and the Indian Ocean. It is very crowded to this day and the waters can be very treacherous, in many senses of the word, including pirates. It would prove to be dangerous to us too.

Chapter 10
Penang and Malaysia

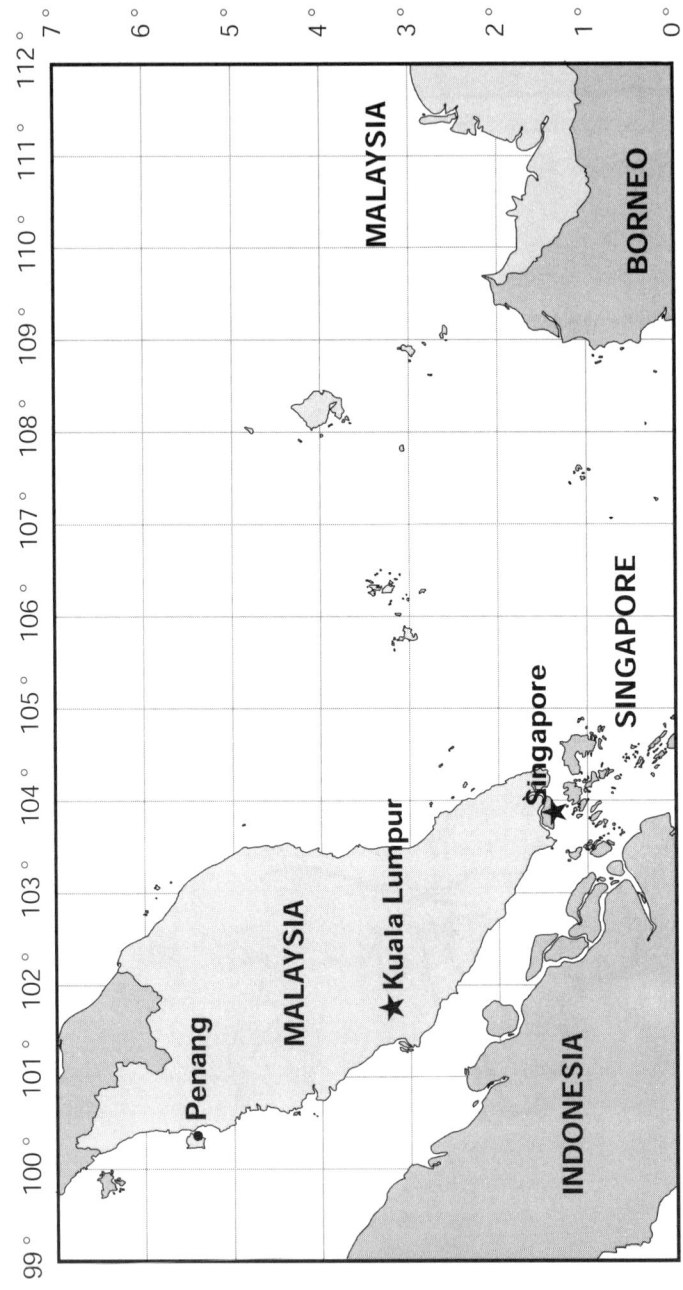

Chapter 10 – Penang and Malaysia

Equatorial Diversity

csr

For the first two days in Penang, Malaysia, we visited places of worship: temples, pagodas, mosques and churches. Although the state religion is Islam, there seemed to be more Buddhist temples and pagodas which represented various approaches to Buddhism - or maybe our guides were Chinese and took us to more Buddhist sites? What these temples had in common with Hindu temples was their colorful and energetic appearance. This is easy to understand since this part of the world is the most biologically diverse and colorful area of the planet, so it seems natural that their places of worship and prayer would have a dynamic rather than a static spiritual quality. Most of the Buddhist temples and pagodas present a form of Buddhism very unrelated to the Buddha's ideas or to the form of Zen Buddhism to which we are exposed in the States. Here ancestor worship or relationships to ancestors is stressed far more, and practices which have to do with lucky numbers, lucky actions, and fortune telling seemed to dominate the scene. Much of this appeared to me to be a form of superstition motivated by fear or hope. But I am sure that Catholic practices of candle lighting and medals and rosaries can be interpreted in a like manner by observers. Most Catholics would be horrified by the comparison. In a recent article by Annie Dillard she states that "The presenting face of any religion is its mass of popular superstitions. It seems to take all the keenest thinkers of every religion in every generation to fend off this clamoring pack." In my experience this is very true. The religion of my growing up years, which I have practiced and took for granted as Catholicism, was different from the religion which I studied in books and lectures on my way to a doctorate in ministry. Or was it? I think after sixty years of practicing Catholicism, it is both. And being a Catholic, or Jew, or Muslim, takes a lifetime of practice.

The routing of the tour group through the merchant stalls as we visited the shrine of the Ten Thousand Buddhas had nothing to do with religious differences or spiritual subtleties. It was all about buying, and more buying. It seemed to be the Mall of Ten Thousand Buddhas. Whether it is in Christian cathedrals and shrines, or shops attached to other religious sites I have visited, I am always critical of this kind of commercialism; but I have seen it from one part of the globe to another. It was very evident on the pilgrimage route to Compestelo in Spain which has seen Christian pilgrims since the ninth century; I have found it in Jerusalem; I have found it present alongside feast day celebrations in Native American Pueblos in New Mexico. When crowds of people gather for whatever reason, commerce is sure to be present. The pressures to buy seem to me very far from fostering meditation and prayer.

Besides all the commercial stalls, the many shrines were not very carefully or artistically done, with the exception of the large, expensive temple near the top, for which we had to pay a separate entrance fee. The temple itself, the carvings and statues were very beautiful, but I don't know if getting there was worth dealing with all the other aspects. Perhaps I'm equating art and spirituality, perhaps I'm being a spiritual snob, or imposing my current state of spiritual belief and practice on those whose needs are met in a far different manner. Observing others at prayer has helped me examine my own tradition and practices. This observing is part of my spiritual journeying, but I think I've reached the point where, for my sake and others, I should visit fewer places of worship.

As I moved from country to country I noted that mosques were very simple spaces and began to evaluate them as better sacred spaces. But they too have had stumbling blocks for me as I observed instances of men sleeping and snoring on their prayer rugs and widespread sales of talismans. There was a huge entrance fee to the Hassan II mosque in Casablanca. The fact is, there is no such thing as a pure religion which is totally spiritual, or one not abused

Chapter 10 – Penang and Malaysia

by worshipers or priests. There are just humans trying to wrestle like Jacob with the divine. We don't seem to be able to hang on to it, much less control it. Call it what you will, when people reach out towards the divine, the sacred, enlightenment, they often look pretty clumsy. It is a messy human business. We have not yet reached the goal, or closed the circle. We are pilgrims on the way to connect with the Other.

As I visited oriental places of prayer and spiritual striving I kept searching for quotes from Lao Tzu, or Chuang Tzu, or clear evidence of the influence of their insights within Asian spirituality. Usually I didn't find them. Then I began to ask myself: were the aspects of wisdom which I value in my tradition easy to observe? My honest response is that it is often very difficult to find them. Throughout the history of Christianity as shown in images and practices, brotherly and sisterly love, equality, justice and mercy and compassion are not what leaps out from walls and pulpits. The spiritual journey in any tradition and in every age requires one to search their scriptures, interpret them, and pass them on to others as best they can.

On our way from the Ten Thousand Buddhas to Penang Hill, we stopped at a small, very simple, unimposing "Katolik" church. It looked like a small Roman Catholic church from a 1950's non-affluent, Midwestern suburb. The church was closed and there were no services going on, but several parishioners graciously encouraged us to visit, and opened up the church for us. There was something very appealing about this place. The people told us that they have services in Malay and Chinese once a month, and have another monthly service for all the groups together. This accommodation of cultural diversity and parish unity, and a modest statue of the Madonna nursing the baby, gave witness to a parish in touch with the people, recognizing differences, and trying to bring them together in God's love.

"Take Care"

csr

As it turned out, Malaysia presented the most physically dangerous challenges of our voyage.

First, there was my experience in a trishaw. I had declined to try various forms of cycle transportation in China and Vietnam, but I decided that I would give this a try. It looked so authentic and colorful. It was. And also more terrifying than I had imagined. It takes a bit more faith than I have to sit in front of a bicycle and be pedaled and propelled into traffic dodging cars, buses, mopeds, pedestrians, burros, trucks and motorcycles. My heart was in my mouth . . . and I have experience riding my own bicycle in traffic in the States, Europe, New Zealand and Australia. Never again. To top it all off, I got in an argument with the driver because, at the end of the ride, he wanted more than the agreed upon price.

Even more dangerous was our snorkeling trip out to one of the uninhabited islands north of Penang. I had noticed an absence of advertisements for snorkeling trips. That should have told me something, or deterred me. But no. One of my worst and best features is my stubbornness. I don't give up an idea easily. I knew I wouldn't be able to scuba dive on this trip because of distances and transportation logistics, but I longed to get into some of the blue we had been on. After a few days of searching, I found someone who could set up a trip for eight or nine of us. It didn't take much coaxing to convince Pat, the assistant librarian, Loretta, one of the

Chapter 10 – Penang and Malaysia

professors, Deirdre, and five students to join me. When I saw the "boat" I hesitated. It was decrepit. I've stepped into some marginal boats, but this was a wreck. I was determined to get into the water; surely the man who had the boat knew what he was doing and where to go.

The weather looked threatening and the water murky, but as we wallowed along, the water seemed to become more clear. As we approached the shore of Song Song Island, the captain held us off for a few minutes. We saw a totally trashed-out beach, the result of neglect and the rather recent monsoons. We also saw a tattered flag on a red and white striped pole, and a couple of guys with some kind of signs in their hands. As we tried to puzzle it out, we received a clue in the form of two gunshots. We were about to swim and snorkel at a military firing range!

The boatman passed out the equipment, but there was not enough for everyone. I was missing fins. I spent time instructing first timers about snorkeling procedures and techniques. The undercurrent was strong and the visibility was about nil. I decided to go farther out to see if it was better away from the shore and the undertow. No, not much. I saw one coral head and maybe five fish. This was the poorest snorkeling of my life. Pat saw slightly more, but then again he had fins and was able to dive down into clearer water closer to the coral heads.

Then it began to rain. *Hard.* We exited the water and returned to the boat where lunch was in progress. It was a fine protein spread of chicken satay, prawns, fish and beef. After lunch I had time to paint and then waited to see if we would try another snorkel site. The weather was deteriorating and the sea was getting rough so we began our trip home. This was not good. The waves were about eight feet and we were being tossed all over the place and shipping water. The other snorkeling boat, as old and decrepit as ours, would periodically disappear behind waves that hit them sideways. I'm sure when the passengers in that boat saw us, we

At Sea At Sixty

looked as endangered as they did to us. The students were pretty sick and also scared, as well they should have been. Our faculty participant, Dee, counted four lifejackets for the lot of us, nine passengers and two crew. At one point the boatman grabbed the sack of snorkels and put it in reach of us, I guess so we could grab them if we capsized - a very possible scenario.

from Song Song Island - Malaysia

After a few hours of this I realized that soon we would have to beach this craft and all would have to disembark. But how? The captain tried to surf onto the beach with a wave. Dee and a student and the cabin boy jumped off and made it ashore. At this point it was decided that the rest of us would not be able to get off, so with a gathering crowd of people pointing down shore, we continued on and tried again, in a slightly less turbulent area about a mile from the first attempt. This time we all made it, but in the nick of time. The boatman and his son got out of there quickly and left us to our

Chapter 10 – Penang and Malaysia

amazed selves. We collected our nerves, had a cup of tea at a luxury hotel outdoor dining area, and returned to our comfortable ship, and to our cautious and capable captain. We later read that the night before a ferry had capsized in the same waters and fifteen drowned. Sobering information. I realized that when activities are not readily available to tourists, this should tell you something. Don't insist or persist. Accept the limits of an area.

Searching for Beauty in Malaysia

pjr

Amazing what people will do for a glimpse of beauty. We were about to snorkel at the trashed-out beach of a freaking firing range!

The visibility was terrible, and there were few fish, but I did get to see a beauty I had never seen before, a colorful fish called the "Moorish Idol," easily identified by the distinctive delicate filament trailing from its dorsal fin. I could barely make it out in the murky water. Straining in poor light to see the beauty of the Moorish Idol - life as religious metaphor again. On the return trip to the mainland, we hit very heavy weather, almost swamped several times, and we wondered at the strength of our rotting old boat. Our captain had to get out of the way of a monstrous Evergreen, the giant Hong Kong based container ship bringing Malaysian electronic stuff to America and the world. Metaphor, metaphor. It will crush your scarred and creaky old boat without a moment of caring. Out of the way, or die, we are coming into your living room. All is metaphor. The young ones onboard seemed oblivious. Then we think we made it, or they did, but Catharine and I saw the trouble coming. The trick is to *get out* of the boat, alive. The captain knew the danger, he pulled away from the first attempt after the cabin boy and two women made it off. This is *all* metaphor, living metaphor, but I don't see it until after India. Trying to get out of death alive, that's what it's all about - good luck. The captain finally disgorged us on the beach about a mile from our original destination, in a slightly less turbulent area, but it was still dicey. As soon as we were all into the water, the captain pulled back out to sea. He was agitated and afraid, but he still managed to give me a proud thumbs up, and I returned it gratefully. A good man, caring, but unfortunately I can't understand a thing he says. I wish I knew his language.

A crowd of people had watched us from shore with grim faces, first at our aborted disembarkation spot, then following us to the second offloading. They were not so dumb - this could have been a tragedy in the making. But once we were safe onshore and crashed a bored hotel poolside scene, we were icily ignored, with averted eyes by hotel staff and guests. The patrons were bored as hell, what with the overcast skies, muddy grass, and nothing to do but ask the obsequious waiters for another drink. Catharine, Deirdre, Loretta and I thought everything was just great. Wow, a freshwater pool, with no waves. Fresh water to drink. A stationary chair. Half naked people. Our own laughter. Children. Paradise. Life is sweet.

The hotel staff finally gave us a gentle bum's rush out of there. Two women students from our snorkel group booked in and spent the night in luxury. I left this Paradise of a hotel on another high point, with a probably (hopefully) pasteurized ice cream bar in a gold foil wrapper. We hired a taxicab to drive us back to the ship, and I sat in the front seat and chatted amicably with the driver, an obviously intelligent and educated man. The taxi was luxurious, new, and clean, and when I finished my ice cream bar, I glanced around for a place to deposit the gold foil wrapper. The driver graciously rolled down my window and said just throw it out. Was he surprised at my reaction! "NO. No way, *never*. This is against my religion. No, no." And I meant it. In Malaysia, Hong Kong, Vietnam, India, and in *most* of the world, the locals are oblivious to trash, and natural beauty is irrelevant except for tourist business, so I always encourage an eco-tourist ethic. Hit them where they live, in their pocketbook. In Belize, where we live part-time, an anti-

Chapter 10 – Penang and Malaysia

litter campaign proved to be successful only when it was coupled with the tourism business. Eco-tourism has its detractors in the environmental movement, but I am convinced that it is the only viable approach for saving some of what remains of this once beautiful planet.

Since we had elected to stay in the Penang area and not take overnight side trips, we were able to talk to our friends at night as we gathered on the ship. From their stories we gathered that those who had gone into the jungles and highlands had really been stretched to their limits; those who had gone to Kuala Lumpur or Singapore had basically seen large, busy, modern cities. Just about all of us were struck by the difficulties of this country religiously, politically and financially. Religious tensions were strong, the current head of the government was losing control of his support, and the former finance minister who had challenged him was on trial. The form of money used, the ringit, cannot be used anywhere else. Just as we were leaving, the Malaysian government announced that it would no longer honor exchanges back into foreign currencies - our ringits are now souvenirs. What does seem to be uniting everyone in Malaysia is a strong desire to avoid the riots of 1969, which shut down the country completely for two years, and to avoid similar problems in Indonesia, which are causing much bloodshed today. Those problems had led to the cancellation this fall semester of the originally scheduled Semester At Sea visit to Indonesia.

Chapter 11
The Adaman Sea and Indian Ocean

Chapter 11 – The Adaman Sea and Indian Ocean

Preparations for the Indian SubContinent

csr

The Adaman Sea is a part of the Indian Ocean, the third largest body of water on earth. It takes its name from the Adaman islands off the west coast of Thailand.

For this leg of our journey we would cross the warm, deep blue sea to dock in India at Chennai, formerly called Madras. The changing names of ports in Vietnam and India are clear indications of general change in these countries. In these cases they point to political changes which seek to identify power with the local native people.

This inter-port time was spent preparing for India. I must confess that I became pretty tired of hearing in the Core Course that "nothing can prepare you for India." What the faculty meant was that even with information about history, sociology, religion, economics and politics we would still have some shocks. My sense was that the faculty didn't want to turn anyone off to this country; they wanted us to appreciate it, which we did, and like it, which some did and some didn't.

What is helpful to know about India is how huge and diverse it is. Geographically it stretches from hot, humid jungles in the south, through some deserts, and high mountains near the roof of the world, the Himalayas. The people seem even more diverse than the landscapes. Officially the country communicates in Hindi, but most don't speak it. There is no language which everyone knows. There are many languages and many beliefs, even though most are Hindu. India has the second largest Muslim population in the world followed by Pakistan. The differences between Muslim and Hindu are enormous. Muslims are monotheists (believing in one God) and allow no representation of humans or the divine in their mosques. There is an emphasis on the brotherhood (and sisterhood) of all. On the other hand, there is very little commonality in beliefs among the Hindus who fill their temples with many gods engaged in so many activities that they have many arms and legs. Despite the fact that officially the caste system went out in the 1940's it is still very much alive. From the original four castes of Brahmin, Warrior, Merchant, and Farmer plus the "outcastes" (or fifth caste) there have evolved thousands of modern castes. This social reality determines most people's lives, job opportunities, marriages and expectations. Westerners, especially North Americans, bring with us a heritage of democracy and independence; we expect people to recognize the private and political benefits of "liberty, fraternity, equality" and "life, liberty, and the pursuit of happiness." We do not believe that our current position in society and our future has been determined by some past life. We do not arrange marriages (although we read some very convincing arguments for maintaining this practice), we do have an ideal of being able to associate with people of diverse walks of life, skin color, education, and place of birth. We surely have problems arising from racist attitudes, but racism is not the accepted, agreed upon norm, much less the goal of the majority. Even in recent time - in my life time - religions in the United States allowed segregated churches and schools. But it is very rare today. People can and do change when they are educated and motivated to change for the common good. There is less racism when people are more educated, whether the locale is the USA or India. But all this takes attitude, time and resources.

My questions going into India centered around these things. I also wondered about issues of population and pollution. Would the images I had in my mind from movies like *Salaam Bombay* or *Passage to India* and *Gandhi*, and books like *Son of the Circus*, *Midnight's Children*, and *The God of Small Things* have a relationship to the "real" India?

How would I respond to crowds, traffic, art? Would I find the beauty I expected?

Going into India, I was all questions.

Chapter 12
Chennai (Madras) and India

At Sea At Sixty

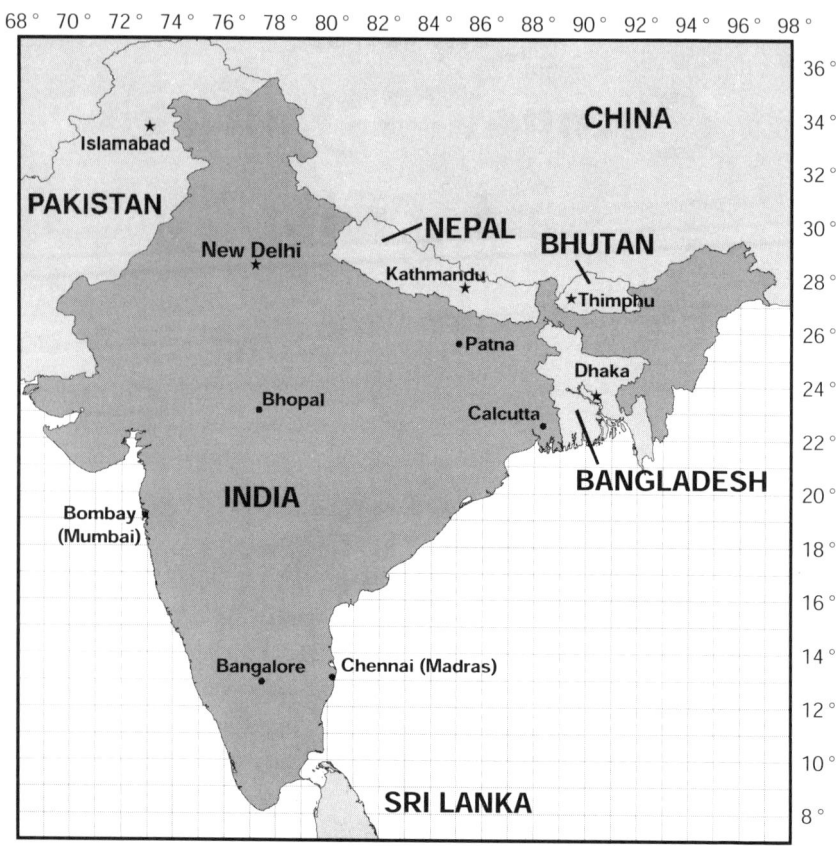

Chennai, India
Latitude 13° N Longitude 80.2°E

Chapter 12 – Chennai (Madras) and India

India, Ready or Not

csr

After clearing customs and exchanging forty US dollars for a very large stack of rupees, Pat and I took off on a bus tour of "Rural/Urban South India." This was led by a woman PhD from the University of Madras. Getting to the university and driving through Chennai to the small rural fishing village was a traffic-jammed, eye-opening experience. My first (and second and third impression) was one of filth. I can't put it in a more polite and yet accurate way. Garbage was littered everywhere and cows, goats and people were picking through it. The sewers and streams beside the road were filled with gray water. The Encyclopedia Britannica says that Tamil Nadu (this southern state of India) has "substandard urban sanitation and drainage." It was scary. The traffic seemed more organized than past ports, but it was heavy.

The "urban" part of our tour was a small factory called "the fishnet making place." The equipment reminded me of the machines we saw last summer in Irish woolen mills. They probably came from the same time period. But they were doing the job of turning out nets of various sizes and types to be used by large fishing fleets and individuals fishing in cooperatives. The persons running the machines creating the nets were young and barefoot; OSHA was not a gleam in the eye of any regulating body here.

After our short visit in the factory we continued on to a fishing village on the coast of the Indian Ocean, 20 or so miles south of Chennai. Looking at the boats, which were more like rafts, I was amazed. They consist of five rough logs tied together which are launched into the surf and travel as far out as ten kilometers. A catch is hauled in and transported back to shore where it is prepared for market and nets are repaired. The fishermen go out twice a day, in the early morning and late afternoon. Besides the raft-like boats, there was a larger boat *stitched* together. The stitching holes were plugged with coconut husks and dowels. Inside and out were decorated, including paintings of eyes on the front of the craft to "see" the fish and the way out and back.

We began to go into the village, moving very quietly because we thought the town might be napping. Not so. The men seemed to be having some sort of meeting, but it turned out they were playing a betting card game. The children and women came out to investigate our strange presence. We spent a very pleasant hour there and then returned to our bus and ship to get ready for a welcoming reception held at a tourist hotel.

The reception was a very colorful affair. We were greeted with flower necklaces, *yum yums* (red and yellow dots on our foreheads for beauty and luck; in a higher religious symbolism, they represent the "third eye" of awareness), a variety of delicious snacks, and many local people wanting to speak to us and sit with us as we were entertained by musicians and a dancer enacting tales from the Bhagavad-Gita. I've followed dance most of my life: ballet, folk, social, and have never seen anything more colorful, complex and artistically demanding. We were a very impressed and enthusiastic audience. What was unsettling was that the Indian audience talked during the performance; I had noticed a similar situation in China at another dance performance. In both instances the guides told us it was not polite or acceptable behavior but "it happens." The dancer in Chennai said sometimes the audience is very quiet and attentive. I wonder what determines this?

A few crafts and clothing were for sale in conjunction with this cultural demonstration. I bought a small blue cloisonné pill box to aid me in one aspect of aging that I don't like: pill taking. You know how folks often think that accidents, or troubles of various kinds happen "to the other guy." Well, pill taking was one of these things for me. I thought I would grow old med-free. I thought I would sail through menopause naturally. Not so. All this is humbling. I now feel more bonded to the rest of the world's pill-taking population. Having the pretty box makes my daily ritual on a trip a

Chapter 12 – Chennai (Madras) and India

little more enjoyable. It is like a mini art show and a reminder of art I found in Indian culture.

The next morning we were up early to go on an overnight to the coastal area to see temples and stone carvings of major importance. The temples are found in Kanchipuram and there are still about one hundred left of the original thousand. There are ten story pyramid-like temple/fortresses from the 16th century and wall paintings in the Kailasanatha temple dating from the 7th and 8th centuries. All these stone structures are highly carved. I can't imagine anyone knowing who all the gods represented here are. Many pilgrims crowded into small internal shrines; many Brahmins blessed them for a fee, many vendors filled the courtyards and surrounded the buses.

Mahabalipuram was the port city of the Pallava kings. For centuries they had elaborate carvings made. The largest bas relief sculpture in the world, Arjuna's Penance, is here. It tells a very involved tale from Hindu mythology. How could this be carved 1200 years ago with such detail and so few tools? I carve in stone myself and I stood there amazed. Equally impressive were the temples carved from huge boulders - no "building" at all, only carving. There were several free standing animals sculpted from these boulders on the beach. Elephants were a favorite subject and it is evident from the work that the artists knew and loved these behemoths.

Our day ended at a seaside resort (do *not* picture an Acapulco type of situation) with local food and folk dance entertainment. I enjoyed it very much; I also liked walking on the beach and watching the waves filled with bio-luminescence come rolling in under the clear and star filled sky. It was a special time to think about all I had seen and share some quiet time with Pat away from tours and students.

The next day was mostly a free day and I chose to hire a taxi to take me back to Mahabalipuram so I could more carefully examine and sketch Arjuna's Penance. This was a terrific day for me. I met a precious little boy who took me all around and joined me in some painting, and I was able to "chat" without words with the sculptors who live and work in the area. One fifth generation sculptor did have some English and I went to his home/shop and saw his very detailed work, mostly in a marble that comes from northern India. He showed me his tools which were finer than those used by most workers in the village and told me he had studied in Switzerland. He also said that even though the traditional subject matter is set, e.g. Ganesh, the elephant headed god, *how* that is expressed can vary widely. Instead of representing four arms and legs, the one he had done (which I bought) had eight and expressed many aspects of the myth of Ganesh.

All this was of great interest to me as a sculptor and made me grateful for every pneumatic and electric tool I have. I realize that having power tools means that I can carve until I am much older; I would not have the strength to do what I do now if I didn't have them.

Sculptors in India are classified as outside the caste system, that is, "outcastes" or untouchables. The current term is "Dalit"; Gandhi called these untouchables *harijan* or little ones of God, but the term is not in current favor. Knowing that sculptors are so low in the social system has been a meditation for me; I look forward to discussing this with other sculptor colleagues. Western civilization has had a very different relationship to artists and those who work in stone. I wonder if painters in India were also "outcastes." And yet some of the most important expressions of Indian art and culture are in stone: the Taj Mahal, temples all over the country, the ornate arch in Bombay.

It was not the first or last contradiction I bumped into in this country.

The worst and best part of my time in India occurred during the next two days. I went with nine students on the Dalit Village trip.

Chapter 12 – Chennai (Madras) and India

The first and worst part was an information stop at an NGO (non-government organization) which focuses on the education of Dalits and tries to keep young children in school who might otherwise be swept up into family businesses. I was interested in this, but I must admit, I was very turned off by the way the presentation was handled. It took all day and was very repetitive. I grew very tired of the propaganda atmosphere, avoidance of questions, and the talking down attitude. I was also disappointed in the students' responses to questions. "What are your impressions of India so far?" brought responses of "colorful," "busy" "pleasant people," etc. Yes, I noticed these things, but no one mentioned the very disturbing pollution, sanitation problems, and very obvious caste system. I thought I was in the middle of *The Emperor's New Clothes* and there was no boy to point and say "the emperor has no clothes." I considered just finding a taxi and going back to the ship. What I had expected and wanted was to meet Dalit people and share what they had to offer rather than the offerings of bureaucrats (albeit Dalit bureaucrats) in the Madras office. But I stayed and am glad I did because the village was very special.

About four in the afternoon we boarded buses for Erusamanallur in the Tamil Nadu state. The sixty kilometer trip through heavy traffic (is there any other kind in India?) was a sobering experience since we saw three overturned buses on the way.

We were given a very warm welcome in this farming village of about a hundred or so. Women and children led the presentation of flowers, *yum yums* on our foreheads and the blessing of the pathway entrance to the village. The men and their drums led the procession through and around the dirt streets. We ended up at a Christian church made of concrete where we were motioned to sit in chairs in front of the building. Then the children began to perform many songs and dances. Next it was our turn. What did we know in common? Not much. Our attempt at the "Star Spangled Banner" was very weak, and our dancing of the hokey pokey brought howls of merriment from the crowd. Percussion instruments indicated that it was time for general dancing. When some called for "Grandmother, grandmother" I got up and danced. This brought much applause and interest. Young and old, male and female wanted to dance with me; it was loads of fun.

Next the men marked out a game court in the dirt and began to play a team game which was some form of tag. The whole town was out to watch; the young Semester At Sea men joined in and it was quite something to see them play a game with no knowledge of the rules. They broke quite a few of them to the enjoyment of their teammates.

Before bedding down for the night on the floor of the church, I went with the three other women to find the "toilet." I knew that, at best, this would be some form of squat toilet; the young women did not. How they had avoided this experience in preceding ports was beyond me. More "beyond me" was the fact that they didn't know what to do, nor *could* they do it. How could you reach the age of twenty and not have this in your background? The answer is: grow up in a big city in the East. The following day was a moment of truth since the luxury of the outhouse was not available and the challenge was an open field. This was the fall Semester's most basic course offering.

The highlight of our visit for the village women was dressing us up in saris. It was like playing dress up fifty-five years ago. They asked for many pictures to be taken and we obliged. With many hearty waves and "good-bye"'s we pulled out and left the villagers to their busy work day.

On our sixty kilometer return trip, we saw four more accidents. This should have prepared us - but didn't - for the tragic news when returning to our ship that Loretta, the assistant librarian for Semester At Sea, our snorkeling companion and buddy of several tours, had been hit by a bus, hit-and-run, on her way to the post office just across the street from our dock, and was now in an inten-

Chapter 12 – Chennai (Madras) and India

sive care unit. In shock and sadness we gathered for a prayer service. Since we were sailing that night, it was decided to leave one of our nursing staff behind to take care of the situation and wait for one of her children to fly out.

It was a sober moment for all as we left India. All of us full of many different experiences, impressions and opinions and feelings.

Flunking India

pjr

"Whehre fhruhm?" His *r*'s were gently rolled as the young Tamil taxi driver looked at me with his friendly, soft eyes. "The United States," I answered, as I usually do, and received the usual blank stare. "America," I said. His eyes brightened with recognition. "Ah, . . . vehry rhich." I did not try to qualify terms, nor ask for definitions or clarifications (do you mean America is rich? or that I am rich? are all Americans rich?). Neither did I apologize any more. People like America, and they want to be rich, too. So I just nodded slowly and said yes. But I was thinking, "Sure, rich. And very *clean*."

I know that rich and clean correlate, but not perfectly. Japan is having hard times right now, but I cannot imagine a Japanese depression so severe that they would stop cleaning their streets, let roaming animals dump all over their cities, inhale coal dust, let dead people lie in the streets, or give up bathing. Catharine visited Nepal in 1987, and found the rural areas as poor as anywhere in the world, but reasonably clean. Also, no thievery. The Nepalese did not have a *word* for stealing until recently, and there was no begging.

India's overwhelming problems are obvious to any visitor. As my gentle Tamil taxi driver takes me back from the World Heritage site at Mahabalipuram to our ship (the great white Mother) in Madras, I see two hours of unrelenting filth, as we did on the three hour bus ride out yesterday. The faculty, good people who tend to the romantic, have advised the students to "get past the poverty of India" and see its beauties. That is good and meaningful advice from a caring faculty, and indeed the great majority of the Indian people we encounter are charming and sincerely friendly, and the religious sites are like nothing else. There are some pleasant breaks in the countryside, but basically, I find that after I "get past" the poverty, the filth, the malnutrition, and the disease, what I mainly see is more poverty, more filth, more malnutrition, and lots more disease. Plus suffocating industrial and traffic pollution, dangerous traffic, incipient violence, religious manipulation, disregard of the environment . . . Peddlers, hawkers, and beggars. From the Semester At Sea faculty's perspective, I flunk on India.

The oft-repeated theme of our pre-port lectures was "Nothing can prepare you for India." This is not my experience at all. I find myself fully prepared, not just by Semester at Sea, but by all my previous second-hand exposures to India through documentary films, dramatic films, novels, geography and history books. The slice of India that I have seen, in the Southern India coastal state of Tamil Nadu, looks just as bad as I expected. I don't think I've learned a damn thing new from India. Actually being here only confirms to me that the documentary films have not been lying through selective editing. Not only are the scenes real, but they are almost all there is to see. In a two hour drive, there was a little open countryside where you could breath, and even though it was overgrazed, it was not an assault on your senses. But most was just as we've all seen second hand - poverty, filth, malnutrition, disease . . .

Everyone says that Old Delhi, Bombay and Calcutta are even worse. Semester at Sea formerly stopped in Calcutta, but it was too much even for the faculty intensity junkies, what with dead people lying in the street. (However, some corpses were seen in Madras on this trip, as well.) And, Oh Calcutta!, where 700,000 people sleep on the streets every night, and Mother Teresa was awarded the No-

Chapter 12 – Chennai (Madras) and India

bel Peace Prize for her saintly ministrations to the dying. She undoubtedly was and is a saint, and will undoubtedly be canonized by my Roman Catholic Church. The good she did was heart-warming, inspiring, and immense; the harm she did is incalculable. By publicly naming birth control as sinful, she reinforced the Hindu and Muslim inclination to religiously enshrined fertility. She believed that the population explosion would be handled by world-wide voluntary celibacy - after all, it worked in her order of nuns. The Pope loved it. He made a trip to Africa and gave religious mementos to a gathering of women each of whom had ten or more children. Personally, I would prefer the Pope to canonize, and the Nobel Peace Prize Committee to honor, a woman like Margaret Sanger, the pioneer for birth control. Not *natural* birth control, the rhythm method that my Roman Catholic Church grudgingly accepts, but what we should plainly call *unnatural* birth control - you know, the kind that works.

Plenty of traffic accidents were evident in Chennai, some involving our shipmates. Of course, reflexive defenders of anything non-American would point out that traffic accidents happen in the States, too. I would go further, and note that you are probably less likely to be hit by a drunken driver in India than in the United States, and certainly than in my home state of New Mexico, whose lawmakers and judges protect drunken drivers like a cultural heritage. But to give an idea of traffic in Madras, consider Catharine's experience in an overnight side-trip to a Dalit village. In the 60 kilometer (35 mile) trip there, she and her Semester At Sea companions saw three separate instances of overturned buses by the side of the road. On the return trip the next day, they saw four automobile wrecks. The only previous instance of fatal SAS traffic accident was in 1994 in India, when four students and a senior citizen passenger were killed in a bus trip. Indian traffic is not funny. At lunch after we left India, Sara, my SAS "grandchild," told of being in an auto rickshaw, a three-wheeled semi-enclosed motorcycle form of public transportation, trying unsuccessfully to slow down the reckless driver when he hit a bicyclist. The driver was angry with her when she refused to get back in or pay him. The young woman next to us at lunch was in an accident when her bus hit a car. (My own gentle Tamil taxi driver was excellent and controlled, in such marked contrast to the surrounding chaos that I was moved to give him a 50 per cent tip, both out of relief at arriving safely, and to encourage such caring and respect for life.)

The hawkers of India - post cards, sandals, carvings - are almost as bad as those in Saigon and China. The beggars are not as difficult to handle, and sadly so, because they just do not have the energy. Truly pitiful. Once you "get past" the initial blurred impression of beggars, you can see more of India. Sure. Like, the woman blocking my way onto the bus outside of a famous Government-approved silk goods store. "Get past" her faintly smiling, horrible saintly face, "get past" the filthy dress she wore, and experience the real India. Take a good look at the begging hand she thrusts toward your face, and notice the one finger that is only rotted off to the first knuckle. The other fingers and the thumb are gone all the way to the second knuckle or beyond. Leprosy. Earlier, Catharine and Semester At Sea students "got past" the beggars outside a temple compound to find a case of fully developed elephantitis.

A land of contrasts, they say, exciting contrasts. Like poverty and wealth. Personally, I have not seen any wealth, beyond a few middle class homes by the shore. Our friends doing Rotarian visits saw some wealth, but I think you have to have such a contact. What the unconnected traveler sees is more and more of the same old crap, not many contrasts and definitely not exciting, unless you would also get excited by freak shows and slumming. I know, I know, freaks are my brothers and sisters. They are, and I love them, but I do not like the freak show *mentality*.

Chapter 12 – Chennai (Madras) and India

There are certainly plenty of contrasts, but my larger impression is that of complexity. Fifteen languages recognized in the Constitution! This does not count English, which is the language of higher education and the professions. In all, 1600 languages and dialects. No language enjoys a mayoralty - Hindi comes closest, as 40 per cent speak it. Like Malaysia, it takes a lot of imagination to think of India as one country. To the lasting credit of the founders, they realistically determined state boundaries not so much by area but by language groups. Of course, there will always be minority groups who get short-changed, but at least there is functional coherence in government. Ethnic groups still speak their own language, just like the Polish and Italian neighborhoods of my youth in Detroit. We had Polish newspapers, I was taught some Polish by Polish Felician Nuns, but no one expected the street signs to be multi-lingual. No Polish separatist movement for Hamtramck. And here in Tamil Nadu, there is no need for, nor paranoia about, an "Official Tamil Movement." Most of the people speak Tamil, so Tamil is the official language for the government. What an idea.

Talk about contrasts and contradictions. India is the world's largest democracy, and not just in the limited technical sense of popular voting in multi-party elections, but in other values of democracy such as a usually high rate of voting, a vigorous and articulate free press, and widespread interest and discussion of political issues. On the other hand, they democratically chose to be governed by a virtual royal family from Independence in 1947 through 1991, forty-four years during which the notable prime ministers were J. Nehru, his daughter Indira Gandhi (no relation to Mohandas Gandhi), and her son Rajiv Gandhi. Indira Gandhi was the first democratically elected woman head of state in the world. She is most remembered for avoiding an election in 1975 by imposing martial law for two years, imprisoning opposition political leaders and censoring the press. She and her successor son were both eventually assassinated. Indian democracy assassinates so many politicians that they should consider writing it into their constitution. Consider June 1991, when they postponed the scheduled election until February 1992, because there were 800 recorded deaths of people going to the polls. In the state of Punjab, 23 of the thousand or so campaigners were assassinated! Democracy, Indian style: One man, One bomb.

Another common saying is that "For anything you say about India, the opposite is also true." Here is one pair of observations that fits the aphorism. "The best thing about India is religion." And, "The worst thing about India is religion."

Thomas Merton said India was the most religious country in the world, and most of it is Hindu - specifically, 83 per cent. Hinduism is fascinating, and, like India, full of contradictions. It is outrageously polytheistic at its popular level and practice. As Merton said, the Hindus worship everything that moves, and everything that does not move. The multiple gods have multiple forms or avatars, just like our Roman Catholic avatars. The apostle Thomas proselytized here, and is (perhaps) buried near Madras. About one quarter of the state of Tamil Nadu is Roman Catholic, and I think that the Catholics and Hindus have more in common in personality (rather than shared scriptures) than the Catholic and other "people of the book," the Jews and Muslims. The more intellectually refined of the faithful of both Hindu and Catholic recognize (at least intellectually, if not in practice) that these avatars are just different appearances of the same being. Like the Catholic Blessed Mother, who is the same as Our Lady of Lourdes, the same as Our Lady of Perpetual Help, the same as Our Lady of Guadalupe, La Conquistadora. That one hurts. To use the mother of Jesus of Nazareth as a symbol and tool of Spanish conquest in the New World! On the high theological end of the spectrum, she is Co-Redemtrix. Unbelievable embellishment, having nothing to do with the admirable woman about whom we know a few things for sure, such as, she had a very hard life, and she deserves our respect and love and at

Chapter 12 – Chennai (Madras) and India

least one title, that of "Blessed Mother." But she was no "lady," a classist term hung on her by later generations to further legitimize their own class control. She was a poor peasant woman who said "yes" and was swept up in mega-history and myth-making, to the point where she even lost her name. Not only was her memory subjected to the incredible indignity of dirty old men (priests and theologians) arguing about her perpetual virginity, but they had to Anglicize her name, from the gently rolling Hebrew "Miriam" that her parents gave her, to "Mary." Take a trip to Mexico, and try to convince an objective party - say, a Muslim - that Catholicism is monotheistic. (This does not even broach the subject of Trinitarian doctrine.)

But Roman Catholicism, even the rural Mexican version, seems monotheistic alongside Hinduism. It out-embellishes them all, even the classic Greek and Roman pantheons and the Mayan underworld. How a land of Hindu temples can accommodate the unequivocally monotheistic Muslims (11 per cent of Indian population), who hold as sinful any artistic representation of human or animal forms, is beyond my understanding. The religious bloodshed before and since India's 1947 Independence has been horrible, and the far north states of Kashmir and Punjab are still spilling blood, but I cannot understand how they manage to co-exist at all. Sure, Americans could do it, but remember that the Indians, both Hindu and Muslim, *believe*.

What this Hindu hyper-polytheism conveys that is true, is the incredible, staggering complexity and richness of the world, of life itself. Especially sexual life, including graphic temple depictions, inside and outside, of godly copulations and sexual organs. As metaphor, and surely religion at this level must be taken as metaphor, the hyper-theism is true. At the higher levels, Hinduism recognizes monotheism. The various major avatars of Vishnu were obviously devised historically to incorporate local gods into one religion. Your group has a god named Lord Krishna, and wonderful epic poetry built around him. So we also accept him, and now reveal to you that he is none other than another avatar (specifically, the eighth) of *our* god Vishnu, who himself is but one of our Hindu trinity, but if that is still not monotheistic enough for you, we go beyond mere monotheism to *monism*, the understanding that all is one. Literally, *all*. Major gods, minor gods, multitudinous avatars, people, you and I, and the creepy crawlies. This Hindu extreme is overwhelming, too, on the *mono*-side, just as the Hindu temples are overwhelming on the *poly*-side, and just like life. And life is getting more overwhelming, not less. Imagine what the Hindu theologians and artists would have created if they had possessed our modern insights into biology (trans-sexual fishes, cloning, microbiology, DNA) and the parallel "zoo" of sub-atomic particles and the measure of star distances in light-years and Hubbell telescope photographs and earth volcanism and tectonic plates and comparative ethnology.

So, "The best thing about India is religion." And as we environmentalists like to say about the benefits of technology, "And now, for the bill."

I think that every one of the universally recognized problems of modern India is institutionalized in its primary religion. Hinduism is more than a religion, it is the philosophy and society and personality of India. Increasingly, it is also the government. Although by constitution a secular state (as contrasted to the officially Islamic states of Pakistan and Bangladesh that border it, and were born in the same bloody time), the recently elected ruling party is the BJP, fairly characterized as Hindu fundamentalists. The caste system is officially outlawed, but inter-caste marriages and (more importantly) an individual's caste mobility are rare. The 4-level caste system (or 5-level, if you include the outcastes) was originally based on race (the old Hindi word for the caste was *varna*, meaning color) and is embedded in the major Hindu scriptures. This is a god-given system, now embellished, in true Indian fashion, to

Chapter 12 – Chennai (Madras) and India

cover several thousand castes based primarily on occupation but also incorporating social community, eligible marriage candidates, and of course color. Reformers like Mohandas Gandhi worked at explaining away the caste system, but it is embedded in the religion. There is one very important thing about India that I learned here from Catharine, which she learned on her overnight visit to a Dalit (outcaste) village. The Dalits are *not* fans of Gandhi, because their leader Dr. B. R. Ambedkar, who led the development of the Indian constitution, recognized that their problems were embedded in Hinduism, and urged his people to drop it for Islam, Christianity, Buddhism, or Baha'i - anything but Hinduism. Gandhi won out. He also refused higher education for his own children, in his romantic yearning for a pure peasant life, but the Dalits believe in higher education.

The Hindu belief in reincarnation includes the concept of *karma*. Your lowly caste position and miserable present life are your own fault, from your sins in previous lives. (Looking around Madras, it is clear that there was a whole lot of sinning going on in previous times, and these poor people are paying now.) This does not help motivate social action, anymore than the Christian view of heavenly rewards did in previous times. The world is an environmental and social mess, but not to worry, because it is all illusion (*maya*) anyway. As for institutional sanction of violence, the *Upanishads* (the core of the Sanskrit mega-epic poem, the *Mahabharata*) endorses it as religious duty. The critical point in the story is that the hero Arjuna has misgivings on the eve of battle about slaughtering his cousins. He is talked into "doing his duty" as a warrior by his chariot driver, who turns out to be none other than Lord Krishna himself. Mohandas Gandhi tried to clean up the interpretation of this story, as all religious reformers do when confronted with key scriptures that become offensive. Maybe Gandhi was right, that the point of the story is misunderstood (it is duty, or *dharma*, not violence *per se*) but he was surely right that it is

At Sea At Sixty

widely understood to endorse, legitimize, and in fact sacralize war, and understandably so. That's what the story says.

On the other hand, Gandhi and Hinduism honor all life, and refuse to kill, most of the time. Vegetarianism is widespread, but certainly not universal in India. So far, so good. But consider the cows. Not that the Hindus should butcher and eat beef, but couldn't they at least get them off the city streets? Every visitor to India has asked this obvious question. How naive, how culturally insensitive we are. Gandhi said the cow was "a poem of pity." End of discussion. And blocking traffic is not the major negative result. The cows turn grass, garbage and cardboard into fecal matter and feed the flies, whose own fecal matter in turn shows up on our menus, Indians and visitors, adults and children alike. Maybe I'm just hypersensitive - in 1970, we very nearly lost our first-born seven-year old child to food poisoning (Shigella B dysentery) and Catharine herself was hospitalized for a week. Or maybe I just flunk India because of my cultural biases, but I reject the value of a religious belief that sacralizes dysentery. Besides cows on the street, other Semester At Sea people saw city-roaming camels, elephants, pigs, goats, and even a bear up north. Then, consider the rats. Call it religion or sick sentimentality run rampant, you have to give them credit for consistency. The Indians loose a lot of grain to rats. A few years ago, a rat-borne plague swept parts of India. The government wanted to kill some rats. The religious people would not hear of it (the very popular elephant-headed god Ganesh was saved by a rat!) so the plague was left to "run its course," that is, people died. Poetry and sentimentality live. However, the Indians are a little less consistent and more pragmatic when it comes to adjoining states occupied by Muslims. The recent test (May 1998) of a nuclear weapon by India enjoyed widespread popular support, the democratically elected BJP party having made it a campaign issue. It brings to mind a 1970's nuclear weapons project in the

Chapter 12 – Chennai (Madras) and India

United States named after Shiva, the Destroyer member of the Hindu trinity.

The government has made brave attempts to reduce the birth rate, and for a while had success (and excesses), but vasectomies are now rare, and female sterilization has become a gender-political issue, understandably so. The annual net rate of population increase (birth rate minus death rate) is again at 2 per cent. At this cataclysmic rate, and starting with almost a billion people now, India will surpass China early in the 21st century. Needless to say, the wealthy and the emerging middle classes, who could pass on a tradition of education and who could afford to support children, have lower than average birth rates. The wretchedly poor and uneducated are burgeoning, with the approval and encouragement of their religious leaders.

The Hindu religion and social system is possibly no more self-contradictory and potentially destructive than (say) medieval Christianity in Europe. The difference now, on the eve of the 21st century, is that the Hindus still believe this stuff. Certainly no one else can help India, but not even the Indians themselves can help India, without changing it. This is axiomatic, of course, but people persist in acting as though they can help a society, their own or another, without changing it. Hindus would have to *radically* change their religion. Or at least ignore it, or take the Roman Catholic approach and "return to an earlier tradition." This is of course hypocrisy in action, but it has its advantages. I am not sure if my Roman Catholic church will ever ordain women priests, or replace the caesaro-papacy with a more egalitarian leadership, or wake up and catch up to its literate laity on birth control, but if they ever do, I am absolutely, 100 per cent, bet-the-ranch sure that they will not say "Sorry, we've been screwing up your lives for generations but we now recognize and admit our error." No, they will "return to an earlier and more honored tradition." Which is actually true. And the Hindu religious philosopher Ramakrishna tried it, in the 19th century, retrojecting an imagined history to reform Hinduism. His disciple Vivekananda traveled to the United States and founded the Vedanta Society, whose publications introduced many, including myself, to the rarefied, idealized Hinduism. They achieved only marginal success in their own home. These reformers flunked India, too.

Of course, if one could magically remove Hinduism, the result would be chaos. As people realized in Africa in the 1950's, the old ways must be replaced with "Something of Value." If there is any hope for India, I think it is the Baha'i religion. It accepts and honors the best of all major religions and philosophies, and could be made palatable to many non-fundamentalists, and I think would not require the temple bashing that would strip India of its cultural Hindu inheritance. (I look forward to visiting the Baha'i World Center at our next stop in Haifa, and finding out more.) The relatively new and gorgeous Baha'i temple in New Delhi, called the Lotus Temple, is now the major tourist attraction in India, surpassing even the Taj Mahal (which incidentally is not Hindu either, but Muslim). I would be delighted beyond expression to be proven wrong in my pessimism for India, but if I returned in five or ten years and found India significantly improved, I would be amazed. As contrasted to Vietnam, for instance, where I would be surprised to find no progress.

I would return to India to see the Baha'i Lotus Temple in New Delhi, a city that our shipmates say it is fairly clean (it was originally strictly British), proving that it could be done countrywide if the people had the will. The other reason I would return to India would be to experience the state of Kerala. If I had known a little about it, I would have foregone the drudgery of Madras and the state of Tamil Nadu, and headed directly west to the other coast of the southern peninsula. From what I read and hear, Kerala is the best. This is the only region of India I want to see. It is India's only fully literate state. It has a high standard of living, not just in an

Chapter 12 – Chennai (Madras) and India

economist's phony measure of per capita income in US$. It looks clean. It has achieved zero population growth! It did not achieve ZPG by coercion. Its natural environment is reasonably intact and beautiful. Our inter-port lecturer, a woman geographer on the faculty at Madras University, says Kerala is always used as an example of modern Indian achievement.

Kerala, this single unequivocal Indian success story, is perhaps the ultimate Indian irony. Kerala sports the world's only elected state *Communist* government! There are two Communist parties, the hard core Marxist and the backsliders. (Not their ballot identifications.) They have been voted in democratically, and voted out democratically, at which time they went to work within the free electoral system and, following the rules as well as anyone, were voted back in. Unlike the orthodox single-party Communist totalitarian regimes, they do not view all religion as inimical. For added irony, the party leader is a Brahmin, that is, priest caste. The tourist brochures brag about the local religious festivities. Apparently, the system works. But no one can think of a way this Indian success story could be exported across state lines. They flunk, too.

I like lots of things about India. I love the warmth of the people. I like modern arranged marriages. (The bride and groom are not coerced, just screened and introduced by caring relatives.) I like temples and monuments. I like the fishing village we visited, on the coast about 30 kilometers south of Madras; it was poor, but not destitute. Their were no evident problems of obesity, but the staring children were healthy and warmed up considerably with a little coaxing from their mothers. The men were too involved in a couple of rummy games, sitting in circles in the shade on the dirt, to bother with us. I like that. They participate in the cash economy enough to be able to take the family into the big city for a movie every week or so. I like the professional people, faculty members from several geography departments, who were generous enough to accompany us to the village. Dr. Suresh told me of his work with a tanning industry operation that switched from "primitive" methods to modern chemistry, and thus destroyed the downstream vegetation and permanently poisoned the soil with heavy metals. If I had more time, I would have accepted his generous invitation to visit his city and university and stay at his home. Likewise, we had a delightful conversation with our guide to Mahabalipuram, a woman almost our age with a PhD in economics. She, our group leader Anne, and Catharine and I shared some good laughs about marriage and men and women.

And there are indeed some wonderful sites in India. Mahabalipuram is the home of "Arjuna's Penance," billed as the largest bas-relief sculpture in the world. In the 7th century, the merchant-king Pallava family supported artists to tear into tough granitic sandstone to create monolithic rooms and the bas-relief depicting the Hindu epic poem *Mahabharata*. It is a monument, not a temple, so the priests aren't running the show. The fine-scale rococo-like embellishments of later temples are not evident, but the legions of characters are, including Lord Krishna (in an inside room) with his arm around the shoulder of Arjuna (I think) in the same casual and intimate show of affection of Tamil men and boys today. If it were not for the godly head-dress, the amazingly naturalistic styled carving could have represented my older brother with his arm over my shoulders when I was a kid, singing sentimental Irish-American mush to our Dad's piano playing. I like this god! And his consort is busty and thin waisted, as all Hindu goddesses are, looking almost corny, like an adolescent boy's mildly erotic vision of a dream woman. Most of the major bas-relief is on an outside wall, and most are human forms arranged in horizontally tending rows, not stiffly vertical but in varying, slightly leaning poses. An eye-catching vertical sequence shows first a cobra with flared head, then right above it another cobra body that develops into Lord Krishna's consort, then right above that another cobra body that

Chapter 12 – Chennai (Madras) and India

develops into Lord Krishna himself, playing his flute, like our Kokapeli in the American Southwest.

But the elephants steal the show. The human and god forms are roughly uniform portrait size, but the main elephant is huge. Another big one is right behind it, and a handful of little guys are underneath, some behind the legs of the big ones. Elephants are wonderful in the flesh. If you ever get a chance, ride one. Better yet, watch a circus elephant work, not in the show, but taking down the tent. Our old Jesuit priest / circus clown friend, Nick Weber, once arranged for us to watch them work. Our favorite was named Barbara. She pulled up the tent stakes on voice command, working in a very confined space, with noisy distractions including men taking down grandstands. She had to back up her entire body length in areas barely wide enough for one of her feet. Grace and intelligence. My one regret in taking the taxi back to the ship was that I missed an elephant. The Semester At Sea tour bus pulled up alongside an elephant in Madras, and Catharine had an eye-level view from the bus window. The Hindu *Upanishads* speak of the characteristics of a desirable woman, saying that she should be as graceful as an elephant. Rent a video of David Lean's film "Passage to India," which we viewed on the ship traveling to Madras. There is a sequence where he tracks the camera with a striding bedecked elephant. Grace and intelligence. I want one.

The elephants in the bas-relief of Arjuna's Penance capture elephant-ness. The overall composition has the huge elephants off in the lower right of the wall, the vertical cobra-sequence towards the middle, and the host of characters arranged above and to the left. It is a daring and successful composition, one that would take a lot of courage to attempt in a water color, let alone in a wall of granitic sandstone using 7th century technology. For me, Arjuna's Penance was worth the two-day scheduled bus trip, and in fact was worth the stop in India.

So why had I taken this taxi ride? I traveled to Mahabalipuram on a tourist bus with other Semester At Sea people, but then I made a mistake. At lunch, at a government approved resort hotel, I mistook a cold salad (slaw, chick peas, and other tasty things) for a hot vegetarian dish. At the first bite, I knew my mistake, but I did not want to spit it out in polite company. Besides, the serving size was only a couple of tablespoons. The strong recommendation had been to not eat anything cold. I'll spare the details, but the next day, rather than wait with my guts churning until our bus departed at 2:00 pm, I decided to hire a taxi to get me back to the ship, pronto. The medical staff said that on previous SAS trips to India, half the ship came down with diarrhea (or "Delhi belly") bad enough to show up at the clinic, and some went on intravenous injections. This does not count those who suffered in silence (or at least in privacy). The shipboard medical staff had urged us to approach India as a health challenge, to beat the diarrhea odds. But in this test, as in the others, I flunked India.

Chapter 13
The Indian Ocean and Arabian Sea

Chapter 13 – The Indian Ocean and Arabian Sea

Time for Some Heavy Thinking

csr

Coming out of India, I was still full of questions. The long voyage after India gave me important time to think.

Crossing the Indian Ocean and the Arabian Sea took as long as the Pacific crossing. On this part of our voyage we reached the half way point of the entire round-the-world journey. For the students and faculty it was time for mid-term exams. For me it was time to an examine life, and my life in particular since I am past half way any way you figure it. I come from a line of long lived folk, but none reached 120. So most of my life is past. What can I imagine in the future? How do I want to spend my remaining time, my life energy, my "fortune" ? Has traveling through these countries altered any of my ideas about my own aging?

To travel light is the first lesson which comes to mind. In the literal sense, it means a paring down of what is necessary to carry with me: take few bags, and use modern materials for the necessities. The new synthetics are lighter and do dry faster than cottons and wools. This is helpful when hand laundering is needed and is all part of not being dependent upon machines. Clothing is an easy place to begin. The intellectual baggage of the years is something else.

I think traveling light may mean throwing out things (including art and papers) from my past which are no longer "me" or useful to me. I can find new homes for some possessions, I can surely clear out files. I have a current practice of giving away clothes or books if I get new ones. I'll continue that, but one senior on the ship has a practice which really got me to thinking. He doesn't buy a new book unless he can read it in the next month. I must confess I have books I haven't read yet . . . years later. Do I think I'll get the contents by osmosis? Work is needed in this area. When I saw how people live with so little, it made me question excesses in my life. Including books.

Symbolically, "travel light" incorporates much more than literally traveling light. Of course I can live out of one or two bags. But the important question is just what are the necessities of life? What excess baggage am I now hauling around?

Through sixty years of living, loving, parenting, being a minister and counselor, I find that love is the most common, persistent, and important of human experiences. It is the most important "bag" to pack well. Being loved as a child is basic if one is to know how to love oneself and others. Things I saw on my voyage brought up this issue of love and children. I was sad and frightened when I saw children asleep on the streets in India with no parent around . . . or none I could see. I put some of my response into these words.

about three years old
sleeping that
deep childhood sleep
on the pavement

above: a sign:
introducing
home loans
Hong Kong Bank

India
you break my heart
and perplex my mind

What of this basic love and that child? Does he, or she, have a chance at a life that includes love? At first I just thought of poverty and said "no." But then I remembered the poor Dalit village. There I did see children well loved by mothers, fathers, sisters, brothers. Love could be there in the midst of poverty, nourishing, sustaining life, making more love possible. But poverty makes care harder.

Chapter 13 – The Indian Ocean and Arabian Sea

Wealth doesn't guarantee it. Some of our shipmates were very financially cared for, not all were well loved. It is good thing for the world that love isn't dependent on money.

I think the basis of love for a child is that she or he be wanted. After that they need care in both word and deed. Sometimes parents don't know how to care in ways a child needs. After examining life, I find that to a certain extent we all fail in this. Our parents did, we did. But the need was still there. Others can fill parent-love roles for ourselves and our children. We can let them.

One of the tasks of aging is to forgive our parents for not loving us in all the ways we needed, and to forgive ourselves for not loving our children in all the ways they needed. We have to let go some of past expectations and hurts. To have expected perfect love from parents, or from ourselves towards our children, can produce a whole lot of anger and/or guilt. It is a heavy burden; in a word, "excess baggage." The baggage we should pack is all the times our parents, ourselves and our children have succeeded in love. This will serve us well as we continue loving children that come into our lives. We can love, but to insist that it always be done perfectly can be a huge stumbling block. The unrealistic expectations of youth do not serve our old selves.

What of all those questions I had going into India? The answers were varied. I think I did see the India of the movies, films and books to which I have been exposed. On the ship I read the Booker Award recipient, *The God of Small Things* by Arundhati Roy and I found that, for me, it symbolized my experience. The writing was brilliant, like the colors of the saris, and the characters engaging, like most whom I met, but the story itself was wrenching, as was my experience. Wrenching in a way beyond experiences I know in my daily living. The book, and India, left me saying to myself, "This is the end? Oh, no."

One faculty member and a student were so upset by all the outstretched hands of the needy that they went out and bought bags of cookies to pass out. I think what they wanted to give was love; they knew how basic it was. And they did give love. But what all those hungry hands need cannot be met by bags of cookies given by Westerners. If tomorrow someone or some country in the world gave billions to India (or any other struggling nation) and if tomorrow the Developed countries cut their consumption of goods in half (which I consider one of my country's problems), the problems of India would still exist. The problems of food, population, pollution are their problems to be solved by them. If and when they do, they will know self-love and the strength that comes from it. I think it arrogant of us to think we can solve all the world's problems. Yes, there is an inter-connectedness among peoples, but like anything else it can be misunderstood. If other countries are perceived as unable to solve their problems, from where will come their sense of life and success?

Can India change? Will India change? Despite the fact that the caste system was made illegal half a century ago, it is still operative. I believe many Indians seek change in education, the rights of the poor, and improved sanitation. The country has a history rich in leaders, like Mohandas Gandhi, Nehru, and Ambedkar, the Dalit who led the writing of the constitution and urged other Dalits to convert to Buddhism or Christianity. These people can inspire in ways not possible by western leaders. They have been catalysts for change. But right now there is a renaissance of Hinduism in an older form. The Hindu National Party (BJP) is the majority party. They claim to be inclusive of all religions, but with a name like that, the claim is not very convincing. There has been a renewal of violence among Indians based on religious and political beliefs.

Other questions remained after our ship left the port. Does India have the time to change given the rapidly expanding population? I don't know. Does it have the resources, financial and others? If you're the type of person who thrives on challenging situations, complex problems, you'll be attracted to India. If not, you

Chapter 13 – The Indian Ocean and Arabian Sea

can be overwhelmed by it. In any case I agree with our Core Course professors, you'll think about it long after you leave port, and you might not ever be the same.

Isn't there anything I think can be given to India? Admonitions of my traditions are conflicted: Isn't it "more blessed to give than receive?" But doesn't "God help those who help themselves" ? All those phrases from the past bombard my present and if I am an old one I must sort out what I believe is true. To say that all approaches are equally good and valid is to side-step the tasks of aging. Just as one must finally decide what I want to be when I grow up, one has to decide "what is it that I believe?"

What I think can and should be given to India specifically, and to anyone in need, is information and access to information, support, encouragement. All this takes wisdom, balance, compassion. I do know it is wrong to assume I can solve all problems; I do know it is wrong to completely withdraw. I'll spend the remainder of my life trying to figure out the details with my own family and my own country.

Exploring the new and making mistakes is the job of the young, sorting out values is the task of the old. After all is said and done, what is valuable? There were those onboard who subscribed to a sort of relativism which implied that all cultural decisions are equally "right." I think in my own life at one time or another I have believed that. I no longer do. I think I can say that I am clear in my belief that slavery is wrong, female infanticide is wrong, genocide is wrong, female circumcision is wrong. I think I can conclude after sixty years that education is good, health care is good, freedom of religion and speech are good. Governments and academics can argue and disagree, but I have the task of reaching some conclusions about life about which folks can argue. To say "whatever turns you on" or " I'll mind my own business" is to shirk responsibility - the responsibility of being old.

Besides packing into my old age suitcase the basics of love for children, self and others (that "random acts of kindness" appeals to me), I think truth and justice need to go along with me. Hebrew scriptures say they "kiss". That sounds good and descriptive to me. I'd also throw in my pack a good bit of beauty: in nature and made by humans - audio, visual - actually, I wouldn't leave out any of the senses.

Finally, I'd pack a large box of humor. I need it when I look back on my mistakes, and see the flubs of those I love, which includes my country and church.

One important thing is missing from my list of what to take with me on my life's journey. It is called by many names: God, religion, things of the spirit (Spirit). This voyage prompted the most reflection in this area. During the time spent in the Indian Ocean I thought and wrote, so did Pat. I wrote to our children, "I think if I lived in India I would become very anti-religious. The Hindu belief system keeps the caste system operative, even though officially, legally, it is supposed to be out. The belief in *karma* makes it easier for people to accept being very rich or very poor, it makes it easier for people to allow injustice, pollution, and, yes, filth. Filth and poverty don't have to go together. In the Dalit village the litter and garbage seemed to be more localized than in Chennai. Those who went to Calcutta, Bombay and Delhi said that Chennai looked cleaner and less chaotic. It is hard to believe. I think despair has invaded many people in the big cities; it stares out from blank faces. I don't believe people were created to despair; I don't believe that is anyone's karma."

I have also thought about religious ideas from my own tradition which I think have done much damage to human beings. I think "the devil made me do it" is as harmful as *karma*. I think believing that I am *chosen*, or that we (Americans, Christians, Jews) are somehow specially blessed by God, is as harmful as *karma*. I am not sure I believe in a personal God (maybe a creative energy, or

Chapter 13 – The Indian Ocean and Arabian Sea

Wisdom, or Love) but if I did, this God would not pick favorites. There would be no Manifest Destiny except that of blessedness for all creatures . . . and I mean creatures, not just humans.

On the ship I played cassettes of Mahalia Jackson singing out her faith. I listened to her songs of belief in a God whose eye is on the sparrow, who is real, who walks with her and talks to her. She sings "If religion were a thing money could buy, the rich would live and the poor would die." But I can't even simply accept all of Mahalia's songs. For me God is not so simple. Surely, Religion is not. The songs I love to hear are *her* songs. I confess to a current love - hate relationship to religions. As I have lived, studied and traveled I have seen much abuse by religions. Certainly in my own Christian and Catholic tradition. I am not convinced that religions have done more good than harm. I see many of them holding on to social and political definitions of the roles and "positions" of people, rather than freeing them to new ways of being holy. I am not convinced that religions have made humans "act justly, love tenderly and walk humbly with God" (Micah) or become more fully human, more fully alive (Augustine).

But I do believe that most people have a capacity for things of the Spirit. Things not bounded by the senses. A capacity for Mystery and the Other. A capacity for awe. And I notice that people from different times and places have a need for ritual. Religions have responded to these needs and have kept a record of the human wrestling match with divinity in many forms. That's important. If by "religion" the Mahalia Jackson song means the grace of God, the tender mercy of God, the pursuit of things Spiritual, I can sing along with the great gospel singer. If on the other hand, she means a specific religion which makes one better than anyone else, I'd have to be silent. Having read of how she lived her life, I know she accepted all prayers of all people. Maybe I will be "walking all over God's heaven" with her yet.

Maybe I am right now.

Dying In India

pjr

Returning to our ship in India was quite different than it was in Vietnam. After Vietnam, shipmates joked "Did you survive Vietnam?" No one said that the morning after we left India. Everyone knew that the Semester At Sea assistant librarian, our new friend Loretta, whom we had introduced to snorkeling in Malaysia, was slipping away in a Madras hospital, the victim of a hit-and-run bus driver.

On our third day out of Madras, at the conclusion of our Core Course, we received the announcement that Loretta had died. No one was surprised. The shipboard community, our floating village of larger than normal egos and usually talkative students, was silent as we drifted out. I find it disorienting to have just met someone seven weeks ago, found much in common including our age, made friends with, shared an adventure with, and made plans for future playing together, and now she is already gone. I wanted to know her better. I learned from her a lesson I already knew, but need to keep re-learning, like drills in sports. Our snorkel trip was poor, but she enjoyed it. I was disappointed for her, and thought it would have been better to wait until she could join us in Belize for excellent skin diving but she knew to enjoy the day's offerings, not to just plan for the future.

Loretta's life was honored by a beautiful shipboard memorial ceremony, with sincere and specific remembrances. It lasted through sunset, with balloons into the air and flowers into the sea, a tall white cumulus peak pointing towards a three-quarter waxing moon and close-by evening star. The ship sounded its horn, and altered it course, swerving a few times over ten minutes or so, leaving a glassy arching wake through the mild chop along the vague boundary of the Indian Ocean and the Arabian Sea. What a strong gesture, to alter the ship's course. Yes, the voyage goes on,

Chapter 13 – The Indian Ocean and Arabian Sea

as our lives go on, but to take a break from goal-oriented pursuits of ship and passengers, and let up a bit, wander a bit, hang out together while pausing to remember and wonder. As I stood on the aft Sun Deck looking down where most of our shipmates were gathered on the Promenade Deck, I saw many faces I did not know seven weeks ago, and who have now crossed their lives with mine. In seven more weeks, we will split up, a few of us will be in contact, but mostly not. In a few decades, possibly much less, Catharine and I will be gone. I wonder if any of the students, then in their early fifties, will remember us. I know they will remember Loretta.

Healing Waters

csr

I think much of the life and life values discussed in the Indian Ocean arose because of our travels in India, but to a great extent they arose because of the death of our friend Loretta who died from injuries sustained when hit by that bus in Chennai. Death has a way of getting our attention, especially if it is someone close in age or interests. The whole ship assembled for a memorial service led by the captain. It was very touching and prayerful.

A group sang "Amazing Grace" and "Let There Be Peace on Earth." As the ship changed course to honor her, we threw flowers into the sea as the strains of Dvorak's "New World Symphony" drifted into the sunset sky.

After the memorial services, I don't think I was the only one thinking of my mortality and my desire to live longer. There are many more things I want to see and do. This moment raised the question "What is a full life?" My dad is in his mid-nineties and it is easier to see his life as full or past the point of fullness. A life ending in the 60's is difficult for me. It seems more like a beginning than an end time. The beginning of retirement, of exploring new interests or goals, of new relationships with adult children, of developing new aspects of old relationships with friends who in the past may have had similar jobs or interests of child rearing. To have the newly discovered work of old age terminated is a loss. I'm not yet expecting friends and contemporaries to die. I miss how they model aging for me, how they help stir my imagination and reflections.

After the service we had to deal with the contrast of exuberant youngsters, children of the faculty and staff, who were knocking on our cabin doors shouting "Trick or Treat." Life had just taught them about some of that, but we were glad to fill their bags and laugh with them for a moment. It was good. I think Loretta would have wanted them to have their evening of fun.

It was also good to let the rhythm of the sea comfort us for many days. To deal with death we walked, ran, wrote, sang, studied and looked out to the far horizon. These waters have an abundance of life - dolphins, flying fish and the best marine life of the trip, a stream of tuna about a mile long. I watched it a long time, and I thought about my connections to life: my children, my ideas, my art. I thought of how all life came from the sea. I felt blest. As the sun set, orange and glowing, it was nice to know that death does not have the power to stop beauty, or the waves.

Chapter 14
The Sea of Aden, Red Sea, Suez Canal, and Mediterranean Sea

Suez Canal – 11-8-98

Chapter 14 – Sea of Aden, Red Sea, Suez Canal, Mediterranean Sea

Imagining the Past

csr

On the third of November I was up early, not wanting to miss seeing the Horn of Africa and our entrance into the Sea of Aden. We would be traveling some very ancient waterways here. The Horn of Africa sticks way out and is the farthest east point on the continent. It is clear geologically that this "horn" was once attached to what is now called the Sinai Peninsula. But now the narrow strip of water called the Red Sea, lying in the Great Rift, separates the continents of Africa and Asia. The narrow passage from the Sea of Aden into the Red Sea is called *Bab el Mandeb* or the "gate of sorrows" because there have been so many shipwrecks in this area.

On the day we moved into the Red Sea it was very, very calm and beautiful. No hints of how rough things could be. I saw lots of sea life including dolphin (about twenty) and a stream of tuna which stretched out about a mile. With binoculars in hand and Mozart in my ear, I enjoyed the day until it fell away with another brilliant, orange sunset.

These seas, the Red and Aden, have an air of the very old about them. The shores are barren and hilly with scattered lighthouses and occasional cities. It was through these waters that early Christianity probably found its way to India, and through them that Islam surely moved east with Muslim sailors and merchants to India and Indonesia. The secret of the changing seasonal winds was the key to trade and, in turn, the exchange of ideas between the Middle East and North Africa and the countries along the Indian Ocean. The overland trade routes were also well established, but the sea routes proved faster and safer.

As we sailed in the Red Sea we began to see more and very diverse sea traffic. We knew that most of these ships would be going through the Suez Canal with us. This passage proved to be very fascinating to me, one of the highlights of the trip.

At Sea At Sixty

First a bit of history. The canal was built over a ten year period under the direction of the Frenchman Ferdinand de Lesseps, and connects the Red Sea and the Mediterranean Sea. Finished in 1869, it has had a changing political history. In the beginning it was owned by French shareholders and the Egyptian king, then in 1875 the British bought Egypt's shares and it was a neutral zone of commerce until World War I when only the British and her allies were allowed to use it. Some changes took place after the war, but essentially the British controlled the area through World War II. After 1949 through various treaties, a greater share of profits and control were given to Egypt. Then in June of 1956 the British left the area; a month later the Egyptian president, Jamal Nasser, nationalized the canal. Shortly thereafter Israel invaded Egypt, with the support of France and Great Britain. The canal was re-opened in 1957 under Egyptian control with the United Nations armed forces maintaining peace.

Scattered along the eastern banks of the canal we saw evidence of previous conflicts. But most of the war remnants were from the Six Day War in 1967 which Israel won. Repairs to the canal took many years. In 1979, restrictions against Israeli ships were ended and since then all ships have been able to use the canal - for a price. For merchant ships particularly, the fee is a small cost compared to sailing around all of Africa.

The canal is about one hundred miles long and cuts through a number of lakes: Lake Manzala, Lake Timsah, and the Bitter Lakes. It took all day to go through it. I kept moving from starboard to port and back again. On one side I saw barracks, soldiers, a satellite dish, and two camels. On the other, an oasis town with several minarets. On starboard, bits and pieces of old wars; on port, military installations. And both fore and aft, ships of all kinds, sizes, and purposes. At times it looked like huge cargoes had been deposited on the sands; a closer look revealed that these were barges floating on side canals.

Chapter 14 – Sea of Aden, Red Sea, Suez Canal, Mediterranean Sea

Although fascinating, the Suez Canal trip was also frustrating, because we knew that the pyramids and temples of ancient Egypt were near, yet oh so far. The original planned itinerary for this Fall Semester At Sea 1998 voyage had included a major stop in Egypt, as it had in earlier years. But in 1997, the people at the front of the SAS group walking to the Great Pyramid heard shots, and wisely turned their shipmates back. Several German tourists just ahead of the SAS group died in the random hail of terrorist gunfire. The SAS administration canceled the next year's stop. This was both prudent and politic, we believe. Even though the incident was now a year old, the cancellation has the effect of an economic boycott. The loss of over 700 tourist visits, it was hoped, would encourage Egypt to improve anti-terrorist security. All the same, we were disappointed to be denied our long-held desire to see ancient Egypt.

It was a rainy evening with no sunset as we neared the terminus of the Suez Canal and, unfortunately, there was no Port Said to see until after dark. Then its lights glowed on the portside as we passed, finally, into the mythical Mediterranean . . . *the* sea of western civilization; the sea of all those books of Roman and Greek history; the sea of the Bible; the sea of naval battles for thousands of years. The sea of fishermen, merchants, and prophets.

As we were sailing through these seas we were preparing for our next country, Israel. The Core Course preparation for this port was controversial and emotionally charged, to say the least. It was controversial on two fronts: the content and the form of presentation. Many of us expected that information and facts outlining both the Israeli and Palestinian claims would be given in a balanced way, or with some attempt at balance. From my perspective, this never happened, not only in the Core Course, but during our stay in Israel. We had to dig for information about Palestinian history. The form of presentation was predominantly emotional. One Jewish professor born in North Africa stated, "I'm not interested in facts ... only Truth." Her "Truth" has caused much confusion, bloodshed, and a stalling in the peace process. Her "Truth" was as absolute, black and white, as the "Truth" of Palestinian terrorists. In writing about the difficulties in Israel and amoung our shipboard community of sorting out fact and emotion, one senior passenger said, "Personally, I'd say the *fact* is that Israel is all about *emotion.*" I agreed with him before we docked and after. If peace is to come in this troubled part of the world, all participants, secular and orthodox Jews, inclusive and exclusive Muslims, as well as the various Christians present, must give up their belief in their absolute Truth, and work with principles of *relative* truth, *relative* justice, and the common good. Both Hebrew scriptures and the Koran (now transliterated as Qur'an) provide ample texts to make this possible. Both value the virtue of hospitality and love of neighbor. Both know from their scriptures that justice and mercy are cornerstones of peace. But, as in Ireland, Bosnia, and many states of Africa, the few extremists determine the fate of the majority. In the history of the world this has been tragically true; it continues to be true today.

West of The Suez Canal 11-9-98

Chapter 14 – Sea of Aden, Red Sea, Suez Canal, Mediterranean Sea

We arrived in Haifa on a bright sunny day. I had not wanted to come to Israel again because of the military realities, but I was hoping that I could poke around some excavations in the Galilee with Pat and show him a few sites that had really interested me on my two previous visits.

Little did we know that we were the last ship allowed into the port. It was closed so that Israel could make preparations for possible attacks from Iraq in retaliation for possible attacks by the US on Baghdad. This focus on threat and fighting has been the Israeli reality for its entire fifty year history.

Chapter 15
Haifa and Israel

CBR
11-98
Ceasarea

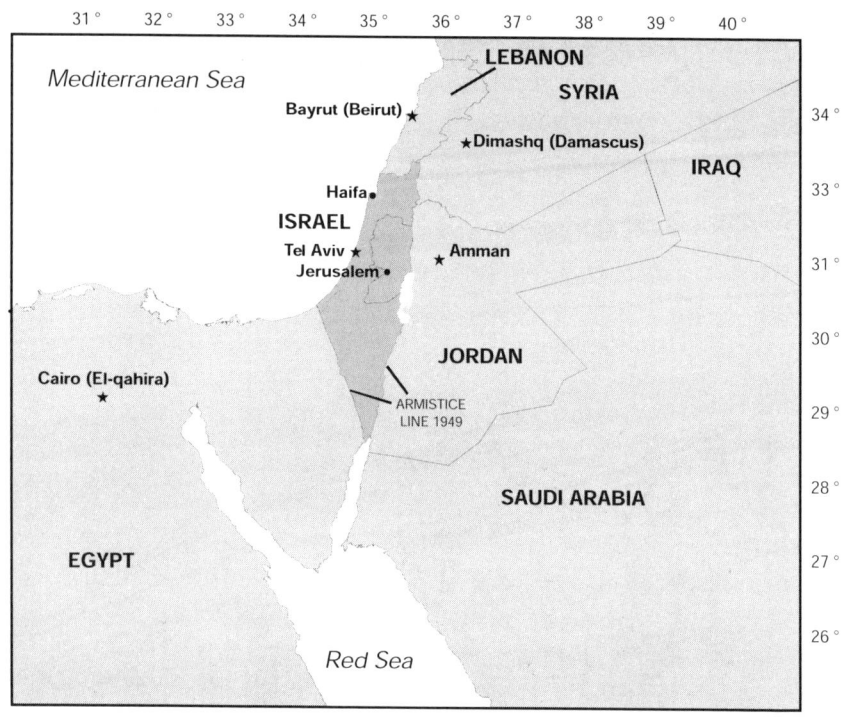

Haifa, Israel
Longitude 32.5°N Longitude 34.6°E

Chapter 15 – Haifa and Israel

Not So Safe Harbor

csr

The ship cleared smoothly in Haifa, in spite of the fact that war rumors were flying. Clinton had threatened Iraq and was moving the U. S. Navy into the area. The Port of Haifa was closed right after our ship docked, out of fear of a shooting war with Iraq. Many passengers and students nevertheless went off on a comprehensive tour of Israel. We had chosen a trip to Caesaria, old Roman ruins of a city built by Herod about the year of change from B. C. E. (Before the Common Era) and C.E. (Common Era). I had wanted to get back to this site ever since I first made a brief stop on a tour in the mid-970's.

Misinformation Galore

pjr

I was apprehensive about Israel to begin with. Tales from Catharine (she had been here twice) and many others had me worried about offensive Christian shrines, Israeli-Arab prejudices, and gruff attitudes. (Israel is, after all, a military state.) The bristling, argumentative atmosphere on board ship since we embarked for Israel added to my concern. Even the Israel romanticizers among the faculty volunteered the observation that people (especially in Tel Aviv) were rude, rather like New Yorkers. Then, of course, there was the little item of possible war, since the Port door had been closed behind us. I tried to keep an open mind - after all, secondhand information like this is the essence of prejudice in its true and only stinging meaning, that is, *pre*-judging. But the worst problem with prejudices and stereotypes is that they all too often are somewhat accurate. Our first excursion confirmed these prejudices. (Let me say right up front that my later excursion, into the Galilee, did much to correct these first bad impressions.)

Our first trip in Israel was to Caesaria, the Roman city and aqueduct system twenty miles or so south of Haifa. Our guide was a font of mis-information, arrogance and prejudice. He made so many factual errors (that we knew of) that at least four of us independently just wandered off on our own at Caesaria, preferring silence and no information to his mis-information.

On the bus ride to and from Caesaria, our guide could identify no flora. Pointing out the Baha'i World Center, a major site in Haifa, he dismissively referred to it as "that new religion" and gave a vague date for the founding of the religion, "about 200 years ago," which is the wrong century. He knew he had the founder's name wrong, but dismissed it saying "I can never get his name right." (Moses, Luther - whatever.) He said the shrine there holds the remains of the founder, which is not true (in fact, the remains are those of another prophet of Baha'i, a precursor of the founder Baha'u'llah.) He also identified a large building at the center as "their Supreme Court," which also is not accurate.

On to the beautiful aqueducts of Caesaria, where our guide gave the conversion from English to metric units as 100 kilometers equal to 70 or 80 miles (actually 61). The funniest one to an engineer like myself was his misinformation on the slope of the aqueduct, "one-half degree in 100 meters." This was not a slip of the tongue - I tried to talk sense to him, but he insisted and kept reciting it. The correct information must bear some resemblance to what he remembered, perhaps "one-half degree," or perhaps "one-half meter in 100 meters," but his mis-information is something like giving the temperature in pounds.

Students of medieval history will be glad to know that, according to our guide, "the Crusaders came to bring order." Some of us gasped, others gagged. He also claimed (on a later trip) that Jerusalem was the oldest capital in the world, having functioned continuously as the capital for thousands of years. Capital of what? In fact, the city has had many long periods of abandonment or ne-

Chapter 15 – Haifa and Israel

glect, including the four centuries of Ottoman rule ending in 1917. The tourist Mark Twain wrote in the 19th century that Jerusalem then was non-functional as a city, let alone as a capital, and was over-run with sheep. Today, the official internationally recognized capital of Israel is Tel Aviv, not Jerusalem. Our guide hardly mentioned the native Palestinians, and then only as though they were all transients. In our guide's narrative, there was no mention of Saladin, by all accounts one of the most enlightened political and military rulers of all time.

Although our guide was extreme, we and other Semester At Sea participants found the general attitude of Israeli Jews to be shocking. I say "Israeli Jews" to be precise; the term "Israeli" alone sounds less harsh and perhaps accusative, but it is not accurate, since there are also "Israeli Arabs." Other terms are sloppily used, much to the detriment of honesty in this part of the world, for example, identifying the native Palestinians as "Muslims," when some in fact are Christians. The Palestinian Arabs became an essentially Invisible SubCulture. On several placards at the site of Caesaria and others, vandals had scratched out the word "Muslim."

Our guide also had the precise count on King Herod the Great's "Slaughter of the Innocents," namely 1500. How could anyone know this? The only mention of the slaughter is in the Christian Bible (and there only in Chapter 2 of Matthew), and no numbers are given. The Roman records do not include the incident, and many historians (rather than Biblical fundamentalists) doubt that anything like it ever occurred. (Later, in Bethlehem, we would be shown the *tomb* of the innocents, under a Christian church, another figment of over-active religious imagination with one scant basis in fact - there are bones inside.) But our guide had the numbers! He also assured us later, in the Druze Village of Dahlit al-Karmel above Haifa, that the Druze are not Arabs. Funny, they *speak* Arabic. The germ of truth is that the fascinating and likable Druze are not orthodox Muslim, but have their own unique and impenetrable religion which split off from mainline Islam in the eleventh century. They also enjoy nearly full Israeli citizenship, including service in the army, which is not allowed to other Israeli Arabs. (Druze villagers in the Golan Heights area have refused Israeli citizenship, and generally would prefer their area to be returned to Syria.)

Amidst all this mis-information, our guide did recite for us, on two occasions, the fourteen Stations of the Cross. This is remarkable. Catharine and I combined have about 40 or 45 years of Roman Catholic education, but neither of us could name the stations as our guide did. Clearly, the Israel Ministry of Tourism has trained their tour guides to cater to Christian tourists. Hence, the whitewash on the Crusaders. Never did we hear one negative word about Christians or Crusades, and we were treated to the most absurd pseudo-Christian beliefs stated as fact. The government is frantically preparing for the onslaught of the year 2000, when thousands of Christian pilgrims will flock to the "Holy Land," especially Bethlehem and Jerusalem, now major construction sites where the government is building hotels and renovating streets and "traditional sites" like Mary's Well, David's Well, Rachel's Tomb, Solomon's Pool, etc.

Our intrepid guide informed us that "Christians believe . . . ," not "some Christians" or "some lunatic fringe Christians" or some other qualifier, but "Christians believe . . . " something that no one in our group had ever heard, nor could we imagine in our wildest theological flights of fancy. He actually said,"Christians believe that Jesus Christ comes back to earth every thousand years." Wow. Better buy your tickets to Israel now. Clearly, this guy is a nut-case, and I did not listen to one quarter of what he had to say. At Caesaria, flabbergasted by his bullshit and attitude, I walked off on my own very early, I thought, but then I saw our friend Bob walking alone - he had given up on our guide way before I did. Shortly after I saw Catharine, then our inter-port lecturer Kurt Wenner, each off by themselves and looking grumpy. Kurt was later totally incensed

Chapter 15 – Haifa and Israel

(he is, after all, a scholar on Islam and the Middle East) and wrote a complaint about the guide to the travel office.

The treatment by Israeli Jews of the Arabs as an Invisible Sub-Culture was clearly evident. We actually heard people say that "the Arabs have no culture." Cab drivers were always reluctant, and sometimes flatly and irrevocably refused, to drive people north of Haifa to the Arab city of Acco (Acre), a unique medieval fortress city, the last stand of Crusaders, the final resting place of the founder of the Baha'i religion, and one of the most interesting cities on our entire world voyage. The guides actively discouraged walks in the Arab sections of Haifa, which were in fact not a safety problem. In Jerusalem, guides actively discouraged or prohibited visits to the Dome of the Rock, one of the religious architectural wonders of the world. (As a consequence, only a few of us experienced this treasure.) On our last day in Israel, in Jerusalem, a few of us bargained to be able to go off on our own. Security was a valid concern, because of the war preparations and rumors. We were in Jerusalem on the Jewish Sabbath, so the Jewish section of the city was inactive. As we prepared to leave the bus for our independent walk, our guide insisted that we not go into the Arab quarter "for security reasons." As though Iraq would shoot a Scud missile into Jerusalem! Or perhaps the Palestinians would bomb the Dome of the Rock?

Did I mention he was also rude and pedantic?

Baha'i

pjr

I had long anticipated a visit to the Baha'i World Center in Haifa. Baha'i friends in Belize had told us the buildings and grounds were beautiful, and I had developed a respect and interest in the religion from shipboard conversations with Heshmat, a new friend and enthusiastic Baha'i on the Semester At Sea staff.

The Baha'i World Center covers many buildings and elaborate gardens, built up the mountainside in nineteen levels overlooking the Port of Haifa. It is still under construction, and one cannot walk the entire length up the mountain because of construction barricades. After years of imprisonment, the founder, known as Baha'u'llah, lived out his years in a comfortable home located north of Haifa, in Acco. Here in Haifa at the Baha'i World Center, there is a truly elegant Shrine of "the Bab" (gate) holding the remains of the prophet (rightly compared to John the Baptist of Christian scripture), who was the precursor of Baha'u'llah and who was martyred in ghastly fashion by the Muslim authorities, to whom he was, of course, a heretic. Baha'u'llah means "beloved of Allah," a title that shows Baha'i can be viewed historically as a reform movement of Islam, just as Buddhism was originally a reform movement of Hinduism, Christianity was originally a reform movement in Judaism, and Islam was a reform movement in both, and on to the Protestant Reformation, etc. Both the Bab and Baha'u'llah were severe critics of the priestly authorities, a dangerous vocation in any religion - the Bab was martyred, and Baha'u'llah spent many years in prison and exile, avoiding death only because of powerful family connections. The Shrine of the Bab, and the entire Baha'i World Center, show the Baha'i inheritance of Islamic art in the emphasis on geometrical and vegetal forms and the absence of human or animal representation, but with a softer modern feel, and no Arabic calligraphy evident. The Shrine of the Bab is not a large building, but an appropriate, human-scale, tasteful, and truly elegant tribute to a brave prophet.

 The Baha'i walk a tightrope in Haifa. Although their World Center is a major feature of the hillside presentation of the city, and their presence brings much needed tourist money into the country, they seem to be "strangers in a strange land." The World Center is here in Haifa, but there is no Baha'i worshipping community here! Amazingly, the staff at the Baha'i Center, who come from all over

Chapter 15 – Haifa and Israel

the world, do not hold the regular prayer meetings that Baha'i communities in the rest of the world do, to avoid the criticism of overt practice in Israel. (I was told that the resident staff meet for prayers informally, irregularly, and in small groups.) You could not convert (in a formal public profession of faith) to Baha'i here, nor anywhere else in Israel. From some questioning, I surmised (from somewhat evasive answers) that there may also be an accommodation involved with the government of Israel. There have been published criticisms by Israeli Jewish orthodox leaders denouncing the Baha'i presence in Israel.

Although the Baha'i do not proselytize or accept conversions here, they do have an introductory slide presentation on the history and themes of the Baha'i religion, presented in a small room that holds perhaps twenty people at most, and with sincere hospitality offered small cakes, sweets, and tea. They accepted questions, but were somewhat diffident about theological issues, which is consistent with their approach to theology - when it comes to theological doctrine, the Baha'i are simply not very doctrinaire. They allow a great deal of latitude in belief, admirably trusting more in the process of individual pursuit of truth than in any rigid statements. A cornerstone of their position is that all religions, or at least all major religions, hold the same truths at their core.

After the presentation, after many discussions with friends, and after reading two Baha'i introductory scriptures, I am still very impressed with Baha'i. In my opinion, they do have shortcomings, but these are small compared to the world's other major and minor religions. Although intellectually enlightened, they still seem a bit too literal, too clinging onto magic words. They almost flirt with numerology - strictly speaking, it is not there theologically, but there is enough to appeal to someone who wanted it. (Lots of 9's and 19's.) Likewise, they leave open the door to the simplistic use of "prophetic" in the sense of secret knowledge and arcane practice and prediction of future events, like fundamentalist Christians,

At Sea At Sixty

rather than prophetic in the sense of social criticism and religious reformation. The questions after the presentation resulted in somewhat evasive answers, that did not yield to my further (too-persistent) questions. Early on in their history, they were somewhat overly concerned with personalities and family line (as are Muslims) and physical relics. But today, they seem to have developed beyond the personality of any present leaders; the governing body is elected for a finite term in this democratic representative religion.

I'm told by my friends that the founder Baha'u'llah wrote in both Arabic (a precise language, they say, good for theology) and Persian (or Farsi, the "sweet language" for poetry). The experts then translated the original scriptures into a canonical English standard. This English canon is used as the basis for further translations, already in some hundred languages. Unfortunately, from my point of view, the English chosen is stilted in the extreme. Not just the "thee"s and "thou"s of the old King James Bible, which never bother me very much, but the strange and artificial "-eth" suffix, as in "he prayeth" rather than "he prays." One or two of these are no problem, but a long prayer or poem which would be difficult to follow in any translation becomes virtually impenetrable for me. The language sounds vaguely religious, but I find it a minor stumbling block (as are the exclusively masculine pronouns) and it has an air about it of Gnostic secrecy, of a special language known only to initiates.

I dearly wish it were true that all the major world religions hold the same truths at their core. Unfortunately, I find it an untenable position, no matter how embracing and brotherly it would be. There are, as the divorce courts say, "irreconcilable differences" between religions, even between sects of the same religion. I certainly do find it true, and of utmost importance, that all major (and most minor) world religions have plenty of valuable insights, and that none have a unique monopoly on truth, and that all would

Chapter 15 – Haifa and Israel

benefit from the exercise in humility that such an admission would involve. But in most cases, such an admission would amount to rejection of some important founding principles, that is, to heresy. I take (or wish) the Baha'i position to mean not that they are blind to the irreconcilable differences between religions, but just that they recognize and honor the common core, and are humble and wise enough to not wage war over the distinctions, and to learn from them all.

The Baha'i sociological values are excellent. An admirable and unique aspect of this prophetic religion is that neither Baha'u'llah nor his followers claimed that he had the final word for all time. His time scale was rather grandiose - a millennium - but after a thousand years, the faithful can look at new prophets with an open mind and heart. Time scale aside, the important point is that the Baha'i recognize evolution of ideas and spirit, or the concept of *progress*. This is a huge step for a prophetic religion, one that would be rejected by the major religions. I think the best thing possible for the world right now would be the spread of Baha'i faith.

Exploring

csr

After the Baha'i World Center tour Pat and I and Kurt Wenner, our most recent interport lecturer, went exploring in Haifa. We looked in vain for an Arabic restaurant, settled for an Israeli deli, and walked back to the ship down, down the steep hill through the *pasha*, or old city, full of buildings from Ottoman Empire times. It was fun to have Kurt with us because he's an interesting fellow and knows so much of the history of this area. Plus, he understands and speaks some of Arabic; he could read posters and respond to clerks. This turned some heads.

When we made it down to sea level Kurt decided to go back to the ship, but Pat and I caught a cab to the ancient city of Acco

(Acre) just up the coast from Haifa - in fact, we could see it from the deck of the ship.

This was a great place to wander through the winding cobblestone streets, visit mosques, and walk along the fortified walls of this crusader town. At sunset the call to prayer echoed across the town: "God is Great." We stood and watched the sun slip away. Then we went looking for some *falafel*, olives and other treats. Even eating a meal has political implications here. The Israelis say *falafel* is their national food; the Palestinians consider it essentially Arabic. In this decidedly Muslim town, we had a beer with our meal, even though alcohol is forbidden by the most strict Islamic law - another example that we humans aren't very consistent in our beliefs and practices.

Curfews

csr

Around six in the morning, as I finished my T'ai Chi Chih, I heard the announcement that all on board the ship were being confined to the city of Haifa because of the threat to Baghdad by the US government, all of which occurred after the weapons inspectors were ordered by Saddam Hussein to leave Iraq. Semester At Sea participants were told to call into the ship every three hours to be told if we were to sail immediately. Those on tours away from Haifa were being called back. Pat and I would not be able to go to Jerusalem, nor hire a car explore in the Galilee area. I had looked forward to this and was as disappointed as a ten year old. I think I pouted. I had recently read a book by John Dominic Crossan, *The Historical Jesus*, which went into much detail about the Galilee and particularly the city of Sepphoris, the principal city of the area and an important crossroads at the time of Jesus. I had really wanted to go to Sepphoris, a few kilometers from Nazareth. Current Biblical scholarship has investigated the relationship of Jesus to this trade center and a different portrait of him has emerged. In-

Chapter 15 – Haifa and Israel

Mediterranean at Haifa 11-13-98

stead of Jesus as a "hillbilly" growing up in a backwater town, one may imagine someone who grew up with the world passing by his doorstep, with information and ideas very accessible to him. I was curious about all this. But I knew that the standard tours would not focus on Sepphoris, so when it was announced a day later that the scheduled tour after all would be allowed to go to Galilee, I passed and opted for a day on the beach, drawing, reading, listening to music. Quiet time alone.

Beautiful Galilee

pjr

I took the re-instated all-day guided bus tour of the area around the freshwater Sea of Galilee with other Semester At Sea shipmates, but not Catharine, who enjoyed a day on her own. Our guide was excellent, and what a difference that made! This will be obvious to most experienced travelers, but I had not traveled much like this before - on busses with tour guides. She was informed and candid on difficult issues, from nuclear weapons to communist kibbutzim. The beautiful Galilee area is modest, open, and pastoral, the blue lake surrounded by mountains and hills. Although the region has been contested and the scene of war in modern times, it still has an air of gentleness about it for me. If any part of this country qualifies for the name of "Holy Land" it would be the Galilee.

In spite of war rumors, our bus was allowed to take an unscheduled (though common) side trip up above the Sea of Galilee to the Golan Heights. We stopped for lunch at a kibbutz restaurant on the heights, overlooking the Sea of Galilee, providing a view of the city of Capernaum partially obscured in haze. I know that I sound knee-jerk anti-Israeli at times, but I think they would be nuts to give back the Golan Heights to the Syrians, as suggested by some peace advocates. Before the six-day war, the Syrians made a game of indiscriminate shelling of civilian traffic and workers on the lake-side road below. When the Heights were captured by the Israeli army, they found half-starved Syrian soldiers chained to their machine guns, delighted to be captured.

The area around the lake itself meant a lot to me. I felt good to be at what is quite possibly Peter's house - it had been marked as such as early as the second century - although I would have liked it better without the Franciscan church built on top of it, and the nearby competing Greek Orthodox church. It felt good to walk amongst the ruins of a nearby synagogue in which (in an earlier version, but same location) Jesus had almost certainly taught - it is the only synagogue known in the entire area. An inscribed plaque acknowledging donors for the new building, erected some 400 years after the time of Jesus, notes the contribution of the local family of Zebedee, as in "James and John, the Sons of Zebedee."

Chapter 15 – Haifa and Israel

A very minor, unmarked little cove is locally known as the "Bay of Parables," referring to Mathew 13:1-3, in which Jesus stepped into a boat and was rowed offshore a little so he could speak to the crowds on shore. The little cove moved me. I know there is no evidence that this is the "spot," but he did it someplace around here, and this sure looks like a good location. Of course, in the intervening twenty centuries, lake levels and shorelines would have changed, but that is not so important to me. The first time Catharine came back from Israel, she shared her insights on the difference between sacred "spots" and sacred "spaces." People like to build churches and mosques on the *spot* where Jesus was born, Mohammed ascended to heaven, Abraham offered to sacrifice his son, etc. Then they proceed to ruin the spirit of the place by building churches, etc. Like the Church at Capernaum, idolatrizing the supposed rock where Jesus began feeding the multitudes, the rock now moved, chiseled down to fit under an altar, taken out of context, and looking like a pretty stupid rock. Or like the Franciscan Church of the Beatitudes, beautiful enough, but erected on the "spot" where Jesus is imagined to have preached the beatitudes - but he *left* the synagogue to preach this sermon, he did not need a church building, he preached outside! Galilee to me is a holy space, an area, a land, not a "spot," and I hope nobody ever builds a church, or even puts up a sign, at the Bay of Parables.

On Our Own

csr

The following day, Pat had his own private time and "rest" day hiking up and down Mount Carmel and drinking Guiness on tap, while I went off with friends to a Japanese Museum. Yes, in Haifa. I did not enjoy the exhibit because it glamorized the samurai, making them practitioners of religion (a form of Zen Buddhism) and presented their weapons and stylized combat techniques as forms of high art. To me this is a violation of art and religion that bends both into the service of the least worthy of human endeavors: death and war.

After the museum my friend Joan and I took off for the Druze villages. The only unenjoyable part of the excursion was negotiating for the taxi. Prices to and from any place varied so much and it seemed impossible to get drivers to simply use the meter. It is an exhausting endeavor and felt like a lose - lose situation each time.

The previous time I had visited the villages they were jammed with noisy election day crowds. But now, all was back to normal and quiet. We enjoyed a leisurely lunch and shopping. On our way back to the ship we became involved in demonstrations near the university. All the universities in Israel, students and faculty, were on strike over high tuition, which had increased by 50 per cent in the past four years. In fact, about a dozen students initiated a hunger strike and were asking that moneys spent on the new West Bank settlements be used for education. That is a bold suggestion which I could not imagine would be taken up by the current government. (It wasn't.)

On our last day in Israel we were told we could go to Jerusalem, provided we stuck with the tour, or close to it. Three of us decided that we would go to the Temple Mount and visit the Dome of the Rock and the al-Aqsa mosque. Our thinking - not the guide's - was that these Arab sites would be the least dangerous places to be in the whole country. Not even Saddam Hussein is crazy enough to bomb them.

I'm glad that Pat was able to visit Jerusalem. It *is* one of the most fascinating cities in the world. For me, it was once more painful to see so many police, military, and check points. I had to remind myself once more that at the time of Christ the country was full of Roman soldiers and the military was everywhere.

Coming from the American West I see so many similarities between the evolving nation of Israel and the old emerging and developing United States. The Holocaust was a bitter impetus for the

Chapter 15 – Haifa and Israel

founding of Israel. No ethnic cleansing policies as severe as that of the Nazis brought immigrants to the US, but many oppressive policies of states and churches as well as famines brought people to the Americas and the result was that a nation was carved out of the lands of the peoples (many nations) who already occupied the land. A policy of "Manifest Destiny" gave almost a religious tone to the movement West, burying tribe after tribe that tried to defend its land and families from the encroaching settlers. Atrocities were committed on both sides; in the end the US forces were stronger and had the force of economic development. I see a similar situation in Israel. I imagine that Palestinian Arabs will continue to attack and resist the claims and power of the state of Israel. I don't know if a State of Palestine will come about, and even if it does it will not become as powerful as Israel. It will have a hard time competing in the market place; it will be hard to co-exist peacefully. This has been the way of the strong and not so strong throughout most of history. "Liberty and justice for all", a concept from two centuries ago, is admired by most countries of the world, but it is a long way from being realized in most of the countries that we visited during our Semester At Sea.

Praying in the Evil Land

pjr

Holy Land? Holy City? On our way up the Red Sea, headed for the Suez Canal and Israel / Palestine, there was a lot of action and controversy in the Core Course on the Palestinian dilemma. To punctuate the problem, we received the news on 6 November that a car bomb had exploded in the Jewish market section of the old city of Jerusalem, killing the two suicide drivers and injuring fourteen others. The Old City of Jerusalem is one square mile of the most hotly contested real estate in the world. With the creation of the state of Israel in 1948, Jerusalem was divided, with the Old City coming under Jordanian rule, and the New City under Israeli administration. As a result of the 1967 war, Israel conquered and "annexed" the Old City.

The city is "sacred to all three major faiths," say the tourist promotions. For my part, leave me out. Don't kill anyone for my sake, I don't have to walk the Via Dolorosa (the Way of the Cross), which in any case is but the figment of Saint Helena's imagination. Likewise for the Church of the Holy Sepulchre, where the "Christian" Greek Orthodox, Armenian, Roman Catholic and Coptic priestly castes are so scandalously vicious that they have different altars and territories within the cluttered and harsh church, and need to have a Muslim hold the keys to the church for them because they cannot trust one another. If (say) an Armenian priest strays over the Greek Orthodox territorial line, the Greeks hit him with sticks. The Ethiopian Catholics arrived a little late, so they live on the roof.

I don't need this. I don't think any enlightened religion needs any "holy land." Whatever is holy about Judaism, Christianity, and Islam is written in their holy scriptures and in some hearts. I'm not into holy real estate, not even the Islamic holy city of Mecca (although I understand that the prayer rituals of the Muslim's once-in-a-lifetime pilgrimage to Mecca are admirably egalitarian). I do believe in pilgrimages, and therefore special religious places. If it were not for Jerusalem, I might even think "holy place" or "holy land" was a good term. But this kind of vicious tension is not worth it. I much preferred to visit the beautiful but unassuming freshwater Sea of Galilee, where Jesus walked and taught.

The Israeli and Christian hype for the "holy city" neglects the other Judaic tradition of the "tenting" God. The Ark of the Covenant was originally *carried* by the Jews, and each night a new sacred space was created with tents by these nomadic people. The prophets (of the Elohistic tradition) warned against building the temple to house the Ark and the Tablets of Commandments, but the Jewish kings did it anyway. (The prophets warned against

Chapter 15 – Haifa and Israel

having kings, too.) The Babylonians under Nebudchadnezzar destroyed the old Temple in 586 BCE, and the Ark and the Tablets were permanently lost to humanity. Herod the Great rebuilt the Temple, and the Romans (under Titus) destroyed the Temple and much of the city in 70 A.D., leaving only a single retaining wall of the Temple. Too bad they were not a little more thorough. Is one lousy wall, the Western Wall (or sometimes, the "Wailing Wall"), worth a protracted war? Isaiah, where are you when we need you? This is not religion, it is magic; it is idolatry.

Of course, the Jews of Israel have a right to the city of Jerusalem and the Holy Land, because *God gave it to them*. Amazing fact: many Israeli Jews practice no religion, and many do not believe in God, yet they all believe that God gave them this land! Never mind that the Arabs had been there since the seventh century A.D., never mind that they kicked out the bloody Christian Crusaders in the middle ages, never mind that it was the Palestinians' own ancestors, the Canaanites, who lived there before the bloody Hebrew invasions described in the Bible.

I can just imagine the scene a hundred years from now, when my great grandchildren are living in Northern California, and Asia finally bursts at the seams. With nothing to lose in a war but their own excess population, the Japanese, Chinese, Indonesians, Malays, and Indians arrive in the Pacific Northwest. "Sorry to have to inform you," they might say to my progeny, "but our Gods have given us your land. In fact, we were here first! About ten thousand years ago, when the Bering strait was still iced over, our Asian ancestors peopled North America millennia before your ancestors arrived. So move over. Or better, just get out. The Canadians and Mexicans should take you in - you are all Christians, right?"

Who, outside the Muslim world, was not thrilled with optimism when Israel was created? After the Holocaust, the fledgling United Nations could not turn the Zionists down. I can't imagine saying no. Now, Israel has an elected Prime Minister who compared the previous PM, Yitzhak Rabin, with the German Jews who collaborated with the Nazis, because he arranged a peaceful agreement with the Palestinians. The extremist Israelis took care of him. Jewish Orthodox groups in Israel did some rabbinical scholarship, and widely disseminated their legal-religious conclusion that it would be good for Jew to kill Jew in this case. Rabin was assassinated, at a peace rally. There were violent responses, and the new government was elected (by a margin of 0.1 per cent). The peace program dragged on, new elections gave renewed hope, but we can expect war in this "holy land" . . . again.

In a really bad mood, I might pray that all Jerusalem residents are removed, and then the earth opens up and the one square mile of the Old City disappears. One less thing to kill over. Better, I pray for all religious egomaniacs to learn humility and tolerance. Which, I wonder, would be the more astounding miracle?

In spite of myself, when Catharine and Kurt and I walked around Jerusalem for four or five hours, I was charmed. If you love history, if you respect religions, if you like archeology, if you like people and action, you can't resist Jerusalem. "Look at those stones, Lord!" Although warned off by our Israeli guide, we cruised the busy markets of the Arab quarter, and visited the al-Aqsa Mosque ("the further mosque" of Islamic myth) and the famed Dome of the Rock, the first grand structure of Islam. It is wonderful architecture, but as we know from an excellent pre-port lecture, it is another example of politicized religion. The Dome of the Rock, completed in 691, was erected on the Temple Mount over irregular rock that may have been the altar of burnt offerings or the cornerstone of Solomon's Temple. Similar to the architecture of the Anastasis Rotunda of the Christian Church of the Holy Sepulchre, which it outdoes in beauty (and certainly in the good taste of its managers and religious devotees), the Dome was built to establish a permanent presence of Islam on the Temple Mount, a claim of Islamic fulfillment of the earlier Jewish and Christian tra-

Chapter 15 – Haifa and Israel

ditions. The huge (240 meters long) inscription inside the Dome is a polemic against Christians, urging them to turn away from trinitarian beliefs back to pure monotheism. Interestingly, the Muslim world did not put much import on the Dome of the Rock unless it mattered politically. The Dome fell into neglect and disrepair, and collapsed in 1016. Jerusalem itself was not of continuous great importance to Islam; for example, a grandson of Saladin temporarily ceded Jerusalem to the German Emperor in 1229 in return for military aid in a family war. For centuries, the Dome and indeed the entire city was obscure, abandoned, and dilapidated. But it was refurbished and re-emphasized during the time of British rule (1917-1948) clearly as part of a politico-religious competition with Zionism. In Israel and the rest of this old part of the world, religion and politics and war cannot be separated. Holy Lands, Holy Wars. Never again will I take for granted the American belief in separation of church and state.

My Last Time

csr

As the mooring lines were drawn into the ship, I thought how glad I was to be leaving this troubled part of the earth. I know that we visited many troubled spots, but this one was personally very troubling to me. I remembered the disappointment I had felt the first time I had gone to Israel in the mid-seventies. I had thought that in the Holy Land I would discover places of holiness. It was not my experience then, nor this time. Instead of sacred space, I had only found exploited spots. Very small hints of prophets, many reminders of earthly powers. As we moved away from the port my heart prayed with the Nazarean: Jerusalem, Jerusalem, you that kill the prophets and stone those who are sent to you. How often I have longed to gather your children, as a hen gathers her chicks under her wings . . . (Mt 23:37)

Jesus was unable to comfort this city, this part of the world; I am not either. We both had such hopes and expectations of spirituality. They were not met for him in ways and places he expected. Instead of a holy temple, he found money changers. They are still there. Ezekiel said humans needed to repent and "make yourselves a new heart and a new spirit" (Ez 18:31). This is a prophecy acknowledged by all the People of the Book - Jews, Christians, Muslims. That prophecy is still waiting to be fulfilled. I believe that the grace is available for this new heart and spirit to come into the world, but humans and nations must want it. I wait; the world waits and hold its breath.

Chapter 16
The Mediterranean Sea and Aegean Sea

Chapter 16 – The Mediterranean Sea and Aegean Sea

My God, Your God

csr

Somewhere at sea, I began to re-read *Moby Dick*, something I promised myself before we began this voyage. Early in the book the character of Ishmael, the storyteller, states, "as everyone knows, meditation and water are wedded for ever." Yes. And in the Mediterranean, the birthplace of three major religions, I realized that it was time to mull over, not only Israel, but matters of Religion and religions.

We had come through many cultures and many religions: Japan with its blend of Shinto and Buddhism, China with many variations of Buddhism, Islam, Christianity and animistic beliefs, Vietnam with many Chinese beliefs and French Catholicism, the Islamic Federation of Malaysia which also included Christianity and Buddhism, and recently Israel with every kind of Christian, Jew and Muslim imaginable. But what *is* Religion anyway? I would define it as a set of beliefs held in common by a group who share not only beliefs but also traditions and often sacred scriptures, and who practice rituals and meditation or prayer. Some religions focus on one god (i.e. Judaism, Islam and Christianity), others recognize many gods or spirits (i.e. Hindu, Shinto), or no god at all (i.e. Buddhism) but have a common goal, such as Enlightenment and common practices. Within a religion over time there evolve many sects (Catholic, Protestant, Shiite, Sunni, Orthodox, Conservative, etc.). This division and evolution is easy to understand since the term "religion" applies only to those forms of commonly held beliefs which have long histories. Religions find their foundations in preceding religions: Christianity in Judaism, Buddhism in Hinduism, Islam in Judaism and Christianity. Yet they all claim uniqueness and some claim divine initiation or intervention.

It seems the way of human beings. At birth we inherit ideas and beliefs of our ancestors; at some point we accept or reject them; we incorporate new spiritual experiences, we move on and pass on our sense of Wisdom and Truth. I capitalize these terms because religions wrestle with something that is not as ordinary as lower case letters would denote, but Something definitely upper case. The "Mysterium Tremendum" (often languages other than the vernacular convey the soul of Religion) - the experience that causes one to bow low, take off one's shoes, be stirred, be filled with awe. Hearts and minds are changed. The spiritual experiences are told in stories, danced, sung, written down and become sacred texts. These texts are then considered sacred literally or sacred but subject to interpretation from age to age.

Some individuals and cultures are more likely to focus on Religion than others. We have a friend who thinks that there is a "religious gene." He may be right and I suppose I have the gene. But it doesn't mean one finds an answer and rests in a state of bliss, or peace. After sixty years of living, and most of those spent pursuing The Other (or is It pursuing me?), I have come to only a few conclusions. I believe that Religion is not in the domain of logic or reason. At the same time, I do not think it is necessarily unreasonable, or illogical. Faith cannot be analyzed or dissected scientifically. Faith is an action of faithful people accepted by other faithful. I think that some religions meet the spiritual needs of their members and others do not; outwardly some rely heavily on superstition and magical acts. I don't see this as harmful and it may meet individual and communal needs. What I have come to believe *is* harmful to a person or a community is to believe that somehow God has chosen me, or us, above all others, for special favors, position, privileges, or to believe that God has saved me or my city from disaster, or that God uses the powers of nature or armies to punish those who do not follow commands of God as understood by a believer or group of believers. These beliefs produce an "us" and "them" mentality, an attitude which divides and antagonizes humans. It can easily lead to violence; it can be used to condone war. This business of being Chosen People is a first cousin to a be-

Chapter 16 – The Mediterranean Sea and Aegean Sea

lief in Manifest Destiny. Both attitudes allow for taking land from people who are there and not very powerful. It has crept into many different religions in many different ages and cultures.

I worked as a hospital chaplain for years and from this experience came away with a sense of profound mystery. Like many before me, I have pondered: why do bad things happen to good people - the innocent, the frail? And maybe even tougher: why do good things happen to bad, violent, dishonest, selfish folks? I am willing to live with these questions until I die. I have no clear, logical, cause and effect answer. I do know that I do not believe that everything is "God's Will," or serves a Divine Purpose we cannot know or understand. What of the raped three year old? The starved masses in Somalia? The children living in the streets of Calcutta? Part of God's mysterious Self? Not on your life! Some religions would suggest that all this is the result of a previous life, but it still is unfair to the one suffering in this life. Our six year old granddaughter knows what *fair* is. My God would be more fair. I have heard many good, religious people say "The Lord has been faithful to me" or "God has provided" or "God has blessed us," etc. This seems to me as objectionable as the caste system in Hinduism, which allows for 700,000 people sleeping on the street and female babies left to die. Why can't (don't) humans give up these particular "religious" ideas? I think that at heart we are really scientists. We *want* (need on some level) a cause and effect. We are uncomfortable with anything random. We want/need to believe Someone (thing) is in control . . . even if it is magic numbers in control as in some practices in Chinese Taosism. When good things happen to us, we say we are "blessed *personally* by God. Then, at best, if bad things happen to others, it is a mystery. At worst, they are being punished, or disciplined by God. If bad or good things happen in the Hindu framework then it is one's *personal* past which made it so. We humans want to make sense of everything. Chaos is scary and we seem out of control and out of the loop. Having Someone in control of this chaos has continued to be a focus within countless spiritual movements which are not religions but which have successfully met spiritual needs of followers. Among these have been Freemasonry, Twelve Step programs, New Age beliefs, and current forms of channeling spirits from other worlds. Acknowledging some chaos is hard; Someone in absolute control is comforting.

I become sad and spiritually nervous when I hear someone say that "God took care of me" when the tornado went by. (And destroyed my neighbor?) I thought many times on the ship of that baby sleeping on the street in Madras near the sign that said "Invest in India's future . . . Hong Kong Bank." What kind of God would not save that baby from the street, disease, hunger, cold, or being stepped on by a sacred cow? Not the God I love and look for in myself and others. The God I know is not involved in rewarding or punishing me or using other nations to punish my nation. The God I know, which I did discover though religious reading and meditation, is an Energy or Presence available to all creation. The image of God which I found in Hebrew and Christian scriptures is One who tents with us. Other images found there are Lord and King. For this One, temples were built and wars fought. But I prefer the One who was not found in the mighty wind, nor earthquake, nor fire, but rather in a soft still Voice (1K19, 11-13). Because we are human we necessarily speak of God anthropomorphically. But I, as a pilgrim in search of the Mystery, can choose the words and identify the relationship. I can call God Love, or Creativity, or Justice or Abba or Mother. There is no end to the names. Muslims pray to one God, but use calligraphy to write one thousand names of this One. I will not call God *mine* in any way which excludes anyone, or anything. For me that would be sinfully arrogant and blasphemous. It is inconsistent with the admonition of the "minor" prophet Micah to act justly, love tenderly, and walk humbly with God (Mi 6:8).

Chapter 16 – The Mediterranean Sea and Aegean Sea

As I stared out into the blue, blue Mediterranean, the womb of so much religious thought, I wondered, "By and large, have religious beliefs and practices helped us?" It is a question Pat and I have looked at in our private selves and which we have discussed with friends long into the night. Sometimes religions have. Pat says that religion and prayer is a way of being grateful. I agree with that. I am a believer in Presence and prayer but I believe that I can pray "Thank you" when looking at the sunset, a school of tuna, or my loved ones without believing that all this is here just for me because I'm somehow special and separate from those who don't notice and aren't grateful. For me, prayer is mostly a matter of just acknowledging the power of life and beauty. In the face of goodness, I am brought to prayerful tears. I resonate with the line in *Les Miserables*, "To love another person is to see the Face of God." I don't blame the devil for the evil in the world. It just is here. I am content to believe that suffering, pain, and injustice is part of the human condition. We are still involved in creation emerging out of chaos, a chaos which is physical, moral, intellectual and spiritual. Using grace (God's energy?) which I believe is abundant, I can deal with more than my needs and desires and reach out "with a cup of water to a pilgrim in need of such" (once more I rely on one of Mahalia Jackson's songs) . . . no matter where that pilgrim is going: Mecca, Jerusalem, Compestelo, Rome.

But religions have fueled many wars and tolerated many injustices. I do not believe that God will bring about Justice through injustice. I do believe that people of all religions have been given commandments (principles, wisdoms) to guide them towards care of selves, others and the planet.

Sea by sea, port by port, I found I needed to think about how the conflicts over religion in many parts of the world affect me as I grow old. Or does it have anything to do with me and how I personally age? I think it does.

I thought about what has been partially achieved among leaders of Arab countries and Israel and how much of it has been achieved because of virtues particular to aging. From the perspective of many years, many sins and mistakes, much suffering, ill health and a sense of "maybe I can go one step further," these aging leaders came up with agreements at Camp David, Madrid, Oslo and Wye. You have only to remember their faces and their lives: Anwar Sadat, Simon Peres, Yassar Arafat, King Hussein, Yitzhak Rabin, and the Palestinian woman, Hanan Ashrawi. From the long fifty years of war, each changed, each let go what needed to be let go, considered new possibilities.

I'm not saying that only the old are wise in ways of peace, or that the young stir up war. The particular sins of the old have also been in evidence in the Middle Eastern scenario, sins of holding on to the injustices and wrongs of the past, never forgiving. I believe that one can remember *and* forgive. Let go the power in the present, let go the injustices and violences of the past. It is hard to forget the intractability of some of the leaders in this part of the world - or anywhere else - where old leaders and old patriots hold on, when what is needed is for young and old to let go of what was done before, and move into the future with new ways of listening and solving problems.

On the ship leaving the port we sensed that with the crisis in the last port, Israel held her breath; Arab nations held their breaths. So few people in this part of the world really want armed conflict. When we were in Israel the information we had was that something like 67 per cent of the Israelis support the peace agreements. This is true also of Palestinians, Jordanians, Egyptians . . . I don't know about Syrians. The point is that the minorities who oppose peace by words and actions often have power far beyond their numbers and elected representatives. The will of the people is hard to implement. If these peace agreements - so slowly and painfully worked out by leaders who have made mistakes, made compro-

Chapter 16 – The Mediterranean Sea and Aegean Sea

mises, and have made steps towards peaceful negotiations and settlements - are not put into effect, then those who have lead their people towards peace will be dead. You can see it in their faces. They are old, and sick, and tired. They want to leave behind a heritage of peace rather than remnants of war and seeds of hate. Several of these old men were at a peace rally the night Rabin was killed. (Since we returned home, King Hussein of Jordan died.)

I am not so naive as to believe that voting to implement the agreements is the end of the story. But it is an important step along the path(s) toward peace. There will have to be more negotiations, more agreements; new agreements will have to be formulated when old ones are not adequate to new situations. There will be violence bursting out, but some patterns of peace will have been established. I do believe that something is better than nothing. Patterns of non-violence were implemented in India in the middle part of this century; Martin Luther King urged non-violence to bring about needed change in the US. Recently, the majority of people in Northern Ireland and the Republic of Ireland have begun to see that non-violence is an effective way to meet the needs of people who seek justice and economic opportunity, which is the only firm foundation for peace in small communities or nations, or world communities. These are all critical steps towards peace. Each generation must work for peace, just as each day a couple works on a marriage.

I personally think that the best hope for a lasting peace in Israel lies with organizations like *Bat Shalom* (a Jewish Israeli feminist organization) and *Palestinian Women in Jerusalem*. These groups work together for peace and social justice. On Fridays they form the core of the Women in Black who demonstrate for peace in Old Jerusalem. They focus on many common goals and work together for new solutions to old problems. For example, they propose sharing Jerusalem as the capitol of both a Palestinian state and the state of Israel. It seems to me that this would be a great witness to the meaning of "jerusalem," that is, "city of peace."

Shalom

csr

In my own aging life I must consider what I need to let go from my past so that I can be at peace, and those around me can know *my* peacefulness. For twenty years I worked with old people in various settings. At first, I expected that all old people would naturally reach the point of being "at peace" with themselves and their world. Not so. Some clung to past hurts as if they were a shawl. I do not want to be an old woman who holds on to the times she was treated badly by spouse, children, friends, church. But letting go takes real work. I can forgive and let go without demanding of myself that I forget. I can honor the truth of past wounds without letting them control my present. I can choose to move into old age with the best memories of spouse, children, friends, church. Only then can I find peace; only then will others know my peacefulness.

Chapter 17
Istanbul and Turkey

Hagia Sofia
Istanbul

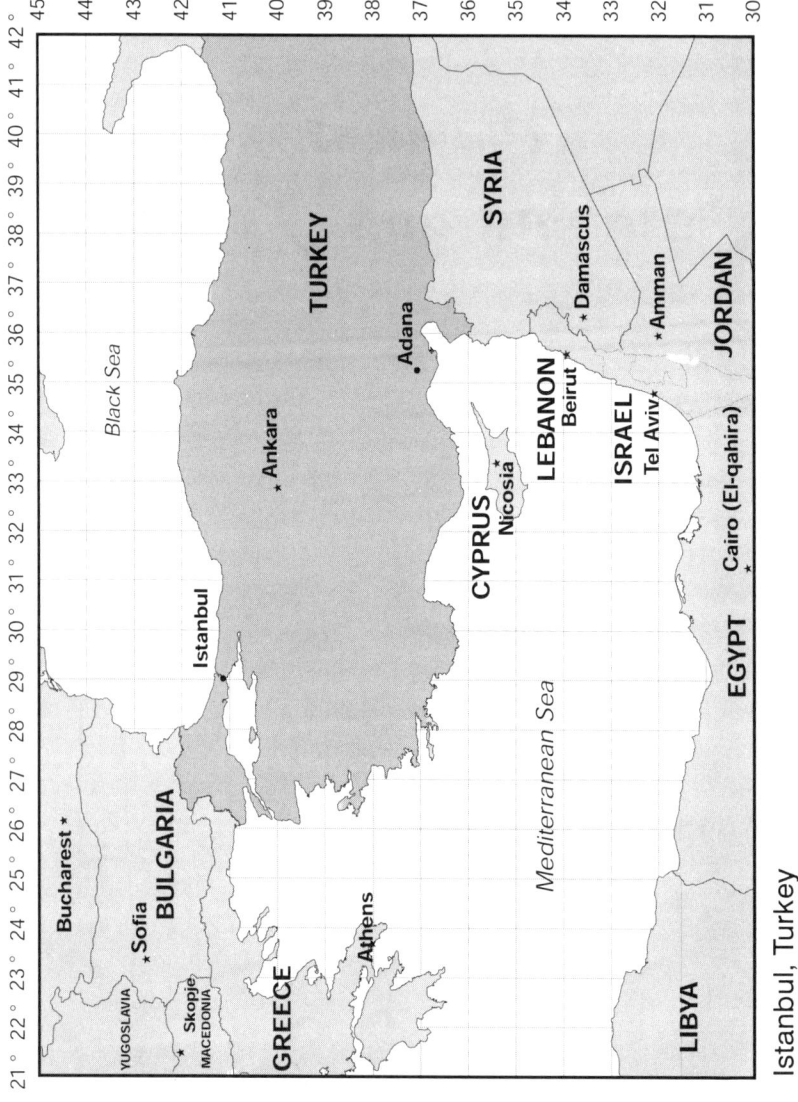

Istanbul, Turkey
Longitude 41°N Longitude 28.6°E

Chapter 17 – Istanbul and Turkey

Crossroads of the World

csr

Sunrise and the skyline of Istanbul! Well, it takes your breath away. The beauty and the sense of history. This is a very distinctive skyline dominated by mosques, a succession of perfectly proportioned domes punctuated by minarets. Sailing in from the Sea of Marmara, past the Golden Horn at dawn and into the very protected harbor, it became clear why an important city grew up in this particular spot. The Golden Horn is an inlet to the Bosporus River that forms the harbor and separates two sections of Istanbul, spanned by the historic Galata Bridge (where the severed heads of enemies were once displayed) and the modern Ataturk Bridge. On this bright clear morning, we sailed just past the Galata Bridge and into our dock, a great location with good food and drink right there. Ferries hurried back and forth between Asia and Europe, both continents in the same city of Istanbul, between one part of the city and another - and another.

Istanbul is the terminus of the famed Orient Express railway, the juncture of Europe and Asia. The Bosporus Bridge, one of the world's longest suspension bridges (3524 feet or 1074 meters), opened in 1973 to link Europe and Asia, two continents separated by a leisurely hour's stroll. Like Rome, Istanbul is built on seven hills. Like Rome, it is a center of institutional religion, being the home (the "See") of the patriarch of the Greek Orthodox Church, one Latin-rite patriarch of the Roman Catholic Church, and one patriarch of the Armenian Church. Much of the city was destroyed by earthquake in 1509, then rebuilt, preserving the legacy of ancient civilizations - classic Greek, Roman, even imported Egyptian.

Three thousand years of accumulated art, architecture, and history beckoned to me. I hardly noticed the rain as I hurried off the ship and boarded a bus for the city tour.

Istanbul was first known as Byzantium and dates from the eighth century B.C.E. It was a very small town in the far eastern

Roman Empire. It had an important strategic location since it was a sheltered port on the European side of the Bosporus and commanded the corridor from the Aegean Sea and the Dardenelles to the Bosporus Straits and the Black Sea. It was, and is, a natural crossroads from North and South, East and West. In the fourth century Constantine conquered it and consolidated all of the Western and Eastern Roman Empire under his rule. Not surprisingly, he changed the name to Constantinople which it remained from that time until the fifteenth century. During the Ottoman Empire it was called Istanbul and has been called that officially since 1930.

The time of Constantine was a remarkable blending in the Roman world. From the western part of the empire came Roman law, but here were also Greek culture, and eastern Christianity. In those early centuries, there was great diversity within Christianity: diverse cultures, theologies, forms of ecclesiastical governing. In the sixth century, the Eastern Roman Empire reached its peak, during the reign of Justinian. He developed the fascinating cistern system which we visited on our first day in Turkey. The cistern was built underground to hold a huge water supply for the city in case of siege. From all parts of the Roman Empire he hauled 336 huge columns to support the ceiling. Some are Corinthian, others Ionian; ancient temples, government buildings and shrines were mined for their convenient pre-cut materials. Two elaborate and beautiful carvings of heads of gods, over one meter on each side, have been used as a base for the columns. These were not used here as works of art, just dross building material for a purely utilitarian public utility project. A head of Medusa with full fleshy features and luxurious wavy hair, once the object of devotion in some long forgotten Greek temple, lies on its side, centuries after being submerged in the waters of the cistern, still holding up the columns supporting the roof. The atmosphere of this walk into the past is eerie. The lighting is soft, the sounds of the echoes, haunting, and the music, beautiful. Before it was cleaned up and made into a

Chapter 17 – Istanbul and Turkey

tourist attraction, we understand it was a very spooky, dark, damp place. Now it is a delight.

Equally delightful was the Mosaic Museum, located in the same hippodrome area as the cistern. The tile work in Constantinople was very fine. It was found in homes where floors showed scenes of animals and harvests, and it in churches where icons and religious scenes were represented. One very famous "Pancreator" (Jesus in a commanding pose) is found in Hagia Sophia (or Ayasofya Museum) on the second floor. I just stood there and marveled at the profound sense of the sacred found in this icon. When the Turks took over Constantinople in the fifteenth century the sultan recognized the majesty of this building and, even though it was changed into a mosque, he did not alter the structure. Because Islam does not allow the portrayal of humans or animals in their places of worship, the mosaics were covered over. With the secular movement of Attaturk in the 1920s and 30s the building was no longer used as a mosque but became a museum ; the plaster was removed and the mosaics were once more visible. Having this available for all to enjoy now is a great blessing; it is a World Heritage Site. This trip showed me the great benefit of having this designation; so much has been preserved and developed as a common heritage of everyone in the world. There were World Heritage Sites in just about all the countries which we visited.

For shear volume as well as excellence of work, you can't beat the museum of Chora. Instead of seeing Jesus and the Virgin in my old art history books, here it was! This was a real thrill. I was glad I had brought along my binoculars so that I could see the mosaics in the dome and high on the walls. The tiles are very small and those with gold make an impressive glow. If I had more time in Istanbul I would have returned to both Chora and Hagia Sophia several times . . . yes, they are that beautiful. They also inspire reflection. Hagia Sophia (Santa Sophia, or the Church of Holy Wisdom) was completed in the fifth century; universally considered to be an architectural marvel, it was designed and executed by two mathematicians. The Hagia Sophia is a remarkable architectural achievement, on a par with the pyramids, but the presence of rehabilitation scaffolding was a serious distraction. It was the largest and grandest church in Christendom and was almost a thousand years old when St. Peter's in Rome was started. I'll take it over St. Peter's any day.

The Sultanahmet, or Blue Mosque, was equally beautiful but not as remarkable in architectural virtuosity. Its "elephantine pillars" are sometimes maligned in art criticism, but we found the effect to be graceful and grounded.

I spent a day with some of the other senior women passengers. We wandered around the Spice Bazaar and the Egyptian Market. These are really hard to adequately describe. Someone said that everything and anything is for sale in the bazaars. I think they may be right. You need a compass or a guide because in the Egyptian Market there are 4000 stalls on 67 streets . . . not laid out in a grid. And you need to have millions of Turkish lira. The exchange rate before we sailed was 167,000 TL to the US dollar. By the time we arrived there it was 300,000 TL to the dollar. A sign at Macdonalds bragged that their Big Mac was reduced from 1,200,000 to just 900,000 TL. One wonders why they don't just move some decimal points. The going interest rate for borrowing from a bank was 145 per cent. One professor gave a class on how this could be *and* Turkey be economically healthy right now. I don't know very much about economics, but it would take a lot to convince me. I'm not ready to invest.

Everywhere in the bazaars there was gold, amber, and precious gem jewelry; everywhere there were spices, many unfamiliar, and huge bags of saffron which in the US is more dear than gold. And in shops above the stores as well as on the streets there were rugs, and rugs and more rugs. Those who had bought rugs in India were now tempted to buy more. Those of us who had not were unlikely to leave this port still "rug virgins."

Chapter 17 – Istanbul and Turkey

As a final fling, a group of us visited one of the old Turkish baths. By old I mean hundreds of years old. I had thought we would have the traditional treatment: marble floors heated by fires from below, cool water fountains, and a soapy massage. We did get the latter (one more gentle than that described by some of the men on board) but the room was not hot, or even very warm. This was disappointing. From what I heard from other Turkish Bath experiences, it was the exception. But the setting was worth the trip. Beautiful pierced domed ceiling and old water taps lining the walls. My imagination easily went back to days long ago when women were pampered, scrubbed, and scented. Going to the baths is still popular today among the residents of the city.

The Bosporus River - Awaiting Armageddon

pjr

On cold and rainy day number three, we boarded a ferry and went up the Bosporus River on a sightseeing side trip. Dr. Bill Orr, Catharine's professor of Oceanography and my professor of Geologic Hazards, was the trip leader. For several hours we cruised the river and gathered information about the geology of the area and the history surrounding the various palaces and fortifications - fortifications that were not able to prevent the Ottoman Turks from penetrating the area in the fifteenth century. The Bosporus joins the Black Sea and the Sea of Marmara, thence the Dardanelle Straits and into the fabled Aegean Sea, an ancient and important trade route. On one side of the river was Europe, on the other Asia. It was a unique and powerful experience.

Unfortunately, the river is heavily polluted with both the obvious trash and scum as well as the less obvious but more destructive industrial and agricultural wastes. The fish vendors at our dock regularly remove unsightly growths and tumors from their offerings. As Professor Orr discussed in our class on GeoHazards, the Bosporus drains the Black Sea, which is one of the world's great environmental disasters, an Armageddon-in-waiting. If you know what is going on, looking upriver feels something like looking up the barrel of a loaded and cocked 12 gauge shotgun.

The Black Sea is roughly 750 miles (1200 kilometers) across west to east, and anywhere from 75 to 350 miles (120 to 560 kilometers) north to south, with a maximum depth of almost 2250 meters (7400 feet). An inland sea, it is the agricultural toilet bowl of Bulgaria, Rumania, northern Turkey, and the western end of the old USSR. These people are not noted for environmental scruples, and this toilet bowl doesn't flush, it just leaks a little, through the Bosporus. The runoff from chemically fertilized fields and animal waste drains into the Black Sea. The northern parts are heavily silted. With very little tidal action and only the Bosporus to drain it, the poison builds up.

The sea has become vertically stratified into two layers of different densities. The upper layer is brackish (low salinity) and heavily polluted by any standards. The lower layer is more salty, therefore more dense, and has little motion. It is also polluted beyond ordinary standards - it is just plain *dead*. There simply is no marine life in this sea below the interface, at about only 20 meters below the surface. The rest of the depths, from 20 meters down to the maximum depth of 2250 meters, is full of dissolved hydrogen sulfide gas. The Black Sea, below 20 meters, is thus a sea of hydrosulfuric acid - of course it is dead! As any high school chemistry student knows, hydrogen sulfide gas is colorless, flammable, and extremely poisonous. It rots silver. It is most known for producing, even in very dilute amounts in the air, the insufferable smell of rotten eggs. It has one other property of great interest - life and death interest. The gas is heavier than air.

The more dense lower layer of the Black Sea is stable, for now. Just as, for example, the lower level of Oklahoma's shallow Lake

Chapter 17 – Istanbul and Turkey

Carl Blackwell is stable, at least in early summer. As Catharine and I discovered during our honeymooning first summer of marriage in Stillwater, sometime in late July the lower level lightens up, through growth of flora, and the lake "turns over." Such overturning lakes are common in temperate zones. The tap water in Stillwater, which uses the man-made lake as its reservoir, turns cloudy, gooey, and stinky. Unpleasant, but not disastrous. Not like Lake Nyos in the mountains of Nigeria, which contained dissolved carbon dioxide gas from volcanic sources. This lake turned over in August of 1986, possibly due to an exceptionally cool and rainy season (which lowered the temperature and therefore the density of the upper layer), or possibly just due to the instability of the gas-saturated lower level triggered by an underwater landslide or a minor earthquake. Whatever the trigger, the saturated lower level was unstable, and the carbon dioxide was liberated violently, like a lake-sized bottle of warm soda. As is the case for the hydrogen sulfide gas of the Black Sea, carbon dioxide gas is also heavier than air, and the gas poured down the mountain slope in a deadly "density current," reaching hurricane force winds that toppled trees. Also because the gas is heavier than air, it does not disperse readily, and animals and hundreds of people suffocated to death. Small peanuts, compared to the disaster potential of the Black Sea.

I do not know how close the Black Sea concentration of hydrogen sulfide is to saturation, but if it becomes saturated and therefore unstable to small disturbances, something will eventually happen. Some trigger will occur - perhaps an exceptionally cold winter, or an earthquake, something. If the Black Sea turns over, the deadly hydrogen sulfide gas will come out of solution, and poison everything in the area. People in seaside towns will die by the thousands.

What to do about it? Why, the same as most of our other environmental time bombs on the planet - ignore it, maybe it won't happen, maybe it will happen after we are gone, we can always plead ignorance. Why didn't those scientists tell us about these things? Of course, they did. I am. But it is hard to push the British Royalty scandals off the front page, and our President, First Lady, and First Slut. And how about those Spice Girls and their babies!

Bosphoras & Faith Bridge

The marine biologist Rachel Carson (now there is a 20th century saint for you!) wrote her "Silent Spring" in 1962, and began a major awareness of industrial and pesticide damage to our environment. Since then, conditions have improved tremendously in the USA, but most of the world is still heading downhill. If the Black Sea turns over, it will be an attention getter, but I still doubt that the world's hearts will change. I cry for the environment.

Sufi Chanting

pjr

The Field Program of the Semester At Sea in Istanbul included a rare opportunity to visit one of several Sufi centers. Sufism is a sect of Islam in which liturgies involve not only prayers and readings from the Koran but also chanting, drumming, drama, and dance. Generally regarded as the mystic branch of Islam, they developed in the late tenth and early eleventh centuries, borrowing

Chapter 17 – Istanbul and Turkey

from Christianity, Neoplatonism, and even Buddhism, and poetically stressing the soul's union with God. Their most well known practice is that of the ecstatic dance of the Whirling Dervishes. On our third night in port, I boarded a bus with shipmates for observation of a liturgy at the Fatih Mevlevi and Sufi Dervish Center. After a long and uncomfortable inner-city bus ride, we walked narrow crowded streets in a cold drizzle to the Center, a somewhat rundown building in an area where we were glad to have a shepherding guide. We removed our shoes at the inner doorway, and the women were separated from the men (and one boy, a child of a faculty member). We men were then seated on the floor of an ante room, where nothing happened.

The Sufis did not seem to know what to do with us. We sat on the floor and chatted among ourselves, talked some trivia and some religion, shared knowledge of Islam and Sufism, and after twenty minutes or so were moved into another room, the air heavy with stale cigarette smoke, where nothing happened again. We occupied about half the room, and local Sufis occupied the other half, talking among themselves. There was no conversation with us, although our presence was being noted - for example, one of the Sufis saw that I was not comfortably seated, and brought me a large cushion. After a long while here, perhaps half an hour, we were moved again into yet another room. Again, nothing happened. The boy in our group fell asleep. The description of this field trip had promised a lecture, and our tour leader tried to give us some background, but it was not very satisfying. He was sincere but somewhat naive. He was at a great disadvantage because he did not know the background of his guests, and was perhaps a little pedantic, although gentle and respectful. Some took him to be a bit condescending and corny, and I could see why, but I thought he was basically a good and caring man who was in over his head. We were able to see the local men interacting with each other, and although we could not understand their words, it was interesting to observe their tender and respectful demeanor with one another, especially when one obviously respected elder entered and sat with a small group of four or five men. They were most respectful, almost obsequious at first, as though in the presence of a holy man, but still were able to converse and relate to him.

Finally, something happened. We visitors were moved to the back of the room, opposite doors opening into another larger room, a small hall, where perhaps a hundred Sufi men (that we could see) were seated cross legged on the floor, facing to our left. Whatever they were looking at was beyond our line of sight. A low chanting began. After five minutes or so, it grew in volume and tempo, punctuated with sharp aspirations, and accompanied by swaying movements of head and upper body. We learned later that our women, although they were somewhat put off by being separated from the men, actually had a better view then we did. We did not see any dancing, just chanting and swaying. It went on for perhaps half an hour, with some rise and fall, became fairly intense at one point, then backed off, and finally ended simply and gently. We could not understand the language, but we knew that the liturgy was simply one of praise, praise to the single God who nonetheless "has one thousand names," whose reality can only be approached through mystic practices.

After the liturgy, we were moved back into one of our previous rooms, where we were served small snacks of fruits, including pomegranates. Again, our hosts did not seem to know what to do with us. Our conversations were among ourselves, with only a little more interaction with our hosts, as we or they sometimes passed the snacks across the borders of our respective territories on the floor, hosts and guests. After another half hour or so, we found our shoes, paid the clerk who had watched them, and trudged after our guide through the cold drizzle back to our bus. On the long ride back to the ship, our guide tried to process the experience for us, but it did not work. His attempts at profound thoughts were not

Chapter 17 – Istanbul and Turkey

well received, with some of the students muttering and almost laughing. I felt most uncomfortable, because I could relate to both the guide and the students, and it was embarrassing. As we exited the bus, I heard one of the faculty trip leaders make critical comments about the entire experience.

I thought about the experience a lot the next day, and when I happened to see the faculty trip leader, I spoke to her and began to defend our tour guide and the whole trip. To my surprise and relief, she was way ahead of me, and agreed. After letting it settle for a night, she too had decided, and so had many of the students, that the experience had been good after all. It was not exactly what we had expected or been told, it was not a deep verbally theological exposition, it was not something on which the students could be tested - no facts or figures or myths or structural concepts or histories. But there was a mood, a manner of relating, a very distant yet genuine hospitality that did not try to bridge the cultural gulf between visitor and host but did allow us a glimpse of another world, a very different world.

What did it mean? Nothing, factually, and yet I still remember it all, vividly and fondly. Just as I remember the chanting of prayers in a Jesuit seminary where I made a private retreat in 1963, just weeks before my wedding. I was shocked that the Jesuits, who have been often criticized throughout their history but never for lack of intellectual standards, raced through the litanies, a leader almost shouting the honorific titles like "Mother most pure" or "Fountain of virtue," and the rest of us in the congregation firing off the repetitious responses like "Pray for us," with no time for reflection, no profound thoughts, no theological hair-splitting, no etymology, no history of heresies, nothing *guarded*. Wordless prayer masquerading as wordiness. Just an outpouring of - what?- love, worship, petition, fear of the Lord - all the above, and more. Just rhythmic prayer. As the fourteenth-century unknown author of *The Cloud of Unknowing* urged, "hammer away at this cloud of unknowing," continue knocking, knocking, "work at it as hard and as fast as you can, I beg you! . . . Short prayer penetrates heaven." Like Feast Day dances at Jemez Pueblo in New Mexico, where I accept the generous hospitality and shared meals of family/friends, then sit in the dirt on the plaza in the stinging autumn sun, surrounded by adobe homes and Jemez mountains, and watch the clans exchange dancers, drummers, and singers, not knowing a single word, yet understanding the prayer and communality, feeling more than hearing the drum after a few hours.

Mysticism - at a Pueblo Indian dance, in a Jesuit seminary, in a Sufi Center in Istanbul - there is not much to say. Hardly any facts at all. No theology, which is just fine. One gift of old age is finally making peace with your own inconsistencies.

Buying in Turkey

pjr

We had escaped India still "rug virgins," but now in Turkey our resistance weakened. We saw some very beautiful rugs around the hippodrome, the Sultanahmet Mosque and the bazaars. We began to think seriously of buying one. But which one? When buying rugs in Turkey or India, you either take a short course to prepare you for the experience, or just go with your gut. We took the latter approach.

The rug merchants of Istanbul are truly ubiquitous. To say "We walked around shopping" is redundant; if you are walking in Istanbul, then you are shopping, no matter what you may have intended. They hustle, but they have so much more class than the street vendors in China and Vietnam. The invitations are to come in and have some tea, "Please, just to look, not to buy, no." After any expression of interest and some pricing, the potential customer's decision to shop around some more, or to think about it, is met with urging such as "Oh, no, you eat while the soup is hot." I love it, and I am not a shopper by natural inclination. One of our shipmates

Chapter 17 – Istanbul and Turkey

said she wasn't sure a large rug would fit in her living room - no problem, call home now, at our expense, and ask your husband to measure, trusting man that he is to allow such a beauty as yourself to wander the world without him.

Bargaining is easy, but takes a little time. After one of the best meals of the entire world journey, in a restaurant on the Hippodrome, we were invited next door to a shop co-owned by the co-owner of the restaurant, and were treated to apple tea, bright conversation, and a show of Turkey's best rugs. After we expressed (genuine) interest in one, the price dropped from $850 to $550 in a quarter hour, with no bargaining from us. All you need to remember is that you have the money, not them.

At another rug shop, the greatest psychology tactic of the trip brought a spontaneous laugh from both of us. At first, the merchant's feelings were hurt, but I assured him I meant no insult, that my reaction was truly in admiration but surprise at his emotional insight and persuasiveness. It was near closing time, and we had said that we liked his rug, we might buy it, but we wanted to return to another shop and compare it again with that rug - we would do it in the morning, and come back here if we decided on his rug. His response was pure *compassion*, in our best interests. If we waited, we would be thinking about rugs all night, it would interfere with our enjoyment of dinner and the evening, we should "Get it off your minds" and buy his rug, now - make the decision and finish this worldly bargaining. (As Catharine noted, can you imagine this technique used in Wal-Mart or a electronic store in the US?) He was so sincere. We really liked him, but we did chuckle all the way back to the ship, and the next day, we bought from another shop.

Our first inclination was to buy a gorgeous room-sized rug, but then the reality of getting it home set in and we settled on a four by six foot Milas rug from western Turkey with unusually light colors for Turkish rugs - soft blues, reds, and earth tones. The merchant's price had come down significantly during our first and second encounter, to $250, and I am sure that we could have chiseled him down to $200, but the guy was very pleasant and had put up with our hassling for three visits. The Milas rug now graces our living room, looking not quite Navajo but not out of place in our American Southwest solar heated home with adobe walls. As we write this, we enjoy it in our home even more than we would have imagined.

Big City Danger

pjr

As much as we liked Istanbul, it had plenty of big city dangers. A student friend told me as we worked out in the weight room that he did *not* like Istanbul, and why. He is from a big city, and is a big guy - a power weight lifter who clearly knows how to take care of himself, definitely not a babe in the woods. He and two other men students were "befriended" on the streets of Istanbul by a well-dressed young Turk, and invited to a bar and restaurant for drinks and dinner at the Turk's expense. My friend became suspicious as soon as they entered the place, with its rough looking clientele. They were ushered to the bar, drinks were ordered, women showed up and drinks appeared for them instantaneously. (Reminds me of Chicago in 1958.) My worldly young friend thought it best to leave immediately, but his companions lingered for another round. Then he convinced them to leave, but their Turkish host took offense. They insisted on leaving, the Turk said he was a gentleman and would keep his word and treat for their drinks. Then he reconsidered, and decided his gentlemanly reputation would remain intact if he paid only for his own drinks. The youngsters were presented with a bill for close to US$300. The clientele looked rougher by the minute. The shipmates wisely decided to pay by credit card, left the bar, returned to the ship, and made a telephone call to cancel the charge and the credit card immediately.

Chapter 17 – Istanbul and Turkey

It could happen in any big city in America, but the image of infamous Turkish jails made it even more threatening.

Last Day in Istanbul

csr

Except for our arrival morning, we had cold and rainy weather, and we never left the city. The cab drivers were mostly cheats, and the street peddlers were pretty intense, but by this time, we had developed sales calluses and could be ruthlessly clear in our rejections. The whole shipload of Semester At Sea people became pretty miserable people to deal with, I think. Those who took side trips to the capital at Ankara, or to the city of Ephesus with some of the most extensive archeological excavations in the world, or to Cappadocia, say we haven't yet seen the best of Turkey. (Those who took the side-trip to the WWI battlefield of Galipoli were dis-

Istanbul
11-18-98

appointed, both in the site itself and in the long and boring bus ride.) Because of these enthusiastic reports of Asian Turkey, and our own many positive experiences in Istanbul, we intend to return to Turkey some day, and explore with more time and the flexibility of a rented car.

On our last day in Istanbul, Pat and I and our new friend, Kurt, first visited an Internet Cafe to pick up our e-mail, then explored more famous mosques and the Topkapi Palace. Because of the movie *Topkapi* (1964) I had expected that this was just a jewel museum. That is only a small part of it. It is a huge complex of buildings which housed the sultan, his staff and family. We visited the hareem, or private quarters, and I was very glad I wasn't a woman in the days of the Ottoman Empire. Their life was very controlled and full of fear. Assassinations, intrigue and debauchery were the order of the day. Sultans feared murder every bit as much as European kings did. The big difference for women was that in Europe they were given in marriage to seal alliances and their preferences were placed second to the needs of the state; here, women were born and bred for the pleasure of those in power. They never left the hareem. It was a place of both protection and extraordinary control. If they became pregnant and carried to term, they had to be concerned about whether they would have power over other women based on the position of their son. Daughters were not deemed very important in either social system.

One of the most impressive parts of Topkapi was a rather small section devoted to illuminated manuscripts of the Koran. Unlike manuscripts of the Bible from the Middle Ages, these have no illustrations involving human figures, but the decorations of Arabic letters and the elaborate designs are magnificent. There seemed to be no end to the variety of ways to fill the spaces of borders and decorate the script. The term used by art historians is *horror vacui* denoting visual discomfort with empty space found in most Islamic art; hence the elaborate and ornate facades on buildings, decorative

Chapter 17 – Istanbul and Turkey

tiles both inside and out, elaborate brocades and treatment of fabrics, exceptional calligraphy, and other visual arts. The previous May, Pat and I saw the Book of Kells at Trinity College in Dublin, Ireland. Pat calls it a miracle. It is hard to believe that anything so fine, so detailed, can be done by mere mortals. But these illuminations of the Koran were of equal wonder; they just have not been publicized as well as European manuscripts. They deserve as much publicity as the famous jewels found in the Treasury building at Topkapi. I think that there are many masterpieces in the world which await the curious and persistent traveler.

A surprising aspect of Topkapi was the two rooms containing religious relics, including two reliquaries made of precious metals and gems, each containing (literally) one hair from the prophet's beard. This is the sort of thing we expect in quasi-polytheistic Catholic traditions, but not in Muslim traditions. In either setting, this sort of thing is not to our taste.

Our final tourist site was the imposing and graceful Suleymaniye Mosque, built by Suliman the Magnificent in the mid-sixteenth century. He really seems to have been magnificent. He is known as the Lawgiver, and had the good sense to hire the genius Mimar Sinan as his builder. Like most mosques, the Suleymaniye is the center of a whole complex of social and charitable institutions: hospitals, an insane asylum, orphanages, schools, "soup kitchens," inns, baths and a library. Happily three hundred Semester At Sea participants returned to this area that final night to experience the interior of one of these impressive old buildings which had been used to feed the poor. Now it was being used to provide us with a splendid banquet and classical Turkish instrumental music and song. The Janiserrie Military Band entertained us outside. History attributes them with "inventing" the marching band. They followed us to the ship where, from our dock, they gave us a send off to end all send offs. The waiters in the restaurant above the street (and at eye level with us on board the ship) lit sparklers and danced and sang to us. We danced in response. Turks gathered at the dock and shouted good wishes. And the band played its vibrant music until we sailed out of sight.

Many of Istanbul's mosques are lit up at night, and I would have to say that the night skyline was even more impressive than the one at sunrise when we arrived. Those images and the music of our Janiserrie Band will be with me as I rock in my rocking chair at ninety. I know I'll smile remembering it all.

Chapter 18
The Aegean Sea and Dardanelles

Chapter 18 – The Aegean Sea and Dardanelles

Sore Throats and Hailstones

csr

This segment of our journey took us from Istanbul back through the Sea of Marmara, the Dardanelles, the Aegean Sea, and into the Mediterranean, through the Straits of Messina to Civitavecchia, Italy.

Only three things are prominent in my memory of this three day period: I was having a serious battle with a sore throat, cold, and cough; there was a spectacular hailstorm; there was an equally spectacular rainbow display.

The ship had come down with serious respiratory illness after India. Instead of the expected intestinal problems, about two thirds of the ship had terrible coughs. I was feeling pretty smug about my health. During the long passage from India both Pat and I had been feeling tip top. But the germs had hung around and clung to banisters and the air and after Turkey it hit me. I didn't shake it until weeks after we were home.

Since we had a cabin on the top deck, our ceiling was the last thing between us and the elements. Early one morning it sounded like Armageddon. We both woke up with a start and tried to identify the sound. It was wind and large hail; one passenger estimated the stones were about three quarters of an inch in diameter. During the night, several seniors went forward to the lounge, which has a bank of windows, and watched the storm rage from there. To their collective horror another ship appeared out of the dark and mist very, very close. This ship was described as "so close you could practically touch it," "two hundred yards at most," etc. In any case they were scared. When we talked to the captain he assured us that our ship was in communication with the other one and that we had passed about one thousand feet from each other. Still, that's pretty close. We were in an area which was relatively shallow and had quite a bit of ship traffic. I have been told that these kinds of storms are common in the Aegean Sea.

Gawking at Rainbows

pjr

It is Monday, November 23rd, in the Aegean Sea. We are headed south from Turkey, in the Dardanelles Strait, called the Hellespont in ancient times, the scene of the legend of Hero and Leander. I am headed down to late breakfast at 8:20 am when Helen, a staff member, rushes by me in an agitated happy state babbling to herself, "Video camera is the only way to go, I just have to . . ."

What is she talking about? "Rainbow," she says, "double rainbow. We are sailing right through it."

I go outside on the starboard Observation deck. An incredibly intense arc plunges into blue sea. Alerted, I look up and see the double part, less intense, but also all the way into the sea. The zenith is still complete in both, as far as I can see forward, obscured by the ship's top deck and superstructure. I run forward, up to the bridge, where a small crowd has gathered. (There are classes going on, after all.) Incredible. The whole thing, a solid arc of vivid color that gets through even to my aging worsening color-challenged vision, both bows in complete semicircles. As we gawk, it becomes more intense, and closer. Thinking of our children and wanting to share it, I take the chance of missing its last seconds, and run back to our cabin for the video camera, and run back to the bridge. Still there, it is yet *more* intense and closer. Both ends drop far below the horizon and into the blue and white-capped waves. I pan the video camera and babble, as does everyone.

Catharine, where is Catharine? Maybe in the dining hall. I run in, and down three flights of stairs, then remember she has an 8:00 am class. Where? I think it might be Professor Rowley's marine biology class, and as I pause to think on the Promenade Deck, I think I hear his voice from Classroom Two. I approach, and it is not his voice, it is Professor Harris lecturing on Islamic Civiliza- tions, and there is Catharine towards the rear of the class, on the

Chapter 18 – The Aegean Sea and Dardanelles

other side of the room. I am a little behind her. Judd sees me, I motion to him to get Catharine's attention. He doesn't understand, but she picks up something of me from peripheral vision or vibes, and looks over to me. I motion for her to come. She hardly hesitates, I knew she would not. Out we go, but the Prom Deck does not have an outside access, so we run up one level to the Boat Deck and outside. She climbs up on the railing to see further forward, and I think I might lose her overboard for a moment. We go up another deck, and a wildly grinning Filipino crewman tells us "We are sailing into the Kingdom of Heaven." Amen. More commotion, I go forward again. Finally, the left half of the primary rainbow fades out, and the second bow dims into the gray. I don't know where Catharine is. It is finally over, and as I head back to the cabin, I see Helen and Jennifer, and we are all laughing at our own enthusiasms. I saw it for at least ten minutes, maybe twenty, and Helen was out there five or ten minutes before me. She says she saw the rainbow's end go into a lifeboat. No breakfast for me today - too late.

After our return home, as I watch my videos of the morning, I am most impressed with a brief shot of Helen and Jennifer, when it was over and we were starting to relax. They are both grinning so broadly, so completely, that I hardly recognize them. Truly a morning to remember.

Grandmother Sea[1]

csr

In 1985, 1 had the good fortune to be a participant in The Cousteau Society's Project Ocean Search (POS). It was the chance of a lifetime to go out with Jean Michelle Cousteau and some of the crew of the Calypso. For ten days, about thirty of us explored the waters of

---

[1] This essay by Catharine Stewart-Roache first appeared in the Summer 1994 edition of the journal *Creation Spirituality*.

the Caribbean. Our primary guide into the undersea world was marine biologist Dr. R. C. Murphy. Dante had his Virgil as guide into heaven and hell, I had Murph as my teacher and friend. During the time on the island and in the water, I don't recall much God-talk, or many theological discussions, but for me it was a time of great spiritual awakening and it has taken me all these years to be able to articulate what I learned of the sacred through my experiences in the deep, on POS, and on many dives since.

In Jewish and Christian scriptures and experience for the most part, the sea has signified a place of chaos, death, and terror. It was inhabited by many horrible sea serpents and was generally unknown except in a surface way. The terror was to be lost at Sea and devoured by a big fish (Jonah). When there are descriptions of water in a positive and/or holy way, the reference is to living, moving water found in streams and *wadis* (arroyos) which one finds in the desert: very rare and very precious. These images were used theologically. I can understand this God-talk because I too live in the desert. It was POS which opened my eyes - all of my senses - my very soul - to exploring a different, and fundamental way of thinking of God and expressing my spirituality with a new anthropomorphism. It is first important to remind Ourselves that all discussions of God (Other, Creator, Higher Power, etc.) are anthropomorphism. No word can completely express this believed Reality. All words are limited to time, place, and culture; all analogies are flawed. But, as far as I know, all theology is either terrestrial or celestial in viewpoint and expression. Volumes have been written about God as a Wind, or Breath of Life; of Spirit discovered more clearly through eagles, bears, all sorts of "creatures great and small," and through gazing at stars and the moon. Wondering. Wondering and sharing those wonderings in stories and rituals. But a new theology emerges as we experience and explore the deep of the sea: marine theology.

What occurred to me when I first dove down into the under-sea world was that I needed a way to exist down there. Being fifty to

Chapter 18 – The Aegean Sea and Dardanelles

sixty feet deep for any period of time was beyond my natural ability. The aqualung developed by Gagnon and Cousteau in the 1940's was a technological breakthrough for ordinary folks to have a way to breathe, a way to exist, in the Deep in a way unknown to people before this century. It can be a catalyst for a theological breakthrough as well. Just as Moses could not look at the face of God (it was too much for him - the sight too awesome and beyond the capacity of his human eyes) so also we cannot breathe and move into the Deep without help. Our lungs (not our eyes) have no capacity for the experience. Because of the aqualung we can now think of God as the Sea of Life, the Source and Force of our being. With scuba (self-contained underwater breathing apparatus), we are now invited into the sea with air on our backs to wander and to wonder. Instead of fearing an encounter with a "big fish," we can dream of swimming with the great sharks and mammals. Who among us has not gone down and come up with a profound sense of "Wow!" Awe. Excitement. Fear. Respect. A different sense of our planet and our inter-relatedness, ourselves and our Creator. Is that not what good theology does? Is that not what good spiritual practice produces?

I was recently reminded of the first encounter of the children with "Aslan," the lion and Christ figure in C. S. Lewis' *Chronicles of Narnia*. Upon meeting Aslan for the first time one of the children asks, "Is he safe?" And the other child responds, "Of course he's not safe, but he is good." Frequently I am asked about my diving, "Is it safe?" that is, always, no accidents guaranteed? Of course the Sea is not, but She is good. And it is good for me to dive in and be in Her and realize that She is in me, in my blood, in my life. I enter her with caution and respect; I must know Her nature and my nature. That we live in God and/or God lives in us is a theme which runs through much of what we call sacred scripture in many traditions, What better experience to connect with this thinking than to dive and (as one epistle says) "live and move [in all directions] and have my being."

In the sea, I found myself spiritually. I don't think I am alone in this. I found my relationship to Something bigger than me and Life-giving to me. Something very fundamental. I call her Grandmother Sea. Before the land was, She was; before the air was, She was. And land and air are interrelated and dependent upon Her. She has the wisdom of ages, which knows no political, religious, or gender boundaries. She is powerful, gentle, and life-giving to all creatures. I am one of the fishes, one of the zoozanthaelae when I dive. Sometimes I float in Her like plankton, sometimes I am as alert as a barracuda. I learn about how I am by going into Her Grandmother arms and being quiet, and receptive, and respectful. This attitude I learned from Murphy, and Jean Michele; from dive masters and dive partners in Atlantic, Pacific, the Sea of Cortez and many places in the Caribbean. Like my spiritual life, the sea waits for my attention and exploration. Through my experiences in the sea I have gained a better grasp of salvation, grace, praise, and awe.

In my studies of sacred scripture, I have noticed many metaphors and similes for God. Frequently the reader explores an aspect of the Other or the Creator when reading the prose and poetry in words like Rock, Cloud, Vine. Shepherd, Lord, Warrior. Not much attention was paid in past biblical scholarship to Hebrew or Greek words for God as Mother, or for the womb-love of God. But in Jeremiah and some of the psalms there is a Hebrew word *rahamin* which is usually translated as "compassion" or "love." But it means "womb-love." It is used to describe one receiving that kind of love and care found in a good womb where one floats, is nourished, and grows. What a good word to describe the Sea and my experience in Her. I used to preach about all of us being pregnant with God. The thought I have now, taught by my wise Grandmother Sea, is that She is pregnant with us . . . we have been and continue to be formed in the watery womb of God.

Chapter 19
Civitavecchia and Italy

At Sea At Sixty

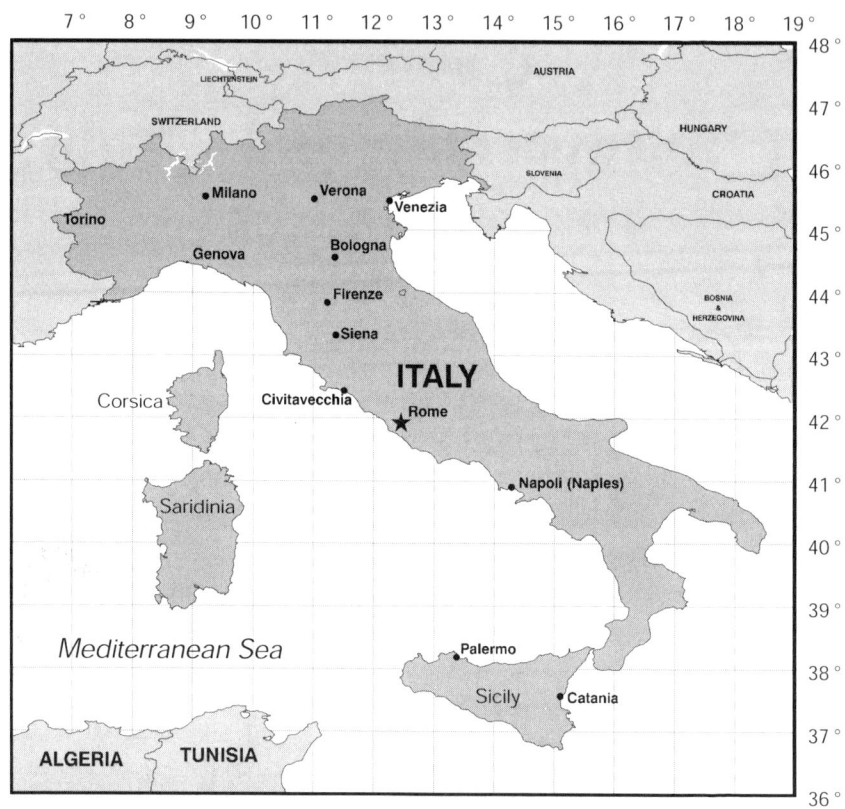

Civitavecchia, Italy
Latitude 42°N Longitude 11.5°E

Chapter 19 – Civitavecchia and Italy

Bon Giorno, Italia!

csr

Civitavecchia is the port used for Rome. It is relatively old, but not particularly historic or scenic. Since Pat and I had both (but separately) spent time in Rome before, we decided to rent a car and drive through Tuscany. We had been advised a few ports back to make car rental arrangements before we got to Italy, but we were unable to do so. We were shocked when the car agent quoted a price of over $800 US dollars for four days . . . with the fifth "free"! As we moved to leave, the price went down. It was still unreasonable, but we did want the flexibility, comfort and privacy of a car for this part of the journey. We had been with groups of people in all the ports. Besides, we hadn't done any driving for a few months.

Our first goal was to get something to eat. We bought a bottle of Chianti in a small village and some bread and cheese from a stand beside the road. Then we were ready for Tarquinia, a center of Etruscan art and ruins. We were just about the only people in the museum, and that was a gem of a museum. It was full of all kinds of artifacts: stone sarcophagi, statues, busts, pottery, and cave tombs brought into the museum from the hills surrounding the town. This was a well developed civilization before and during Roman times. The citizens had a strong sense of pleasure and beauty, although they were rough on their slaves.

After spending quite a bit of time in Tarquinia, we continued on into Tuscany. It was a pleasant time to be in this province. The roads were not crowded, the pace was slow, and accommodations were not difficult to obtain. As it began to grow dark we looked for a place to stay. I had left our Italian phrase book at home (as well as our Japanese, Chinese and French ones which would have come in handy in other countries) but I did remember that *albergo* was an inn. We pulled in. The price was good and the soup delicious.

Next morning, breakfast was the usual Italian fare of bread, butter, marmalade and *cafe latte*.

Off we went through the November country side, stopping when something caught our attention, like a Benedictine *abbezia* with marvelous frescoes and a special devotion to Mary as "La Bambina." I thought I knew of all the Marian devotions, but seeing her as an infant was a new one for me. I was very happy for Pat to be able to see Siena and Florence, I think they are a must on travelers agendas. My patron saint, Catharine, came from Siena. I have considered her life throughout my own and I have found her to be someone very rooted in the spirituality of her own time. What is emphasized in the shrines devoted to her life is the spectacular. This sort of devotion tends to keep saints distant from people. What they did, how they lived seems impossible and, I might add, safe from ordinary folks. (Dorothy Day, the socialist founder of the *Catholic Worker*, once said "Don't call me a saint. I don't want to be dismissed so easily.") In reality, Catharine was a woman very involved in the politics of her city and her church. She was not afraid to assert herself, and confront the leaders of her day, even to confront the pope. I don't agree with the specific actions of her life (she supported armed conflict and also just about starved herself to death), but I do celebrate her example of really dealing with her times and living out what she believed was holiness. She gave the Sienese and Roman Catholicism a lot to think about. She was an example of a prophet. The Hebrew word for prophet is *nabi* and it refers to one who applies the Word of God to a particular moment in history. Often this term "prophet" is used to refer to one who foretells the future. That is a soothsayer. I think prophets have a tougher job. They are the ones who say what needs to be said to bring about needed change. People like Martin Luther King, Gandhi, and Elizabeth Cady Stanton were prophets. They were often not accepted by their religious leaders or their governments. Someone like Mother Teresa is considered to be a saint, but she was not

Chapter 19 – Civitavecchia and Italy

a prophet. What I like about Catharine of Siena is that she had a very intimate relationship with her God, but she did not limit herself to personal spirituality. She moved out into her community and took the flack that it entails.

We moved on towards Florence and stopped for a few hours at San Gimiagno. This medieval town is impressive but it is preserved for tourists; people actually live and work in Siena. Many books have been written about Florence and its importance in Renaissance art cannot be underestimated. I was glad that Pat did not think that I had exaggerated its beauty and important pieces of art like Michaelangelo's David and one of my favorite paintings, Simone Martini's "Annunciation." I think it touched me more when I saw it this time than when I saw it in the 1980's. In this painting, Mary frowns in thought and pulls away from the message of the angel. She is not the sweet compliant maiden; Martini's Mary has questions to be answered before her "Yes."

On my previous visit I had gone to the baptistery next to the Duomo but it was closed for renovation. This time it was opened and we could see the mosaics. We were staggered by their splendor. They were every bit as impressive as those in Turkey.

After Florence we went to Carrera, the mecca of stone carvers everywhere . . . well, Western sculptors, any way. Someone had told me they thought the quarries were being mined out. This is a humorous thought after having been there. There are mountains of marble and it would take several millennium to finish them off. There are so few artists working in marble today that there is no danger. I was amazed to see twenty ton blocks of the stone for sale lining the streets of the town. Selling marble is a backyard business. I knew I couldn't haul a ton back with me, but was very glad to pick up a few pounds to carve someday and remember this part of my trip.

Motoring in Italy

pjr

It was fun, though expensive, to rent a car. I had not driven in almost three months. We did not drive in Rome - we weren't born yesterday. Besides, we both had been there, and both were turned off by St. Peter's. Instead, we toured Tuscany. Contrary to first impressions, Italians are actually very good drivers - not overly literal in their interpretation of traffic laws, but highly skilled.

Our first real stop was in Tarquinia at the Museum of Etruscan art. I had seen a documentary film on Etruscans the previous year, and I was attracted to them and their story. At the time, I remember thinking that I would never see their art, yet here we were. The Etruscans actually built the basic city of Rome, before what is now identified as the Roman culture. Many features of "Roman" culture and engineering are in fact Etruscan, including naturalistic sculpture, aqueducts and sewers, and the chariot. Their distinctive culture had emerged by the eighth century BCE. By the sixth century BCE, they peaked, and had spread their civilization throughout much of what we now know as Italy. They had no central government, but a loose confederation of city states based on religious ties more than politics. A great maritime power, they were experts at iron work, and their gold and bronze artworks are among the finest in antiquity. They enjoyed music, games, racing, and sex - all of which are depicted in their frescoes and on their distinctive black *bucchero* pottery. A major feature of their religion was the Etruscan cult of the dead, which was similar to the contemporaneous Egyptian practice, and which produced distinct sepulchral art. On clay sarcophagi, the lids commonly represent in a amazingly naturalistic style a person or even a couple in a noble, reclining position on a couch.

Their tender, human, and natural sarcophagi carvings, pottery and jewelry were engaging. Most notable were erotic paintings on pottery. These were hard-lined, very realistic, and very explicit -

Chapter 19 – Civitavecchia and Italy

like, genitalia in action. They also displayed some humor. One light-hearted copulation depicted the woman in abandon, with her uplifted feet resting comfortably but incongruously on the circular border of the pottery bowl itself. You would have to say these depictions were pornographic, if that word were not meaningless today. But I found it very touching to think of these people enjoying erotic love as I do, 2500 years ago. They are gone. After the Roman culture itself developed, and wars began, the Etruscans were gradually defeated and their culture was absorbed and lost.

Siena was a great experience, in spite of a driving fiasco. No one should drive inside this medieval city of wandering narrow streets, but certainly not when one leaves the city map in a hotel room. There were no deaths or injuries, nor any real arguments or accusations. I am disappointed in myself that I could not manage to laugh it off right then, rather than now, but at least I did shut up and refrained from asking stupid un-answerable endless loop questions, like "What in the hell were you thinking of?" Older is better. After a bit more than an hour, we parked outside the city and walked back to our hotel, then had an excellent though expensive meal.

On the other end of the driving spectrum, we totally finessed driving in Florence. We followed a major one-way towards the city center, and as things were becoming uncomfortably tight, Catharine spotted an *albergo*. We checked in, parked for good, and walked a few blocks to the famed bridge over the Arno River, the Ponte Vecchio. When we left the next day, we could not simply back-track because we had entered on a one-way spoke of a wheel pattern of roads. As we squeaked out of our parking lot through an incredibly narrow alleyway onto the one-way, Catharine spotted another promising alleyway across the street. We deliberated a bit, tried it, and soon emerged onto another one-way heading just where we wanted, out of Florence towards San Gimiagno. It was flawless driving and navigation, a painless entrance and exit, like sneaking a rapids on a white water river trip.

After Florence, we drove on to pay homage to the Marble gods at Petrasanta and Carrera. As a sculptor, Catharine could not possibly have missed the famed mountain full of Carrera marble.

We continued on to the north, out of Tuscany, to La Spezia. Professional friends had told me of the beauty of La Spezia, and several years previous we had tried to set up a research sabbatical visit for a few months at a NATO ocean research center there, but we could not work out the logistics. The drive into the city on a Saturday night was terrible. We could not read street signs, did not have a map, found ourselves on one-way streets going the wrong way several times, and could find only expensive hotels. I seriously considered just bugging out and heading back south, but we finally decided to stay the night. We rented a video from the desk, and watched a horrible bloody violent foul-mouthed Hollywood film on Mafia murders - as thorough a romantic mood buster as I have ever experienced. After sleeping a fitful night cringing with bad dreams on a hard and narrow bed, we awoke to a bright Sunday morning. A hotel brochure bragged about the nearby towns of PortoVenere and CinqueTerre. I really wanted to forget the whole thing and just start driving back south to the ship, and we almost skipped out. But, it was turning into an exceptionally beautiful morning, and I wanted to take some good experience of the La Spezia area home with me, so we decided to drive out to PortoVenere. Good choice.

The drive along the winding coast road was a pleasure in itself, with little Sunday morning traffic, and lovely inlets. PortoVenere looked too good to be real, almost Disney-esque. Everywhere you turned, there was another trite scene of beauty: an almost ridiculously idyllic bay, an island, a grotto commemorating Lord Byron's swim to Virici, surf, the Alps, another church, a flowered and manicured graveyard, a fortress, a medieval village, a church choir

Chapter 19 – Civitavecchia and Italy

singing three part harmony. It was perhaps the most beautiful and romantic scene we had ever experienced. There was a single touch of negative history - a plaque in the church that we made out to commemorate the church's restoration through the patronage of *Il Duce* himself.

We spent much more time in PortoVenere than was in our "plan", if our vague intentions could be called that. The next time,

PortoVenere, Italy

we will visit CinqueTerre as well. Then we drove a straight shot to the ship in Civitavecchia, on Interstate-grade roads with no speed limits, cruising at 140-150 kph (above 90 mph), being crowded out of the left lane by motorcycles and BMW's on our tail, shooting past at easily 200 kph. We made a couple mistakes and exited inadvertently when highways changed, but basically we enjoyed an easy though long 400 km drive.

We were lucky in Italy. More people were robbed here than anywhere on the trip. Cameras were stolen by pairs of thieves working the railway station, video cameras and bags were stolen from locked train compartments, and there were pick-pockets galore. Apparently one well known tourist bus to the Vatican is known to be half-occupied by tourists, the other half by pick-pockets. One even dipped our security guard Derek, a rather imposing body-builder who is a campus cop in Canada. He caught the pick-pocket and got his stuff back, but it was not worth the hassle to prosecute. Nobody on board our ship could believe a pick-pocket would go after him. Our friend Geraldine feigned, "Hey Bruno, watch me get the big guy!" All our shipmates agreed, these Italians pick-pocket are macho guys.

Pick-pockets notwithstanding, it was enjoyable and relaxing to spend some time in a non-third-world country, and to enjoy the beauty and serenity of the Tuscany mountains. We definitely want to return here for a bicycle trip some day.

Chapter 20
The Mediterranean Sea, Again

Chapter 20 – The Mediterranean Sea, Again

Enduring Sea, Enduring Art

csr

For the third and last time we sailed into the Mediterranean Sea, this time headed for Casablanca, Morocco, on the northwest coast of Africa. To do this we sailed some very old waterways on a very old and changing sea. From my oceanography course and Pat's GeoHazards course we learned how the sea has been closed by land and opened more than once. What is now the narrow passage at Gibraltar was once closed. All of this body of water and the Black and Caspian Seas were once part of the ancient Sea of Tethys. In the times when there were only two continents, the Tethys Sea separated them. This mother of modern oceans (in Greek mythology, Tethys was a Titan, and the sister of the wife of Oceanus himself) left its distinctive chalk and Tethys limestone around the world, from the Temple Mount and Western Wall in Jerusalem to the Matterhorn in the Swiss Alps to the sacred wells called *cenotes* of the Yucatan Peninsula. There is nothing else like the Tethys Sea. It lasted 150 million years, and the Mediterranean Sea is just a left-over shallow puddle of the Tethys. The Mediterranean is so familiar to those of us who are part of Western civilization. Its name is like a family name, yet being on it three times was a very new experience for me. I found out that it takes a long time to cross it, even from Italy to Gibraltar (five days) and that its weather can be unpredictable.

Having been exposed to art as an art major, as a practicing artist, and now having seen art treasures from many cultures - *and* being old - I have observations to share. My opinion is that the enduring art, the gift to a culture and to the world, is that which has some universal qualities and universal appeal. I bought small pieces of sculpture in Vietnam and India and two lovely brush paintings in China. They were pieces which appealed to me personally, but also appealed to people from other countries and cultures. I think good art communicates beyond the particular. As an art student I philosophized with other artists and came to the conclusion that foremost, art had to express the soul of the artist. While I don't think the artist should sell her soul and be produced for whatever is the current fad or taste, I do think that others (viewers and buyers) are a legitimate part of the whole picture. I think that visual artists, poets, musicians, playwrights, and architects express themselves and their culture to others outside of themselves. To a large extent I think much of current art has become very self-indulgent and very heady. This is especially true of much of post-modern sculpture. It has become an intellectual exercise with little regard to tried and true principles of form, texture, or attention to materials, much less crafting skills. Long explanations are posted by pieces of work. I recall someone asking the great modern dancer Martha Graham, "What does it mean?" Her reply was, "If I could tell you, I wouldn't dance it." She expected that she had to dance in a way that the audience would get it, or get *something* meaningful. When I show people the small marble "Ganesh" I bought in India they can enjoy the form and the fine workmanship evidenced in the piece.

Recently some of my sculpture was shown along with the works of four other visual women artists. Our works had content, beauty, and truth. One observer was heard to say, "I really like this show; it is so beautiful . . .and no dismemberment." I am tired of dismemberment, and of presentations that are only shocking. The visual arts have a counterpart in the world of music which is so often loud and "in your face." Of course there is a place for visual art that gets our attention and makes us think about much that needs attention. But Goya's paintings and Picasso's *Guernica* also paid attention to line, value, composition. Much of what I see in art magazines and in galleries pays attention to none of this. It seems that often the bigger, the more obscure, the less accessible, the better it is considered. I think there is a difference between ugly and truthful. Some current works are just plain ugly and shocking. I

Chapter 20 – The Mediterranean Sea, Again

think that the world of art should have room for some pieces that are simply beautiful. I don't think that beauty should be the only criterion of a piece, but work should not be excluded because it is beautiful.

On a world scale, on a historic time scale, I think this trend will pass away. Good riddance. Remember Warhol's *Campbell Soup Can*? Duchamp's urinal *Fountain*? People have not traveled across continents to see this "art." It may be interesting, clever, thought provoking. But I would not classify it as art. Around the world I saw art from past millennia, from ancient civilizations, and from the turn of the century which spoke to my heart *and* mind. I think great art will always involve both. I think traditional themes can be approached in new, fresh ways; I believe that they always have, and that they must. I also think new ideas and materials can be used to express that which links the human family. They can be used to express where there are breaks, but all this must be comprehensible. By paying attention to principles of form, composition, line, color, values, etc., art will do these things. To exclude most viewers from the processes of art, to produce work which few can "get" does not serve art or people very well. Ideas and religions have both unified and separated us, but music, art, and sport, or play, have been great unifiers allowing individuals to touch other people in areas that nourish themselves in important ways. One of the big gifts of the trip was discovering the *dan bau* instrument in Vietnam. I listened to the music and enjoyed it. It was music produced on an instrument completely unknown to me, with unfamiliar sounds and scales, but it was accessible to me. The water puppets of that country also reached out and tickled my spirit. "More, more" I shout to the world.

Do I think art should communicate to everyone all the time? No, that is ridiculous. People can become educated in the principles of art, and then apply them. Taste will be a factor. I will readily admit that Melk Abbey in Austria is a work of art and filled with art, even though the Baroque is not to my taste. Right now there is a trend towards the shocking, offensive, and thrown together, that does no honor to the world of art from the past and which has been sustained in many forms by many cultures. Yes, I know, the *point* of current art work is often that *nothing* is enduring. I have heard artists say that stone is a moribund material for sculpture. I don't believe it. And I don't believe the world is finished with the true, the good, nor the beautiful.

Well, I got that off of my chest. I surely do sound like a cranky old artist. But these are my opinions gathered over a lifetime and I believe that it is as valid for me to express them as for the young to express theirs. Surely the world of art has room for us both.

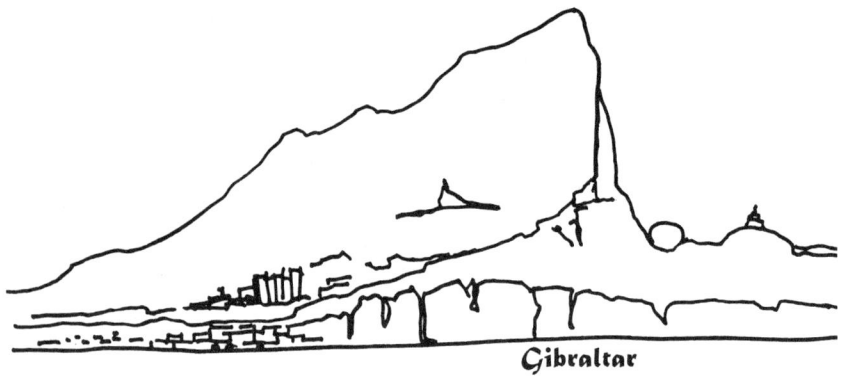
Gibraltar

Landmarks

csr

There it was, Gibraltar. An insurance ad no longer. In fact, having the shape so familiar really didn't prepare me for its splendor. This is a terrific hunk of rock . . . even if you are not a fancier of stone. We had time to enjoy looking at it and the town which lies at its feet because we were refueling. It seemed that there had not been enough fuel for us to buy in Italy. Passengers and crew were warned that smoking had to stop; the tanker pulled along side,

Chapter 20 – The Mediterranean Sea, Again

and the captain said "Fill her up." This was enough fuel for twenty two days of sailing. The ship used something referred to as heavy fuel at the rate of 4.5 tons *per hour*. From this, steam is produced, which in turn drives turbines. The ship is technically called the *T. S. S. Universe Explorer*, standing for Turbine Steam Ship, and is one of only a handful of steam ships left in operation. They have advantages and disadvantages. The primary advantage is that the *Universe Explorer* can go where luxury liners can't. Like the North Pacific. I'd hate to have missed all those typhoons.

A surprise for some while we were refueling was a close encounter with a submarine doing surface exercises. Pat and others saw it only a few hundred feet from our portside, but I was in class at the time.

After going through the narrow passage between Europe and Africa called the Pillars of Hercules, we sailed south and west to Casablanca. On the way we looked north and saw the Sierra Nevada of Spain. I was surprised to see that it was already snow covered. We were told that Europe was having an early winter. It turned out to be a very severe winter, too, with many deaths from avalanches.

As we sailed through the passage I was very aware that we were entering our last ocean and approaching our last port, one with a magic name - *Casablanca*.

Chapter 21
Casablanca and Morocco

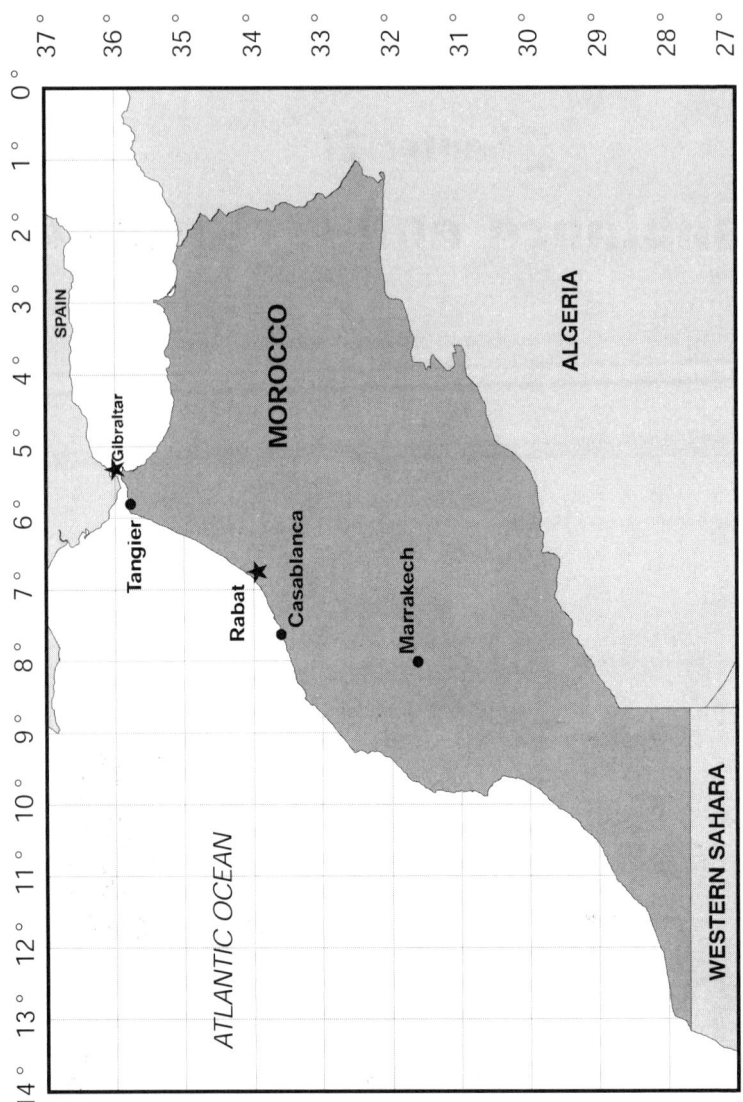

Casablanca, Morocco
Longitude 33.4°N Latitude 7.4°W

Chapter 21 – Casablanca and Morocco

Last Port and New Continent

csr

As we sailed through the passage I was very aware that we were entering our last ocean and approaching our last port, and for both of us, a new continent. Neither Pat nor I had ever set foot on Africa.

Casablanca, on the northwest coat of Africa, was the last foreign port of our around-the-world journey, and ironically is the newest port of our travels. Until the early 1900s it wasn't a port of note at all. With the coming of the French it developed and is now a city of three million, largest in Morocco and second largest in Africa. It is the most modern city in Morocco and reflects the French impact of this century. Most people speak French as well as Arabic, and those who speak English are few.

The film *Casablanca* is a landmark to movie goers around the world. It was a movie not to be forgotten. The city is forgettable. It was almost all built after the 1940's (except for the white house, or *casa blanca*, which no longer exists) and there is no longer a real *Rick's* nightclub, only a commercial use of the name. But we didn't realize all this as we docked in Casablanca on a bright, sunny day in December.

Disappointing Casablanca and Moroccan Manners

csr & pjr

We had been warned by our nephew that Casablanca would be disappointing, and his assessment was accurate. On a guided bus tour introduction to the city, our shipmates literally could not understand why we were stopping at times, with nothing to see. The huge Hassan II Mosque, the largest religious monument in the world after Mecca, seemed at first look to be worthwhile, but on closer look was very disappointing. It is enormous, but dull - an offensive modern mosque, completed in 1993, and built in obviously computer-generated planar modules, big and tasteless, with pseudo-three-dimensional art work. It is a computer designed knock-off of historic Muslim architecture, bigger than St. Peter's in Rome and even colder, as soul-less as a parking garage. It was closed for prayer when we were there, but at other times they charge US$11 just to go in. (They have to pay for it somehow - it cost US$800 million.)

Our bus tour guide in Casablanca also rivaled his counterpart in Israel as a font of misinformation. His whopper was identifying a Roman Catholic church we visited as the Cathedral of the Sacred Heart. There is indeed such a famous Cathedral in Casablanca, an instance of French influence in the city, but as we walked up to the entrance, we noticed another French theme, an artificial grotto, reminiscent of Lourdes. The interior was beautiful, with tall and elegant stained glass windows, but the devotional art of the *Sacre Couer* was nowhere to be seen. Instead, there was lots of Mariology. Furthermore, the style of architecture was more recent than our vague notions of the date of the cathedral. Clearly, this was not a cathedral, but a parish church dedicated to Our Lady of Lourdes, a conclusion substantiated by some brochures. Our guide could not be dissuaded - he insisted that this was the cathedral. We panicked when we were told that he would be our guide on a two-day trip to Fes, leaving in the morning.

In the evening of this first day in Morocco, we participated in a Welcome Reception at an American College. The affair was uncomfortable, being crowded and chairless (Catharine ended up sitting on the floor) with long lines to reach snacks, no real meal. Conversation was strained and difficult. We did enjoy a brief slide presentation on the Berber tribes, and it was interesting to hear a short address by the Moroccan Minister of Health and Sports, the woman who created such a stir in conservative Muslim circles when she ran in shorts (and won a gold medal) at the 1984 Olym-

Chapter 21 – Casablanca and Morocco

pics. But overall, the reception, like the rest of Casablanca, was disappointing.

We thought we heard people being sloppy in their pronunciation of Morocco, losing the first syllable. But that is the way the locals say it, and we have even seen it transliterated more accurately as "M'rocco."

The street vendors and hawkers of Casablanca and Fes were not the most aggressive we had encountered around the world, but they were the meanest. Some literally cussed out little old ladies in language they had not heard in their youth (or since their last PG13 movie), telling them to go home if they were not here to buy. Pat got into a kicking contest in Fes with a street seller who was merciless in crowding and pestering a friend, another woman senior passenger. Our young women students were harassed the most - some advances were romantic or erotic, but most were just a case of domination via sexual advances. Several were *handled*. On our last day in Casablanca, we escorted two women, one a senior passenger like ourselves, another a young student, through a tour of the largest souk, an open-air marketplace. On a previous attempted trip to the same *souk*, our young woman friend had turned back, disgusted with the men of Casablanca. On our outing together, we found, as did other groups of our shipmates, that the sexual harassment/domination ceased with any male in the group. It seems that the men are punishing the foreign women for appearing in public without a male escort. Curiously, we saw several local women who were unescorted and were not being hassled. Whatever the rationale or underlying sentiment, Morocco is an unpleasant place for women tourists.

Roman Volubilis, on the Way to Fes

csr

Our travels in Morocco took us inland to the ruins of Volubilis, a far western outpost of the Roman Empire built in the second and third century CE. These are extensive and reveal a very sophisticated city of about 15,000 people who designed a metropolis with running water, temples, lovely houses with courtyards and fountains, solariums, baths, and toilets. The mosaics were as fine as those we had seen in the mosaic museum in Istanbul.

After Volubilis and another stop for a traditional meal of Moroccan salads, *couscous*, chicken and delicious tangerines for desert, we went on to Fes, the oldest of the imperial cities.

You Must Remember This

csr & pjr

Not Casablanca, but Fes. Now *this* is a fascinating city for history buffs. Getting there took some time and effort.

In Fes, the "modern" part of the city dates from the 16th century. The "new" city is from the 13th century, and the old city (*medina*) was founded around 790 CE. Fes is widely acknowledged by scholars to be the last true example of a typical medieval Arab town, and its character is preserved under strict building supervision of UNESCO. Fes is not a place to visit on your own. Our guide, though far from ideal, had been born in the *medina* and knew how to move through the labyrinth of streets and *souks*. There were amazing things to see around every corner of the twisting streets and alleys: a pottery factory and shop (we did buy), smelly tanneries, weavers, metalsmiths, food markets, all sorts of clothing from modern jackets with "Chicago Bulls" on the back, to Moroccan leather jackets (we did buy) and traditional caftans and *jallabahs*. Since it was rather cool, most men and women were wearing traditional *jallabahs,* long monk-like garments with hoods. The streets were often literally tunnels, with residences and shops built overhead so that no sky was visible. Several alleys were crawl-throughs, perhaps three feet high. When we did catch a glimpse of sky, it was a wonderful clear blue, a sky and a cool day with intense sun that reminded us of our own autumn climate in

Chapter 21 – Casablanca and Morocco

New Mexico. The tannery and wool dyeing operation was just fascinating, reached through narrow stairways that forced you to crouch, extending across several rooftops on several levels, with hides laid out in various stages of curing and processing, barefoot boys stomping on hides in thousand year old pits filled with dyes and chemicals, truly a time capsule.

Our guide, the same font of misinformation from our Casablanca city orientation, had been born in Fes and knew his way around its incredibly complex streets and alleyways. But he was still exasperating, especially to our faculty trip leader, Germaine, who had to deal with his pushiness. He was full of droning double talk, and kept us away from real bargains on the streets, acting as a shill for his buddies and cousins. He even badgered us into visiting a walk-up rug shop, full of rugs that, in our opinion, could not hold a candle to Turkish or Indian rugs. Nobody bought. Still, he was a good navigator, and as fascinating as Fes is, you could be lost forever in there without a guide. We turned down his recommendation on an over-priced restaurant for lunch, and instead enjoyed inexpensive and delicious street food (with no after-effects). But all our guide's shortcomings were forgiven based on his arrangements for an evening banquet.

In the early evening, from the crowded streets jammed with people, carts, heavily laden burros, and quick paced mules, we turned into a gate and entered a beautiful and quiet courtyard. This had been the home of a wealthy vizier, built early in the 20th century with careful detailing of past glories. The tile work was finer by far than that on the new Hassan II Mosque in Casablanca. Now this lovely setting had become our restaurant for the evening. Such luxury. Such food. Such music and dancing.

Nothing else in Morocco came close to being as special as that night.

Leaving for Home

csr

At eleven pm, we brought in the gangway for the last time. I was ready to be finished with ports o' call. I was ready to be on this last ocean. I was looking forward to the Sargasso Sea and all the marine life found there. I was beginning to miss the green chile, the roadrunners, and the sandhill cranes of New Mexico. I was ready for home, but first I had to figure out how to get all this stuff in one carry-on and two bags. I wasn't tired of the ship, or the water, or the passengers, but I was tired of being a monetary mark, port after port. On other travels to developing countries I had found out what it was to stand out, to look so foreign and have no way to conceal it from hawkers and merchants. It was like having a big sign that said "Take me for all you can get." I have never liked this feeling. I don't mind a little bargaining from time to time, but now I was exhausted with it. I was looking forward to a fixed price . . . fair or not. But I chuckled at the thought of going into Wal-Mart and saying at the checkout, "Is this your last, best price?"

The map showed a straight course across the Atlantic, and home.

Chapter 22
The Atlantic Ocean

Chapter 22 – The Atlantic Ocean

Crossing the Deep in Tranquillity

pjr

At last, we depart from our final foreign port, Casablanca. After a few days on the ship, enjoying beautiful weather and calm seas, all the more enjoyable because everyone thought it would be a rough and cold ocean crossing, we decompress and relax. We all know we are heading home, with not very mixed feelings at all. Everyone we talk to is ready to go home - not grumpy about the voyage, just ready to go home. The sailing is very enjoyable, and I would enjoy perhaps as much as another week at sea, if the weather would hold. Some others agree, but *no one* is ready for another foreign port. Fascinating, yes, but we are port-ed out. Catharine and I add it up - including our travel earlier this year, in Germany and Austria on a group bicycle trip, in Ireland on our private bicycle trip, and in Baja California on a whale watch, sea kayaking and camping trip, we had to deal with 16 languages this year. We are zonked out from learning hello, thank you, where is . . . We are depressed with environmental nightmares. We are totally out of patience or even pretense of patience with street peddlers and hawkers. We are tired of being tolerant, excusing rudeness, greed, and environmental amorality. We yearn for the land of fixed prices and free coffee refills. We miss America.

The Last Ocean

csr

This Atlantic, the "other" vast ocean, was relatively unknown to me. Of course, I had flown over it, but does that count? I had bicycled near it up the east coast, that counts for a little. But I hadn't spent time staring at it, meditating, wondering. This was my chance. And I was just finishing *Moby Dick*. How different was this reading from the other time when I was in high school. Although Texas doesn't prepare you very well for *Moby Dick*, I had enjoyed the book then; but now I savored it. This time I was a different person in ways of the sea. I had become a diver and a student of oceans and marine biology. I could read *Moby Dick* and I could gaze at the Atlantic with a little more knowledge. Added to this, I had lived enough years to have experienced human nature more fully. *Moby Dick* is about human nature, as well as whale nature. Most importantly, I have seen and smelled whales. In reality, they are like the ocean in that they are a more awesome experience than can be imagined from reading or even motion pictures. The sound and smell and activity of both fill all of the senses. Reading that book was better preparation for experiencing the Atlantic than a night flight dropping me on land and then driving to a coast for ocean gazing. This voyage convinced me that sailing is the most enjoyable way to cross the "ponds" and arrive on another continent. It changed my perspective on the shape and content of the planet. Before, my experiences of the earth were primarily land, especially desert and mountain. Now I realized, more than intellectually, that we are a water planet. I realized thoroughly that all life not only came from water, but depends on it and on it remaining full of life. My life will still be a land based one, but the context of those lands will be different.

Searching for a Mobile Sea

csr

The last bit of land we saw before Florida was the Madieras Islands. I was surprised that they were so far from the African coast. My only knowledge of them was through their namesake wine and an old comedy act from the 60's. They were a group of hilly islands covered by fog. From now on I would just see ocean and look for sargassum and the Sargasso Sea. This sea is a moving one composed of seaweed-like material that hosts many forms of marine life, many I have never seen, but the streams of it which I

Chapter 22 – The Atlantic Ocean

expected to see never came into sight. This was one of the few disappointments of the entire voyage.

As we crossed this final ocean I spent even more time out of doors. It was a long good-bye to the Big Blue. I could have continued to sail the seas, but I was ready to give up ports. I had reached my limits on shopping, bargaining, being culturally alert and sensitive. I was ready to relax in the familiar. I am not comfortable with all that is familiar in our US culture: materialism, environmental violations, "more (and bigger) is better," violence, and aggressive behavior, but I am comfortable with the ideals of equality, democracy, fairness - and that free refill for a cup of coffee.

I thought about the Semester at Sea. There had been some very extraordinary experiences and some very ordinary ones. On the ordinary, and yet important matter of *food*, there was much that demanded out attention..

Degenerating Diets: Food and Other Fads

csr & pjr

In the Atlantic, heading home, we missed good food, also. The food on board the ship had been good - not cruise cuisine (although sometimes it was very tasty indeed), but 95 per cent good. That is, until we left Casablanca. There were two causes for the catastrophic drop in quality and quantity. We heard that a container of food was somehow left on the dock in Casablanca. Maybe it was a mistake, or maybe it was just housecleaning, because the second cause was that this lovable but aging ship was going into dry dock for extensive and much needed repairs and upgrades. It was to sail directly from Miami to the shipyards at Newport Beach, Virginia, for seven weeks of renovation. The cavernous pantries and freezers, which hold enough food for almost 1,000 people for weeks at a time, were being emptied. Even before Casablanca, the breakfasts were taking on an all too familiar look. After Casablanca, all the meals deteriorated. Breakfast cereal was All Bran, take it or leave it. We used to like honeydew melon, but after seeing it served as the side-dish, dessert, and/or vegetable for two and sometimes three meals per day for a week, it lost its novelty. Fortunately, they finally ran out of honeydew. Previously, main courses of fish had been *identified*, as in "salmon, baked halibut," etc. Now it was "fish." Strange, odorless, mealy, dry, at-long-last-thawed "fish."

We had never been around so many vegetarians or met so many different kinds of vegetarians in our lives. For a while it seemed that food was the topic of most of the young people's conversations. Despite the fact that pre-sailing information clearly stated that no special dietary needs would be accommodated, many vegetarians came trying to get good nutrition from what was served. Our meals were heavy on rice, pasta and potatoes; there were always salads and vegetables. But protein was difficult to come by for those not eating meat, especially those also not eating eggs, cheese or milk. A lunch of french fries and catsup is somewhat lacking in nutrition. As older folks, we worried about the condition of their bones thirty years down the road. Our parents had worried about our lack of good nutrition fifty years ago as well, and for good reason. Somewhere along the way, we made the connection between good nutrition and good health and good life. Most of the senior passengers were omnivores, and for us, the fare for most of the trip was good. But as we neared Miami, *everyone's* choices were down to very few.

Anytime you want to strike up a conversation with undergraduates, use an "opener" by asking about their diet. Vegies, vegans, fruitarians. Male and female. We saw one woman student make a breakfast of a soup bowl full of pineapple rings. A lunch consisting of a heap of french fries and a small bowl of catsup caught our attention more than once. We predict a wave of osteoporosis in the USA in twenty to thirty years. These idiots can't keep living forever off the stored minerals in their bones. The tiresome conversation suggested the following -

Chapter 22 – The Atlantic Ocean

New Irish Curse: May all your house guests be Vegans!

After our return, our virtual daughter Dr. Cynthia Metoyer reported this popular question. If we aren't supposed to eat animals, why are they made of meat?

Sorry to offend our vegetarian friends. Of course, we recognize that vegetarianism can be a firmly grounded philosophy, based on respect for life, with major positive environmental impact if it were widely adopted. And it can be healthy indeed, if (but only if) it is based on the very best of nutritional science and experience, as it is in the case of Seventh Day Adventists, who know what they are doing. But one cannot attain a healthy diet by simply removing meat and all animal products from a typical American diet. It is not rash judgment for us to say that almost all that we saw on board the ship was simple fadism, just like the other food fads anyone our age has lived through (and admittedly have occasionally followed) - steak diets (*the* way to lose weight in the 1950's), low (or high) fiber diets, sugar free, dairy free, margarine, low (or high) carbohydrates, cabbage soup diets, wheat free, high protein, grapefruit and eggs diet, brown rice diets, three-day liquid diets, buttermilk and beef broth diets, yogurt, rye crisp and black-strap molasses diets, pineapple and cottage cheese diets, The Renal Gourmet, . . . In mental health: guilt, anger, sin, co-dependence, and intensive truth weekends all have had their days and been discarded for something more *balanced*. Now there is an un-American concept!

Among the students, this fad vegetarianism was in the same category as the widely popular physical disfigurements, in the forms of tattoos and body piercing, from nipple-rings to eye-brow rings to our favorite, tongue studs, which one student said "gives me something to play with during boring lectures."

The language fads were funnier for us older folks, but more exasperating. We know that we had our own language fads in our student days, but now it is fun to hear new ones, to know how arbitrary and meaningless they are, and how dated this generation will sound in just a few years. Presently, there are only three linguistic positive reactions possible: the mildly approving "cool" (a hang-over from the fifties), the ubiquitous "awesome" (which was once a meaningful and powerful word until it became applied to everything from vanilla frozen yogurt to a basketball free-throw), and "totally awesome," reserved for major life experiences such as *chocolate* frozen yogurt.

But oh, the worst of this college generation's language fads, the curse of these youths on us aged ones, is the word "like."

May the Saints preserve us from "like", especially in the interrogative voice, as in "like, y'know?, like, like, . . ." Like WHAT, for God's sake! Spit it out! Surely they do it on purpose, punishing us for being as old and literal as their parents are. When they ask a question in class, they must see us old ones cringing, squirming in our seats, glancing at each other in communal misery, hoping against hope that there *is* a point and that they will somehow *get to the point*, the professor's eyes glazing over, breathless in anticipation of some noun, *any* content, trying to mentally re-phrase a long paragraph of stammering "like-like-like, y'know, like . . ." to edit it down to whatever germ of a thought it might contain. *Elder Abuse*, that's what it is. Cruel and unusual punishment, just for being educated and having lived six decades. On a two-day bus trip in Vietnam, we heard a young man behind us jabber to a woman student in a *patois* of "like"s that was truly incredible. Much more than three quarters of his conversation was content-free. We could not look at each other for fear of breaking up, but it was beyond funny, it was embarrassing. We wanted to shake him to snap him out of it, but he really needed electro-shock therapy. As the students would say, "He was all, . . .you know . . .like . . ."

We take some comfort in knowing that this, too, will pass. But who knows what the next generation's fads will be?

Chapter 22 – The Atlantic Ocean

Eating and Exercising

pjr

I ate a lot onboard the ship. Regular, healthy meals, with plenty to choose from. For carbohydrates, a choice of potatoes, rice, or pasta at almost all evening meals, and most mid-day meals. I usually took some of each. Near the end of the journey, I had gained ten pounds, to 195, and I'm surprised it is not more. It was not quite *all* fat - I had been weight lifting - but most of it was. Nevertheless, I felt great. This had been the most regular meal and sleep schedule since my freshman year at college, during which I also felt great. (Is there a lesson here?) Towards the end of the trip, talking to a woman student in the weight room, I was surprised to hear her say she thought she was eating about three times as much as she did at home. I was surprised because I had heard that number from someone else, and because it agreed with my own independent estimate. By concentrating on carbos rather than fats, having a large breakfast, minimizing deserts (no real sacrifice for me, since I don't have much of a sweet tooth), and keeping regular hours for food, sleep and exercise, the gain had not been severe. In fact, I think I had leveled off by the end of the voyage, and could probably go indefinitely like this without going much over 200, about ten per cent above my ideal weight. Calorie counting in the old-fashioned way of women's magazines is clearly not the whole story. Catharine did not gain on the trip, but curiously put on some pounds shortly after we returned home.

Exercising on this trip was a challenge. We had been forewarned that it would be so, and that it would not be possible to maintain a high level of fitness, so our goal was minimal. We hoped to not lose it all. Catharine and I are both physically active. We ride bicycles a lot, from casual 15 to 20 mile Sunday rides, off-road mountain bike climbs, competitive road races, long distance touring, to rather extreme endurance events such as "century" or

100 mile supported group rides. (We even rode one double century with lots of mountains, when we were younger - in our late forties.) We also play racquetball competitively, walk, jog, swim, hike, and row, and do some weight training. Life on board the ship was different.

Bicycling was problematical. There were half a dozen stationary bikes (or exercycles) on the ship, but at their best, I hate them. I have never been able to endure more than half an hour on a stationary bike. *Boring.* Besides, they are not designed by bicyclists, and they fit poorly. You can hurt yourself permanently on a poorly fit bike. These bikes were not at their best. Salt air and abuse had taken their toll. By the end of the journey, one bike remained in minimal operating condition. It lived in the weight room, and I used it for 20 to 30 minutes on days when I lifted.

The weight room was pretty good, with some free weights and benches, and some machines including leg curls, lat pull downs, and leg press. Shipboard life added another dimension to weight lifting - like, typhoons! Even without the major storms, one frequently had to exercise considerable caution with free weights, and "spotting" (assisting a lifter) was a more than usually serious job.

Many of the students and staff played half-court basketball and volleyball outdoors, aft on the Promenade Deck. These are also quite challenging on a pitching ship, and some, thankfully minor, injuries occurred. Catharine and I did not get into these, nor did we participate in the aerobic dance classes, also held outdoors. We had intended to pursue this - aerobics classes can be excellent fitness activities - but the atmosphere was not to our taste, with too much shouting, clapping, military-style orders and calisthenics, and insufferable music. In short, we were too old. Catharine practiced her T'ai Chi Chih, and I was very pleased to return to some *hatha* yoga practice, after many years off. Our fellow senior passenger and friend Geraldine led a few classes, and gently moved me back into it. A staff member also led yoga classes in the morning, but they

Chapter 22 – The Atlantic Ocean

were held in a cold room (air conditioning control on the ship was poor) and too early for my tastes.

Walking-running-jogging on the ship was a strange experience. The most used "course" was on the Boat Deck. For the sake of those with cabins on that deck, jogging was not allowed until after 8:00 am, but a dedicated group of walkers typically started about 6:30 am, weather permitting. At most any other time of the day, there would be people running, walking, and jogging. The "course" was an *obstacle* course. It was horseshoe shaped, and no more than one eighth of a mile long. In this distance, a jogger would typically encounter ten to twenty other exercisers, either passing them or being passed by them, dreamy-eyed people writing poetry in their journals or looking for dolphins, crew members washing or painting, leaking hoses, deteriorated outdoor carpeting (I tripped on the same upturned section three or four laps in succession), puddles (from rain or maintenance), heavy doors suddenly opening out onto the course, narrow squeezes around two outdoor staircases going to an upper deck, and blasts of wind and spray on the windward side of the horseshoe course. The corners of the horseshoe were most dangerous - signs urged people to stay to the outside and slow down, but the runners would become zoned out and forget, leaning into the turn instead of out, and sometimes crashing into another exerciser coming from the opposite direction. Just before and after the two horseshoe corner turns, the runners would have to squeeze around the staircases, involving hesitations, jockeying, and stutter steps - mumbled "Scuse me" and "Thanks" and "Sorry" and "Oops" and "Aah!" and "Heads up!" with an only occasional expletive formed the background mantra to the experience. Half the people never heard any of this, because they had on headphones and tape players, listening to their own music. More than half the time, the decks were pitching, sometimes heavily. The situation did not allow all-out running and compromised high quality exercising, but it was fun. It was communal. I was surprised and pleased how tolerant everyone was, how accommodating, even *courteous*! My own jogging regimen included use of light weights, which added to the danger of any collisions, and stair climbing. After I was well warmed up, rather than just stick to the Boat Deck, at the ends of the horseshoe I would bound up two or three flights of outdoor stairs to higher decks, taking two steps at a time. This was in fact a terrific workout, but if anyone else had been trying it at the same time, it would have been dangerous. I always dropped to a walk and tried to look casual whenever crew members appeared, because I did not want to be the target of new regulations.

The best strength exercise (rather than aerobic exercise) of shipboard life for us came automatically just from living on the top Observation Deck. We seldom used the two elevators, which were cramped, slow, and by understanding were generally though not exclusively reserved for injured or less mobile passengers. The closest dining room was six decks (floors) down (and back up!), the other was five. My class in the theater was six decks below our cabin. Bad enough, but it was always near freezing in that room, and I would have to go back upstairs to the cabin to fetch a coat and cap. After three plus months at sea, I finally got this through my head, but by that time I had built up my quadriceps considerably. On at least one occasion, I made the trip three times, having forgotten my book or notepaper or pen. With three meals a day, two regular classes, daily Core Course, evening lectures, card games and socializing, visiting the infirmary to pick up seasickness medication, and just wandering around to avoid cabin fever, each trip involving three to six flights of stairs, and we probably climbed something on the order of fifty flights of stairs each day on the ship. When I returned home and went for a bike ride, I was pleased and surprised - I was not ready for any long distance rides, but I did twenty miles without struggling, and my hill climbing was better than ever, thanks to my stair-built quads.

Chapter 22 – The Atlantic Ocean

Unfortunately, I lost it *all* when I contracted pneumonia a month after we returned home. Catharine observed that we should simply resign ourselves to a life of continually reclaiming our fitness from interruptions of travel, or illness, or time-consuming commitments, or just plain laziness. Nothing is static, and we might as well give up the illusion, even as an ideal. Besides, our inevitable deterioration due to aging is probably less noticeable, and therefore less discouraging, when we experience these ups and downs on top of the aging process.

Panning the Crowd

pjr

December 11, a big day. I was coming down with a cold, but "*the show* must go on." In the morning, the senior passengers staged a (faculty pre-approved) coup and took over the Core Course for 15 minutes. At the direction of Sally, who put the skit together in a day and a half, we presented a Politically Correct, cross-culturally sensitive Christmas pageant. We lampooned the faculty, especially their preoccupation with political correctness and occasionally air-headed approach to college education. Most of the humor was gentle enough, but a couple of impersonations on gender issues and interminable poetry, though deserved, were a bit barbed. Later, we heard that the targets of the lampoon took it well, much to their credit. The students were unbelievably responsive. They roared, they cheered, they applauded, they finished with a standing ovation! We obviously struck some responsive chords. It was most enjoyable.

The presentation in Core by the senior passengers and the students' response to us was terrific and represented what had happened after almost one hundred days together. We enjoyed each other. We appreciated each other. And we knew how to have fun together. We don't know who began the idea of having some older people as part of the Semester At Sea, but students, faculty, and ourselves were glad for the inclusion.

In the early afternoon, I proctored two more (for a total of six) course evaluations. In an uncharacteristic burst of civic responsibility, I had volunteered to distribute forms and pencils, read instructions, collect everything and bring it to the registrar's office. It was surprisingly stressful, especially in the first class where several students were insolent. I felt like telling off one guy, but my standards for student behavior are clearly four decades out of date, so I just got on with it.

In the late afternoon, I presented a guest lecture in the Geological Hazards course taught by our new and good friend, geologist and paleontologist Bill Orr. My lecture was on hurricanes, which fit in with my career research area of fluid dynamics. The opening was on Hurricane Mitch, which had occurred during our voyage. While we were worried about contracting diarrhea in India, the worst natural disaster in the history of Central and South America occurred, eleven thousand dead, twice as many still missing, economies devastated. I thought the lecture went well, and several people said so, but there were two students who were openly sneering at me in the last twenty minutes or so. It was distracting, to say the least. I could not guess if they were bored, if I was speaking above their heads (I had not given an undergraduate class lecture in a couple of decades), or if they just didn't like me personally.

In the evening, the ship's crew put on a talent show, working for tips. They went to a lot of effort, most of which was for mildly suggestive drag acts. (They are, after all, sailors.) It was done in good spirit and was fun, even though the genre is not my taste. The pleasant surprise was Safety Ron, the ship's safety officer. This poor guy is cursed with absolutely gorgeous good looks. (Everyone thinks so but Catharine, but then, she is spoiled.) The aggressive women students had been merciless to him. Every time he had ad-

Chapter 22 – The Atlantic Ocean

dressed the group, they had hooted, given cat calls, shouted sexual invitations and suggestions to him. The less aggressive women would just moan and sigh - I'm not kidding. Now Ron is a good guy, but perhaps a little up tight. You don't keep a job training Filipino busboys in emergency fire drills and running 640 college students through lifeboat drills without being just a tad rigid in your personality. When he and his keyboard accompanist came on stage, I thought he was going to sing some innocuous song. Instead, while the female invitations started up, he turned and opened up his clarinet case. The women started oohing, even the usually raucous ones. I could just hear them thinking, "Oh my God, he even makes music! The guy is too good to be true." He was. He gave a beautifully evocative rendition of the "Wedding Song," so soulful that even that crowd of lascivious females were respectful in their applause. Music doth indeed have charms to soothe the savage breast.

After the first act, I had gone back to our cabin to fetch our video camera, just to catch something on tape to remind us of the evening. During Safety Ron's performance, I scanned part of the crowd that was within the stage lighting. With the 16x zoom, I saw now-familiar faces. I was taken aback at my own reaction. After three months at sea together, I now had some significant relationships with these people. There were people who were friends, there were people who had been friends but now were not talking to me, there were people who had been friends, had turned to ice and scorn and shunning for no reason I could figure, and then had softened to a polite and mildly cordial relationship. I had thought of confronting them when things went bad, but decided not - after all, maybe they had good reason. I had done the same thing with a professor whom I had admired and liked and defended with other senior passengers; but then he gave such an offensive pre-port lecture that I was too angry and disappointed to even talk to him about it or about anything else, I just avoided him. Sad. But the looks I had received were the kind I would reserve for child molesters or mass murderers. Ultimately, I decided I did not want the stress of confrontation, of dealing with hate and perhaps gossip. I'll never find out what went wrong, but then, who can understand what goes right, why people suddenly take a liking to one another? We'll all be gone soon enough.

As I panned the crowd, I saw my heroine, May. A classic little old lady in sneakers, frail at 89, stooped with osteoporosis, scares the hell out of everyone with every step she takes on a pitching ship. She gave the big punch line skit in our morning playlet, lampooning a woman professor who overdoes poetry reading. Early in the skit, May walked to the chalkboard to point out a "New Word," part of the in-joke of the course, and as she turned to step off the stage and return to her seat, the ship lurched. About 700 hearts leaped into 700 throats as she buckled, caught herself up, staggered back to her chair, and immediately launched into her over-baked reading of "Oh, Little Town of Bethlehem." Counting our rehearsals, it was the fourth time I had seen it, and every time she totally cracked me up. The students and faculty were even more swept away then I was. May rose to the occasion, broadened the ham with every wave of laughter, ended in her sobbing mock tears, and the lecture hall collapsed in convulsive laughter. Heart of a lion.

Maybe I'll see her again, but very probably not. Probably not many of these people in the zoom lens, but a few. I felt good panning the crowd, I was touched, lucky to share a round the world voyage with them, and to share real relationships, for better or for worse. As John Denver sang about life, "It's really fine to have the chance to hang around."

Chapter 23
Port of Disembarkation: Miami, Florida, U.S.A.

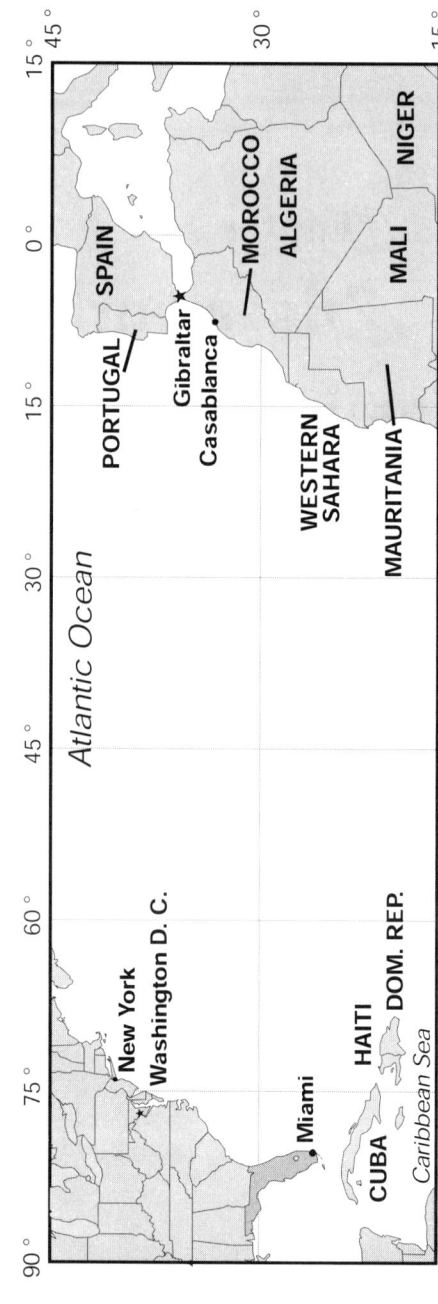

Miami, Florida, U.S.A.
Latitude 25.4°N Longitude 80.2°W

Chapter 23 – Port of Disembarkation: Miami, Florida, U. S. A.

Docking in Miami

csr

As we gathered on the bow decks, sailing into the beautiful Miami docks, I saw people I had never seen during the whole trip! Amazing. I also saw many people who had become very familiar to me. One student, Brett, was a person we always saw a couple of times a day. On this final morning he was on the topmost deck with his saxophone. As we drew near to the dock he played a very heartfelt version of *The Star Spangled Banner*. I don't think I was the only one swelling with emotion. For being home, for having shared so much with some pretty special people, for having been lucky enough to be on this voyage. It was a time of emotion and gratitude.

Then the fun began as we saw and heard cars driven by parents whizzing by and honking on their way to the port to greet us with welcoming signs. The students were very excited. After a hundred days of experiencing some America-bashing, it was good to see the kids cheering, with "Born in America" playing over the ship's public address system. One woman student was singing her alma mater's fight song, the Michigan Wolverines, and we thought of our own Notre Dame. Most of the students were glad to be home for Christmas or Hanukkah. I too was looking forward to seeing family and friends.

What would I tell them? How do you respond to "How was it?" It was not simply "fine," or "great," or "awesome, totally." It was a huge, complex experience. The honest answer would be, "I'm thinking about it all."

Chapter 24
Afterthoughts

Chapter 24 – Afterthoughts

Missing Our Floating Village

csr & pjr

Our first thought about this voyage is "How lucky we are to have seen and experienced so much of this watery planet." On this voyage, we had sailed all but two of the traditional Seven Seas (North and South Pacific, Indian, Antarctic, Arctic, Atlantic and Mediterranean) and many so-called minor seas and gulfs. In our lives, we now have been on all but one of the seven continents (North and South America, Europe, Asia, Australia, Africa, and Antarctica) and we visited four on this voyage. All this has changed us and we think it has changed us for the better. Books, television documentaries, movies, conversations with people from other countries can only go so far in educating us about what is "out there." Travel, especially ship travel, brought to us an experience for all our senses, at once. We smelled the "perfumes of Araby", we tasted the spices of the East, we heard the rhythms of the Gamelon and the strains of the *dan bau*, we felt the hands of children, we saw more than "The Seven Wonders of the World." We had a chance to draw and film what we saw, talk about it, listen to other's experiences. For one hundred days, we shared pleasures, annoyances, waiting lines, meals, fears, hopes, dreams, amazements, wisdoms, purchases, and stories. We all passed the time of day and enjoyed each other's wisdoms and talents.

All this resulted in, for us, a unique and complete sense of community with our Semester At Sea shipmates which was unlike a village or city community back home, or a church community, or a special interest community such as cycling, politics, or art. Catharine had experienced a powerful sense of community when being involved in the Women's Ordination Conference, but it was a group formed around a particular focus. Pat also had experienced a tight knit group on a two week raft trip down the Colorado River. But never before had either of us been so bound to a thousand people. By the time Brett played *The Star Spangled Banner* on his saxophone in Miami, we were a unique shipboard community. We were dependent upon each other in striking ways. All were dependent on the captain and crew as they set our course, provided food, established safety, and insured comfort to the best of their abilities. They too were dependent on us to provide their jobs, practice those life drills, obey warnings, proceed with caution and obedience. Semester At Sea went beyond the limits of a common interest, or passion, and included the ordinary, the extraordinary, life and death, beliefs and goals, and destinies. It was a *large* experience.

The faculty and staff provided structure and education. The students were sources of inspiration, amazement, puzzlement, and because of their ages, provided a time line for those of us who were old (or very old) by comparison. What had happened to us before they were born, and what our assumptions were, were a part of daily reflection. The smallest sub-group on the ship were the forty-two senior passengers. Having us aboard with all those young people was a very good idea, and excellent policy of the Institute for Shipboard Education. Our presence gave them other viewpoints, other physical types, other backgrounds to consider. We were surprised at how many signed up to be an "adopted" grandchild. This did much to span generation gaps. Taking classes together, becoming ill, exercising, watching sunrises and sunsets, and dolphins and rainbows and ships at sea . . . all these things, day by day, wove us together. We miss being with so many people who thrived on moonrises, sunrises and sunsets. We remember time spent one night just staring at the sea as it rolled and splashed along; another passenger was with us, in silence and awe. It is rare in our day-to-day living to be able to share such moments.

Perhaps the most pleasant surprise of the journey was our impression of the students. When we bicycled the west coast from Canada to Mexico ten years earlier, an unanticipated reward was our improved opinion of America. Like non-US residents, much of

Chapter 24 – Afterthoughts

our own impression of America is formed by motion picture and television images which focus on big cities and low life. Bicycling is a great means of meeting people, real people, and exploring small towns. We completed that trip very upbeat about America. The same thing happened on Semester At Sea in regard to the present college generation. Sure, we tease about their language and food fads, and there certainly were more serious problems with some of the students. But we also met *fine* young people, surprisingly many good young men and women whom we feel privileged to have known. We participated in serious discussions on serious issues, in classes and out. We laughed together, played games, shared travel stories, dined together, gossiped, worried and planned. We celebrated and even mourned together. This was not superficial contact, and we left the ship in Miami feeling more positive about these young adults and the future of our country. We are indebted to the Semester At Sea program and the Institute for Shipboard Education for providing us the opportunity to know these people.

After leaving the ship we found that we were "seeing" shipmates in our home town. We imagined we saw those who we had been seeing for three and a half months. Their images were in our heads, and were hard to let go. It was a strange phenomenon. We missed our shipmates. We missed being at sea and watching and smelling, and wondering about all of that wet world.

Back home in New Mexico, we savored being able to have green chile whenever we wanted; seeing roadrunners on their morning jaunts, sandhill cranes flying in clear blue skies, mountains reflecting pink sunsets, and family and friends welcoming us home. We enjoyed shopping without bargaining, obeying traffic lights and stop signs. We were glad to hear Spanish spoken, and to not be hustled.

Would we do it again? We don't think "it" could be repeated, even if we had the same itinerary, time, and money. From this journey we know that there are parts of the world we want to revisit, like Turkey, and others we have not seen, like Greece, Egypt and other parts of Africa which we hope to explore. We learned that we *are* tourists, whether we like this title or not. It is inescapable. We trust we will always be informed and sensitive ones. Right now we think the term "traveler" is being used to drum up business for the travel industry, which sees a new market in people who don't want package deals in hotels with North American standards and food. We do like some independent travel options; we like to try new foods, hear new sounds, see local art and connect with other folks who have grown up with different ideas, religions, and attitudes. But we know we are still tourists to local folks who see us as "American" and "rich." We can't change that anymore than we can change our gender or color or age.

"Extreme" Lists and Currencies

csr & pjr

We visited ten foreign ports on this voyage round the world, listed below along with the currency exchange rates. (Rates change rapidly, so the conversions given below are not to be taken too literally.) Following that is our very subjective list of extremes that we encountered in these somewhat exotic locales.

Vancouver, British Columbia, Canada (1.3 C$ = 1US$)
Kobe, Japan (120 yen = 1US$)
Hong Kong, China (7.26 Hong Kong$ = 7.89 PRC yuan = 1US$)
Ho Chi Mihn City (Saigon), Vietnam (13,903 dong = 1US$)
Penang, Malaysia (8 ringits = 1US$)
Chennai (Madras), India (41 rupees = 1US$)
Haifa, Israel (4.36 shekels = 1US$)
Istanbul, Turkey (300,000 lire = 1US$)
Civitavecchia (Rome), Italy (1665 lire = 1US$)
Casablanca, Morocco (9.1 dirham = 1US$)

Chapter 24 – Afterthoughts

Best Food: Vietnam, Turkey, Morocco - too close to call, we need more field work.
Richest: Japan, close second, Italy
Poorest: India, followed closely by Vietnam.
Most Hopeful: Vietnam
Least Hopeful: India
Most Fabricated Nation: Malaysia
Most Coherent Nation: Japan
Lowest Crime Rate: Japan
Best Country to Visit: Turkey (no contest)
Most Aggressive Peddlers: Tough call - People's Republic of China, Vietnam, Morocco, Turkey are all in the running.
Most Polite: Japan (no contest)
Worst Country for Women to Travel (especially alone and/or blonde): Morocco, with Honorable Mention to Turkey
Most Aggressive Taxi Drivers: Israel (no contest)
Least Culturally Sensitive Taxi Drivers and Tour Guides: Israel (no contest)
Wildest Traffic: Ho Chi Minh City (Saigon), Vietnam (lanes and one-way signs mean little; they have a statistically insignificant effect on the actual direction of traffic)
Most Dangerous: India
Best Drivers: Italy, specifically Tuscany. (Skilled drivers, but not overly literal in their interpretation of traffic laws, etc.)
Best Pickpockets: Italy, specifically Rome.
Most Outrageously Idyllic Scenery: La Spezia, Italy
Most Beautiful Skyline: Istanbul, Turkey
Most Incongruous Sight: Electric "Happy New Year" sign at Internet Cafe in Bethlehem
Best Psychologists: Turkish Rug Merchants (no contest)
Most Self-Deceptive: People's Republic of China (Problems? What problems?)
Most Self-Serving Newspapers: People's Republic of China

Most Surprisingly Candid Newspapers: Vietnam
Easiest Country in which to Travel: Italy
Most International: Hong Kong
Most Ominous: Israel
Cleanest: Japan (followed by Italy, except for Rome)
Trashiest: Vietnam
Filthiest: India
Most Exotic City: Fes, Morocco
Most Beautiful Natural Scenery: Tough call: Guilin River in the People's Republic of China, or Halong Bay in Vietnam, or La Spezia in Italy.
Most Surprising: Vietnam
Most Impressive Stone Carvings: India
Most Impressive Architecture: Istanbul, Turkey
Best Shopping Bargains: Stanley Market, Hong Kong Island
Best Value: Hanoi, a 20 minute herbal sauna plus 45 minute massage for US$6
Most Interesting Shopping: the bazaars of Istanbul., streets of Fes
Most Hopeful Social Movement: Baha'i Religion

Action Items

csr & pjr

- Return to Turkey in some early autumn, wars permitting, and explore Ankara, Ephesus, and Cappadocia.
- Sign up for a bicycle tour in Tuscany.
- Once a week, eat in such a way that nothing has to die.
- Consume less.
- Join the Green Party, a *world-wide* movement for environmental politics.
- Return to our "great white mother," the *S. S. Universe Explorer*, for one of its summer sailings up the inland waterway to Alaska.

Chapter 24 – Afterthoughts

Confessions of An Optimist

csr

When asked "Well, how was it," my soberness surprises me . . . as much as my hiding in the Rex Hotel in Saigon from all the pollution and congestion surprised me.

Family and friends know me as an optimist and one who doesn't give up easily. What can I say, I started out as a Brooklyn Dodgers fan. I hung on through loosing seasons at Notre Dame. I've been involved in feminist Church reform and I started playing racquetball in my late fifties. But after this voyage around the world I have to confess that I am not as upbeat about, nor as casual about, the future of our planet, physically and politically, as I was before I sailed. (Neither is Pat.)

Intellectually, I knew there was a need for environmental attention to be paid to land and sea and air so that these would be viable for future generations. But then the world seemed less immediate to me. The Semester At Sea brought me to the world. After seeing environmental degradation on each continent, I now realize emphatically that I must become more involved than I was to effect change. I am motivated to consume less of the world's resources. I realize vividly that the United States is the greatest consumer of resources in the world. I don't know if the country can turn around on that, but I can as an individual. While on the voyage, experiencing the commerce of "stuff" and "more stuff," I recalled that book from the early 1970's *Small is Beautiful*. What ever happened to this concept? It has been lost somewhere. I can develop an attitude more consistent with this than the current "bigger is better" advertised everywhere we look. "All you can eat," bigger homes, cars, more clothes, more, more, more. Making all this stuff uses up resources and energy which could be used elsewhere. At least I can use my resources and energy more consciously and wisely.

So! What About Aging?

csr

What did I learn on this voyage that affects my aging? First of all, I can choose *some* aspects of how I age (attitude, focus) but not everything. Just as storms came up at sea, and violence struck gentle, careful people, so too, storms and violence (physical, emotional, monetary) can knock me over and I will have to deal with this. In this business of growing old, I might not act the way I thought I would, or think I should. Traveling, I learned to be more accepting of others; I want to continue this until I die, and I want to be more accepting of myself. I want to become as patient at home as I was on the ship and port by port. To develop the habit of saying to sales people, waitpersons, postal clerks, "I'm not in a hurry."

The skills I will need in old age are similar to those I needed as a young mother, as a wife, as one confronting issues in my life. Four come to mind: knowing my limitations, setting realistic goals, being flexible with myself and others, and once I have succeeded (or failed), moving on. I developed the latter skill as I traveled around the world. I knew I couldn't "see it all"; I learned to be very satisfied with whatever a country offered, in whatever form it was offered. Then I moved on to the next port without regrets of what I wish I had done in the last one.

During the rest of my life I want to change what I think I can, but not despair if it proves to be difficult, or unrealistic. My voyage into aging has already had surprises. I can't stop the unexpected, but I can develop an attitude that the "heart-ache and thousand natural shocks that flesh is heir to" (*Hamlet*) is an unavoidable part of the adventure of being human and having life. Life is precious in itself. It is the source of awe and is to be lived, season by season.

I'm confirmed in my belief about traveling light, literally and figuratively.

This voyage continued to teach me about learning from mistakes (such as insisting on a snorkeling trip in Malaysia), and tak-

Chapter 24 – Afterthoughts

ing preventive measures seriously. I think attending to prevention is part of becoming a bit more wise.

Having a loving heart and being loveable I have always thought were the most attractive and important quality of human beings at any age. I still have a few more years to work on that.

Although I have confessed that I am not so optimistic about the condition of the planet, I do think that an optimistic attitude about life is something I want to take along into old age. I don't want to have the main focus of my life be on what went wrong in the past and what could go wrong in the future.

The experience at sea made me more conscious of my connections with all other life. I see my life as part of a vast whole. I was more able to have a sense of the vast whole by being on the seas and reflecting about all those drops of water. They are part of the whole vast ocean. I am a drop of life in an immense universe. I find this comforting and expanding. In a real, molecular way, I am a part of the past and future. My age, my life and death is *not*, and yet amazingly *is*, significant.

My final thoughts on our voyage at sea are best expressed in my following poem.

Sea Moods

csr

sea moods: I thought people were moody
   until I embraced the sea

   more than seven there are
   these times seventy moods

   long rolls to feel in my throat
   hard chops to feel in my knees

   flat, glass making me glad for
   steam power

   God's light bursting through clouds
   sundogs, rainbows; distilled beauty

   steel gray heavy hung clouds
   reflecting nothing but dark

   black silt-filled depths
   like black bean soup

   waves curling frothy over
   sea green patches

   sun winking back through
   clear transparent water

   inviting a forbidden plunge
   into cavernous depths

Chapter 24 – Afterthoughts

roiling night waves
catching full moonlight

typhoon tempest thrilling
and chilling my soul

a dominating mood
a humbling moment

sunsets making long golden
highways on the surface

giving up cloud making moisture
in search of land for shrouding or caressing

I watch alone

I watch with giggling gawking crowds of young
    with those carrying years and thoughts

I watch with sober mourners
    stunned by death

I watch with new friends
    with lifetime lover
    with crew cook and captain

For what do we watch and wait?

for beauty
for life
for surprises
for comfort

for answers
for new questions
for grace

for one more sunrise
one more sunset.

Visit Hermosa Publishers Web Site

Copyright © 1998–1999 by Hermosa Publishers

For immediate purchase of this book please go to the Hermosa Publishers Web Site at

http://www.hermosa-pub.com/hermosa/

Here you will find the *Table of Contents* for all Hermosa Books, *Secure*[†] *On-Line Credit Card Purchases*, *Errata and Addenda* to all Hermosa Titles, a *Customer Feedback Page*, an *Author Citation Index Service* for all Hermosa Titles, author's resumes, excerpts, reviews, and sculpture gallery.

Visit Us Today!

[†] Secure transactions provided through Authorize.Net Secure Services. To provide the utmost security in all your transactions, please use the 128-bit Strong Encrypted versions of Netscape Navigator (Version 3 Gold or higher) or Microsoft Internet Explorer (Version 3.02 or higher).

Netscape Navigator Gold, the Navigator Logo, Microsoft Internet Explorer, and the Explorer Logo are the copyright of their respective owners.

ORDER FORM

Postal Orders: Just return this Order Form with your check or credit card number to
> Hermosa Publishers
> P. O. Box 9110
> Albuquerque, New Mexico 87119-9110
> USA

FAX Orders: Just FAX this Order Form with your credit card number to
> (USA) (505) 866-5323

Web Orders: For Table of Contents, other information, and to **Order by credit card (secure)** visit
> http://www.hermosa-pub.com/hermosa

At Sea at Sixty
Reflections from a Round the World Voyage
by Catharine Stewart-Roache and Patrick J. Roache

To celebrate their sixtieth birthdays, the authors signed on for a round the world, 100-day Semester at Sea program, visiting ten foreign ports in the company of 640 undergraduate students plus faculty and other senior passengers. This book records their reflections on world religions, politics, environmental issues, education, the search for beauty, and their own aging. 310 pages, Soft Cover.

Your Name: _____
Address (line 1): _____
Address:(line 2): _____
City: _____
State or Province: _____ ZIP (Postal Code) _____ Country: _____

At Sea at Sixty
Number of copies ordered [___]× US$15.95 =   US$ ___.___
Shipping and handling charge per order (We pay any sales tax)   US$ 3.50
                    Moneyback guarantee   US$ ___.___ Total

Payment by enclosed check [_] or credit card: VISA   [_]
                                                MasterCard   [_]
                                                American Express [_]
                                                Discover   [_]

Card Number: _____
Name on Card: _____ Exp. Date: _____